LEARNING TO TEA

SCIENCE

IN THE

SECONDARY SCHOOL

Science is now one of the three core subjects for all pupils in secondary schools alongside English and mathematics, and is taught to most pupils up to school leaving age. This handbook presents a comprehensive introduction to the process and practice of teaching and learning science. It is designed to guide student teachers through the transition from graduate scientist to practising science teacher, focusing on personal and professional development.

Chapters cover the place of science in the curriculum; pupil learning; developing schemes of work and planning lessons; classroom management and managing learning; Special Educational Needs in the science classroom; the role of language in teaching and learning science; assessment; and using information technology in science.

Tony Turner is Senior Lecturer in Education at the Institute of Education, University of London and **Wendy DiMarco** is Head of Science, Swakeleys School, Hillingdon. Both the authors and their institutions have been involved in school based initial teacher education partnership for many years and in research projects.

ST MARTIN

Science Dept
Bowerham

Learning to Teach Subjects in the Secondary School Series

Series Editors
Susan Capel, Canterbury Christ Church College; Marilyn Leask, De Montfort University, Bedford; and Tony Turner, Institute of Education, University of London.

Designed for all students learning to teach in secondary schools, and particularly those on school based initial teacher training courses, the books in this series complement *Learning to Teach in the Secondary School* and its companion, *Starting to Teach in the Secondary School*. Each book in the series applies underpinning theory and addresses practical issues to support students in school and in the training institution in learning how to teach a particular subject.

Learning to Teach English in the Secondary School
Jon Davison and Jane Dowson

Learning to Teach Modern Foreign Languages in the Secondary School
Norbert Pachler and Kit Field

Learning to Teach History in the Secondary School
Terry Haydn, James Arthur and Martin Hunt

Learning to Teach Physical Education in the Secondary School
Susan Capel

LEARNING TO TEACH
SCIENCE
IN THE
SECONDARY SCHOOL

A companion to school experience

Tony Turner and Wendy DiMarco

London and New York

First published in 1998
by Routledge
11 New Fetter Lane, London EC4P 4EE

Simultaneously published in the USA and Canada
by Routledge
29 West 35th Street, New York, NY 10001

Typeset in Ehrhardt by
J&L Composition Ltd, Filey, North Yorkshire

Printed and bound in Great Britain by
T.J. International Ltd, Padstow, Cornwall

British Library Cataloguing in Publication Data

A catalogue record for this book is available from the British Library

Library of Congress Cataloguing in Publication Data

Turner, Tony, 1935–
    Learning to teach science in secondary schools/Tony Turner and
  Wendy DiMarco
      p.   cm.—(Learning to teach subjects in the secondary
school)
    Includes bibliographical references and indexes.
    1.   Science—Study and teaching (Secondary)   I. DiMarco, Wendy.
  II. Title.   III. Series.
  Q181.T855 1998
  507′.1′2—dc21   97–29077
                                                                            CIP

ISBN 0–415–15302–6

Contents

Introduction to the series

This book, *Learning to Teach Science in the Secondary School*, is one of a series of books entitled *Learning to Teach (subject name) in the Secondary School: A Companion to School Experience*, covering most subjects in the secondary school curriculum. The books in this series support and complement *Learning to Teach in the Secondary School: A Companion to School Experience* (Capel, Leask and Turner, 1995), which addresses issues relevant to secondary teachers. These books are designed for student teachers learning to teach on different types of initial teacher education courses and in different places. However, it is hoped that they will be equally useful to tutors and mentors in their work with student teachers. In 1997 a complementary book was published entitled *Starting to Teach in the Secondary School: A Companion for the Newly Qualified Teacher* (Capel, Leask and Turner, 1997). That second book was designed to support newly qualified teachers in their first post and covered aspects of teaching that are likely to be of concern in the first year of teaching.

The information in the subject books does not repeat that in *Learning to Teach*; rather, the content of that book is adapted and extended to address the needs of student teachers learning to teach a specific subject. In each of the subject books, therefore, reference is made to *Learning to Teach*, where appropriate. It is recommended that you have both books so that you can cross-reference when needed.

The positive feedback on *Learning to Teach*, particularly the way it has supported the learning of student teachers in their development into effective, reflective teachers, has encouraged us to retain the main features of that book in the subject series. Thus, the subject books are designed so that elements of appropriate theory introduce each behaviour or issue. Recent research into teaching and learning is incorporated into this. This material is interwoven with tasks designed to help you identify key features of the behaviour or issue and apply these to your own practice.

Although the basic content of each subject book is similar, each book is designed to address the unique nature of the subject. In this book, for example, the reasons why science is regarded as a key subject in the curriculum are discussed, including its contribution to explaining the origin of humankind and of the Earth. Science is now one of the three core subjects for all pupils in secondary school alongside English and mathematics. There is an argument that science is part of our culture and is important for that reason. Science is taught now to most pupils up to school leaving age, and the problems this poses for student and qualified science teachers are addressed. Science is taken beyond the science curriculum; we look for ways in which science can be taken outside the classroom and links made to the whole school curriculum.

We, as editors, have found this project exciting. We hope that, whatever the type of initial teacher education course you are following and wherever you may be following that course, you find that this book is useful and supports your development into an effective, reflective science teacher. Above all, we hope you enjoy teaching science.

Susan Capel, Marilyn Leask and Tony Turner
April 1997

Illustrations

FIGURES

TABLES

TASKS

Contributors

Alastair Cuthbertson has taught science and physics for eighteen years and lectured in science education at the Institute of Education, University of London for four years. He is currently Head of Science at Ivybridge Community College in Devon, with interests in effective science teaching and management of science departments. Alastair was a member of the team that developed the science teacher competences, see Appendix 4.

Wendy DiMarco began her teaching career in schools in south-east London. She is currently head of science at Swakeleys School, Hillingdon. She has been an active teacher representative for chemistry at Examination Boards including the MREB, LREB, ULEAC, EDEXEL and has been involved in writing a GCSE science course with the City and Guilds. She has taught many INSET courses for teachers in Hillingdon schools. She has worked in partnership with several Institutes of Higher Education (IHE) in initial teacher education courses, working with student teachers in science, as a professional (educational) studies tutor and as link tutor between the school and the IHE. She has been a member of the PGCE initial course (secondary) committee of the Institute of Education, University of London. She has worked with the science department of the same institution, lecturing to student teachers and has been involved in research projects. Wendy has led school based science research projects for pupils in association with the Royal Society. Her faculty has received financial support for curriculum initiatives from the Institute of Physics and, more recently, with Imperial College, University of London, from British Telecom for a project to build a chemistry virtual reality library which is due to go on to the net in 1997.

Ian Hogg is a science teacher at Swakeleys School, Hillingdon. He is a member of the Institute of Biology and the Institute of Physics. Ian has responsibility for the Information Technology (IT) in the faculty of science at Swakeleys School. He is keen to promote IT as a teaching tool for use by staff and pupils. He is particularly interested in the use of the Internet for teaching purposes. He has recently been involved in the installation of an ISDN Internet link directly into the science area. Ian has acted as external marker for Key Stage 3 SATs examinations, and very recently was involved in a project called 'Explanations in Science', a joint schools and Institute of Education, London initiative (see Ogborn *et al.*, 1996).

Gill Nicholls is currently a Senior Lecturer and Research Fellow in Education at Canterbury Christ Church College. She teaches on the PGCE secondary course and is actively involved in school based curriculum developments in secondary schools. Her doctorate is in science education and is currently in collaborative research in school based teacher research in science. Her professional interests include the use of prior conceptions and cognition in the development of computer software for science teaching, with current research in cognitive adaptation. She recently produced three modules plus software for Key Stages 2–4 in the Energy 9–16 project. She has contributed to *Learning to Teach in the Secondary School* and *Starting to Teach in the Secondary School* books in this series.

Sheila Turner is a Senior Lecturer in Education at the Institute of Education, University of London where she has worked since 1978. She is currently co-ordinating tutor for Continuing Professional Development at the Institute of Education. Sheila teaches on a variety of courses at the Institute: she is a PGCE science tutor and contributes to both the primary and secondary courses; she is also involved in MA and courses for primary teachers, including the Advanced Diploma for Primary Science Education. Prior to coming to the Institute, she taught in schools and undertook research in parasitology at the University of London. Her doctorate focused on nutrition education and she continues research in this area; current projects involve collaborative studies of young people's ideas about diet and health with colleagues in Greece, the Netherlands and Sweden. Her publications include articles and books on aspects of nutrition education, such as *Diet and Health in School Age Children*. Other research interests include studies in biology education and, with Tony Turner, research that focuses on issues of equity in the selection and recruitment of science graduates to initial teacher education courses.

Tony Turner is Senior Lecturer in Education at the Institute of Education, University of London where he has worked since 1976. He has been a science tutor on the PGCE course and currently is involved in

MA, NQT INSET courses and research. He has been involved in the planning, organising and implementation of new school based PGCE courses; he directed the secondary Articled Teacher Scheme for the Institute of Education and was Area Co-ordinator for several years for the secondary PGCE course. He has worked on curriculum development projects both at the Centre for Science Education, Chelsea College and for five years at the University of the West Indies in Jamaica. Current research interest and publications include the issues of equity in the selection and recruitment of science graduates into science teacher education. He co-wrote *Learning to Teach in the Secondary School: A Companion to School Experience* and *Starting to Teach in the Secondary School: A Companion for the Newly Qualified Teacher*. Other published work includes 'Circuses' in Frost (1995) *Teaching Science*, London: Woburn Press. Currently he is co-editing a book series called *Learning to Teach (subject) in Secondary Schools* for Routledge; this book is part of that series.

Acknowledgements

The ideas within this book have been influenced by the many teachers, tutors, pupils and students with whom we have worked. In particular, we wish to acknowledge the debt we owe to our colleagues, both past and present, in the Science Faculty, Swakeleys School and the Science and Technology Group, Institute of Education. Whereas we have tried to record that debt at specific points in the text, we recognise their greater influence through many years of working together in teacher education. Equally influential are the many pupils and student teachers with whom we have worked and who have helped to shape our thinking.

We thank several colleagues for their contributions to specific chapters and for their co-operation in responding to our brief. We are grateful to Janet Maxwell for the several sketches in the book and, with Alan Barrett, for the photograph in Figure 10.1. The lines of the poem that open Chapter 6 are reproduced by permission of Frederick Warne & Co. We are grateful to our close friends and family members who have supported us throughout.

There has been a long-standing partnership in teacher education between Swakeleys School and the Science and Technology Group at the Institute of Education. Without such a relationship, this book would not have been possible. Writing this book has been enjoyable, and we hope it will be useful to others.

1 Teaching and learning science in secondary school

INTRODUCTION

On 16th January 1958, a cartoon appeared in the *Daily Express* newspaper that showed several pupils in a science laboratory, one of whom is heating material in a test tube. As he does so, tiny replicas of the pupil pour out of a test tube on to the bench. The scene is a Giles interpretation of cloning. The comment of the pupil and the image of the laboratory capture a stereotypical image of school science and hints at the controversy between religion and science (see Figure 1.1). The cartoon was published again in March 1997 just after the announcement of the cloning of a sheep.

In the 1950s, some leading scientists dismissed the idea that manned space travel was possible or that a human being would land on the Moon. Yet within a decade a programme was underway and, in February 1969, Neil Armstrong set foot on the Moon.

Science teaching not only has to help pupils understand the world around them but also has to prepare them for developments in science and technology, some of which many scientists and science teachers cannot imagine. Science teaching is both a daunting and exciting task; what makes it fun and important is that so many pupils (and their parents) enjoy science, especially that which they hear and see about in the media. Unfortunately, the image of school science is a duller version of that outside school. The challenge to science education is to devise a curriculum that captures both the imagination and intellect of all our pupils. That we have not done so for many of our pupils is a measure of the task that you face as you enter science teaching. One difficulty is the attempt in recent years to write a curriculum for a wide spread of ability from 11–16 years – science for all. It is only twenty-five years since the school leaving age was raised to 16 and so all pupils were given the opportunity to study for GCSE. That period of time is not long in terms of educational change.

Figure 1.1   'Never mind what the archbishop will say – here comes Chalky.'
Source: Express Newspapers plc

OBJECTIVES

By the end of this chapter you should be:

- able to discuss the reasons why science should form part of a general education for all;
- able to identify the current issues in science education;
- aware of the implications of school based initial teacher education for your progress as a student teacher;
- introduced to the standards expected of a student teacher and how to use them;
- aware of the contents of this book.

TERMINOLOGY USED IN THIS BOOK

We call school children 'pupils' to avoid confusion with 'students', by which we mean people in further and higher education. The important staff in your life are those in school or college; we call these people tutors. Where appropriate, we use 'he' and 'she', 'her' and 'him' equally and not 'her or him' or '(s)he'.

WHY TEACH SCIENCE?

TASK 1.1 WHY TEACH SCIENCE?

Make a list of reasons why pupils should have to study science as a compulsory subject from age 5 to 16. Classify answers as cultural, economic, utilitarian or 'other' category. Do not read on if you want to tackle this task from 'cold'.

This question is one for which you should have an answer, at least by the end of your course of initial training.

Science is the success story of Western civilisation. The developments arising from fundamental research and understanding of the natural world have **transformed the way in which we live**. Science is as much a part of our culture as is music, literature or parliamentary democracy. For this reason alone science can be justified as a key part of any school curriculum that claims to **'transmit the culture'**.

A further reason lies in the stories science tells about **the nature and origin of human beings and of the Earth's history**. Humans are regarded by most people as members of the animal kingdom, with the capacity for speech and to reflect upon their own condition. The story told by evolutionary theory has brought science into opposition with traditional teaching about the origins of life. Furthermore, the way in which science progresses, through public evidence and debate, contrasts with evidence based on tradition, faith and respect for the past. Thus, not only have the facts and theories that emerge from scientific inquiry affected our beliefs and values, but the very methods of going about such inquiry have affected human relationships and society.

Science and good science teaching can address the nature of the differences between **different groups of human beings**. It is important that those differences that are cultural, i.e. learned, are distinguished from those that are genetic. Carefully taught, science teaching can help pupils to understand the common heritage of different ethnic groups and to look beyond the superficial differences of colour and gender. Good science teaching can help to improve social harmony (Thorp *et al.*, 1994).

Another reason for studying science is the relationship **between science and technology**. For many people, science and technology are seen as two sides of the same coin. Traditionally, science teaching in the UK has focused on the academic, teaching the fundamental principles of science. This has been done on the assumption that, through a grasp of the fundamental principles, technologies and the applications of science emerge. However, some technologies emerge in their own right and the relationship between science and technology is complex and not clear cut (Black, 1993, p. 17). Technology is practised in a different manner from science. Whereas science seeks knowledge and understanding, technology utilises knowledge for problem solving. Technology is essentially a task oriented activity where the solution is more important than the reason for the solution.

There is a case for **teaching technologies** and their associated set of skills and attitudes. The importance of technology in our society is under valued, taken for granted or even hidden. The UK does not have a tradition of valuing its engineers. As a society we are dependent on technology, e.g. giant power stations for electricity; oil platforms in the sea for sources of fuel and chemicals; the microchip in our washing machine; continuous heart monitors for hospital patients; the capacity to clone and grow plant and animal cells. The National Curriculum in England and Wales is merely a collection of academic subjects and lacks a cohesive framework or clear philosophical underpinning. It is, therefore, not surprising that there is conspicuous lack of success in developing a technological dimension to the curriculum that integrates the wide range of skills and attitudes needed for its success, including science skills.

The relationship between **scientific knowledge** and **useful knowledge** is not clear. By useful knowledge we mean knowledge that can be applied in a practical situation. It is one thing to know the properties of conductors and insulators, how to measure these properties and to explain them in terms of particles and structures, but quite another to design, construct and fit double glazed windows. The electrician who wires your house may not know Ohms Law, but the graduate who does is not necessarily able to wire a mains circuit. Layton has discussed in some depth the problem of how scientific knowledge has to be transformed in order to be 'useable' knowledge (Layton, 1993).

Learning to plan, carry out and analyse scientific investigations teaches pupils many **skills which, if they can be retained and transferred** to other situations, can be useful to pupils in many walks of life. Equally important is **confidence**; that is, science lessons should help pupils to realise that it is possible to make sense of many aspects of science and to have some understanding of the ways in which scientific knowledge is gained and accepted. If this happens then it may spark a continuing interest in science into adulthood where they may feel able to address issues that have a scientific dimension, e.g. euthanasia, irradiated food.

An appropriate science education should help pupils to be **comfortable with technologies**, e.g. to maintain and repair some machinery or equipment or to be aware that skills can be learned and acquired when needed. The drive towards a vocational element in education is, in part, a recognition of that need (Dearing, 1996).

An important reason for pupils to study science is **to maintain the flow of qualified scientists, engineers and technologists** into industry and business. However, there is a limit to the number of qualified scientists we need, and that is a subject of continuing debate. There does not appear to be a shortage of scientists except in teaching. If demand for scientifically trained personnel is limited and small, then a science education for all cannot be justified on the grounds of personal career or economic need.

It is clear, therefore, that a major concern for future curriculum change is to decide **why** we are teaching science to our young people. When that is answered, the **how** may follow.

Science is thought to be a hard subject and physics is perceived by many pupils as the most difficult of all. This finding is matched by the low level of entries for advanced physics courses, e.g. at GCE A level. The proportion of pupils studying only science subjects at GCE A level has declined in recent years (Havard, 1996). Whereas the gender differences seen in science in the 1970s and 1980s have been largely eliminated, the differences appear now at GCE A level where boys outnumber girls. The compulsory science curriculum for all to 16 years has allowed girls to demonstrate that they can do science as well as boys. In a recent study of pupil's images of a career in science or technology, gender differences were not seen as important, i.e. careers were not viewed as masculine or feminine. Rather it was the pupil's perceptions of the workplace that mattered and whether the working practices in that career reflected society as it is now. Courses of study beyond compulsory schooling and workplaces with traditional images did not attract students; some careers in science are viewed in this way (Lightbody and Durndell, 1996).

HOW SHOULD SCIENCE BE PRESENTED TO PUPILS?

Science graduates are usually specialists; your education from school through post-16 courses to university has led you down an increasingly specialised road. For some, specialisation has become very tight, narrowly bound within a discipline, e.g. genetics, microbiology or astronomy. The price of interest and personal enthusiasm is a widening ignorance of the rest of science. This is fine if your career stays within this focus, but if you should turn subsequently to science teaching, the deficiencies will matter. At which point in the educational flow should a broad science course be compulsory and when should choice and specialist science subjects enter the curriculum?

Science in **primary school** for pupils up to 11 is essentially a general science programme, with an emphasis on **process**, that is the planning, execution, analysis and reporting of investigations coupled to building a body of experience and familiarity with a range of phenomena and concepts. In England and Wales, the primary curriculum is governed by statute (DFE, 1995b). Recently in the UK specialist science teachers have been appointed to the post of science co-ordinator in primary schools. An important feature of secondary school teaching in the 1990s is the recognition by science teachers of the increased knowledge and understanding that pupils now bring to secondary school.

Some 80 per cent of maintained schools in England and Wales enter pupils for double science awards at the GCSE. The importance of a general science course for most pupils has been recognised for many years in mainstream schools. It is mainly in independent schools (i.e. fee paying schools) that the separate sciences are retained, mainly for pupils of high academic attainment. Independent schools are not legally required to follow the Science National Curriculum. There is no doubt that there is a mismatch in the sciences between the GCSE and GCE A level. This has come about in part because the GCSE is based on the National Curriculum, which is a science course for all, whereas the A level course is highly specialised, leading to university entrance (Smithers, 1994). Again, the issue of purpose in science education arises: on one hand, the drive to educate most pupils in and through science, and on the other hand, the need to prepare a relatively few pupils for a career in science or a related discipline, such as medicine.

Despite many attempts to replace GCE A level with a broader and less specialised course, the qualification remains as the centre-piece of government educational dogma.

The Science National Curriculum (DFE, 1995b) is written in such a way as to identify the separate sciences, and schools are free to choose the way in which to organise their teaching. The Programmes of Study (PoS) list knowledge and skills under headings barely disguised from biology, chemistry and physics. Despite the opening rhetoric of the PoS (so called Sc0) for each Key Stage of the National Curriculum in England and Wales (DFE, 1995b, p. 14 and pp. 24–5), the syllabus is so full and the assessment pressures so great that opportunities are scarce for science teachers to explain, discuss and explore the relationships between science, society and technology.

Should a science education be about an education *in* science or *through* science? What are the implications for content and pedagogy of the adoption of either of these alternatives? The ending in 1999 of the Dearing five-year moratorium on curriculum change should see a renewed action on this issue (Dearing, 1994). Science education has been here before (Association for Science Education [ASE], 1981).

Two central questions arise for school science education. Should there be a choice between a common curriculum for all pupils or separate curricula for pupils intending to make a career in science and another for pupils with different aspirations? In both cases a second question arises: should science education focus on the disciplines of biology, chemistry and physics or should an integrated approach be adopted that embraces social, technological and economic issues of science and society? In a presidential address to the members of the Association for Science Education, Sir Brian Follett identified another dilemma for science education:

> If we stick to the core, say the laws of electromagnetic induction or the anatomy of different groups of animals then we risk losing our students who want to learn about space flight and molecular biology. But if we teach only the latter then can our students really understand physics and biology? I feel genuinely concerned for young scientists: the shop window is too dazzling! Somehow we need to stitch our scientific stories together in a cohesive manner.
>
> (Follett, 1997, p. 15)

A SCHOOL BASED COURSE OF INITIAL TEACHER EDUCATION

Since 1994, initial teacher education has been bound by the legal requirement that student teachers spend two-thirds of their course in school (DFE/WO, 1992). Similar legislation is in place in Scotland. Unlike Scotland, schools in England are paid by the Institutes of Higher Education (IHE) to take student teachers. This financial exchange of money is an integral part of the partnership through which your training as a student teacher is shared between the IHE and the schools.

Schools choose to take student teachers and may work with any and as many IHEs as they wish. Most IHEs work with a limited number of schools and often place several student teachers in one school.

Role of tutors

You can expect to work with several tutors, including a subject tutor from your IHE, a subject tutor in your school and, in many cases, a school based general tutor responsible for broad educational issues. The general tutor may act as liaison between the school and the IHE. Each IHE and its partnership schools have their own names for tutors, e.g. some use the term 'mentor'.

The emphasis on school experience, which includes a substantial period of practical teaching, ensures that the course is based firmly on practice. You should gain experience in at least two schools during a one year course of initial teacher education, and wider experience on a longer course.

There are several advantages to spending a sustained period in one school. One advantage is the opportunity to get to know the pupils in the school, which helps your teaching and classroom management; another advantage is the chance to develop good working relations with staff, both in the science department and more widely. Third, sustained teaching with classes enables you to monitor and develop your teaching and to gain advice in a sustained and planned fashion from tutors and contemporaries. A period of close contact with a school allows you to ensure that teaching is, in fact, the job for you.

The responsibility for your progress lies with your school subject tutor and your IHE tutor. In practice, it is the school staff who build up a picture of your progress, and their judgement, based on evidence collected over several months, is a vital factor in the decision to award a pass in practical teaching. Your IHE tutor also has some evidence of your teaching, but his role is to ensure that the decisions made by the school about you are matched by evidence. This includes evidence about observation of your teaching and of the support and guidance you are given. Notes compiled by teachers from classroom observation are key documents in support of those decisions and you should have copies of those notes. Additional evidence comes from your end of term reports which contain a summary of progress, profiles of your strengths and weaknesses and target setting. Commentary and summary of progress about your teaching performance should relate to the standards expected of you (see Appendices 1–4). Tutors have a dual role, of both guide and friend on one hand and as judge on the other. This dual role is difficult

for tutors and made harder on those occasions when they have to recommend that their student should not be granted Qualified Teacher
Status. It is important that you, as student teacher, recognise that
school teachers have a duty to both you and the pupils, but that their
overriding responsibility is to the profession and, through it, to the
pupils.

Science teachers are often seen as a race apart. Many science teachers
spend their breaks and lunch times in groups of like-minded individuals
discussing issues or trying out experiments. The tradition of coffee in
the prep. room is strong. In most schools you are made welcome as a
member of the science team; this is important as you are not isolated and
communication is enhanced. There is, however, a danger in following
this pattern every day because it can cut you off from the wider body of
staff. Try to balance allegiance to the science team with your need to
know and understand the whole school.

School life is hectic and all staff are working under pressure; staff
teach to the bell and you must plan your lessons with that fact in mind
and understand that staff cannot stay talking to you after the bell, except
by arrangement. Try not to ask staff for help at inappropriate times, e.g.
when they are supervising a class practical.

TASK 1.2 YOUR COURSE HANDBOOK

Locate and read your course handbook and the school staff handbook.
Identify the advice given about developing relationships in the school
with science staff and other staff. Locate the statements of standards
you are expected to use to describe and monitor your progress. Discuss these statements with your tutors and clarify the ways in which
you are expected to use them.

Your passage from student to teacher

Most students choose to follow a postgraduate course of training. For
some, the course is an extension of three years' undergraduate work.
Nevertheless, a majority of candidates for an initial teacher education
course have worked or done other jobs. Whatever your background, you
arrive on the course in the expectation that tutors (at least for some of
your time) teach you and that you learn. You have expectations about
your role as student and of your tutors as your teachers. Simultaneously
you have to learn to act as a teacher towards pupils in school. In other

words, there is a duality in your roles on the course. You are required to act as both teacher and student in the same institution. If you pause to think about your relationship to your tutors as, e.g. an undergraduate, you quickly realise that a similar relationship might exist between your pupils and you; see also Chapter 13.

As a colleague once put it, 'As a student, the teachers were "them" and we were "us"; as a school teacher you become the "them" and the pupils take on the "us" role.' Handling the 'them and us' transition for yourself during the course can be a difficult task, carrying with it notions of emerging professionalism and responsibility. It is important to realise that a course of professional training requires you to adopt more and more responsibility for your own learning and to act with the same responsibility that you will *expect* of the pupils in your charge in your first post. For example, the same rules apply to your course work as do to pupils' homework!

This book is designed to help you through the transition from graduate scientist to student teacher to qualified teacher. It is a process of personal development in which you will find out a lot about yourself both as a teacher and as an individual. The important factor is that you should play a large part in the developmental process.

ABOUT THIS BOOK

This book is designed to help you address some of the demands made on you during your period of initial teacher education by providing supporting knowledge, theory and ideas for practice, all interspersed with a range of tasks to help you link practice to theory.

School based initial teacher education (ITE) courses do not leave much time for students to concentrate on the theory and practice of education as an academic exercise. There is some strength to this approach because it enables you to understand the issues and problems of teaching and learning at first hand before turning to explanations. We suggest that theory should arise out of practice and that theory before any practice is of limited value. When the need arises, you can turn to discussion, reading and reflection to get other views of the problem. Most problem areas have been written about and researched, and you should become familiar with some of the literature.

A difficulty with the school based course is that, as a rule, teachers do not have the time to discuss teaching and learning problems at length, largely because of timetable restrictions and often because teachers have not the time or opportunity to keep up with the literature or the product of research. It is the role of the IHE to provide the link between **theory** and **practice**, to give you the opportunity to read key documents and books that relate directly to your teaching and learning. In part, this is what this book and the generic book *Learning to Teach in the Secondary School* are for.

Your ITE course provides you with a reading list and we suggest further readings at the end of each chapter. You should start to develop your own theory of teaching and learning through your own teaching, organised reading, structured observations, focused lectures from tutors and teachers and, most importantly, from taking time to reflect on your experiences. The tasks in this book are designed to provide focused opportunities for inquiry and reflection arising from the school context. There is a danger in school of taking on more and more jobs as though you are a full member of staff. We suggest that you keep time for yourself to broaden your understanding. More teaching, by itself, does not lead to a better teacher.

Following this introduction, Chapter 2 addresses two issues: first the nature of science and its place in the school curriculum and second the Science National Curriculum in England and Wales. In Scotland, a different system of education is in operation, but the principles concerned with teaching and learning that are examined in the remaining chapters apply equally well throughout the United Kingdom. Chapters 3, 4 and 5 address how to get started in your teaching and include lesson planning; each has relevance to all students learning to teach science. The following chapter is on Special Needs and includes a large section on differentiation. The remaining chapters are designed for you to widen your teaching, once classroom management and teaching have become secure. We have taken the view that you cannot attend to pupil learning until you are comfortable in the classroom.

The chapters in this book can be dipped into for information and advice and read separately. We do not expect the book to be read sequentially from cover to cover. We do, however, expect you to integrate the different ideas addressed in each chapter in order to build a coherent but personal teaching style and to accumulate a set of strategies to deploy as needed.

This book is part of a series. The generic book, *Learning to Teach in a Secondary School* (Capel, Leask and Turner, 1995), contains general information about teaching and learning and we make reference to it on numerous occasions. Where issues are dealt with in the generic book, you are referred to it for further information. We advise you to have both books as part of the resources for your course.

Each chapter has a set of objectives. Many objectives are realised through **tasks** that are to be carried out in school. The tasks are embedded in classroom practice and are one way in which we link practice to theory. Most completed tasks need to be shared with someone else, such as a tutor, other student teachers in school or a group of science students, e.g. in your college; most benefit is gained by sharing data and information and by responding together to its implications.

Each chapter has a summary and suggestions for **further reading** that contain several references. The full references to all books and articles cited in the text can be found in the **bibliography**. Appendix 5 contains a list of **addresses** of science organisations and associations that support education.

Finally, in Appendices 1–4 are the standards expected of Newly Qualified Teachers (NQTs) in England and Wales, Scotland and Northern Ireland. An expanded and modified list of knowledge, skills and attitudes required of science NQTs is given in Appendix 4, designed to help you interpret the statutory standards.

KNOWLEDGE, SKILLS AND ATTITUDES REQUIRED OF NEWLY QUALIFIED TEACHERS

All students qualifying as trained teachers are expected to have reached certain standards to enable them to take up a first teaching post. These standards are expressed as generic terms for all teachers and need to be interpreted for subject specific teaching. The standards (sometimes referred to as competences) are set out in Appendices 1, 2 and 3, for England and Wales (Department for Education and Employment (Circular 10/97), 1997a), for Scotland (Scottish Department for Education, 1993) and Northern Ireland (Department of Education Northern Ireland, 1996). The standards identify the minimum knowledge, skills and attitudes you are expected to achieve by the end of your course and are used to report on your development as a teacher, through observations of your practical teaching, through your response to working in school, in your IHE and by examination of the quality of your written assignments.

Throughout your course you should, with the help of your tutors, monitor your own performance on a regular basis against the appropriate requirements. As an aid to this analysis of your teaching performance, we include an expanded set of statements of the knowledge, skills and attitudes needed by science teachers now and later in their career (Appendix 4) (Frost and Jennings, 1995). These statements are not statutory requirements to be met by student teachers; nor are they intended to be used to prepare official reports of your progress. Furthermore, these statements may not meet in every detail the requirements of your particular course and you must refer to the guidance from your IHE or school.

The standards expected of NQTs described in Appendices 1, 2 and 3 provide a framework for the aims and objectives of your ITE course. The statements of standards provide a valuable way of focusing the evaluation of your lessons, of monitoring your development and for the construction of your Career Entry Profile. The documentation you receive from your IHE or school addresses the way in which the generic statements are to be interpreted in subject terms.

We suggest that monitoring your own development as a teacher and awareness of the stages of your progress are important skills for your professional development. At the end of your course your tutors recommend that you have the necessary knowledge, skills and attitudes to be awarded NQT status. However, this achievement is not an end in itself but more the beginning of a lifelong process. New contexts raise new challenges; new learning gives deeper insights – both of which lead to better teaching and improved pupil learning.

One of our aims for you is that, by the end of your course, you can make judgements about your teaching and seek ways to improve your performance. This reflective process must start now and not wait until you are deemed competent to teach by others. With the help of tutors and colleagues, we hope you develop the capacity to monitor your own teaching, i.e. to become an autonomous professional. Appendix 4 is designed to help you achieve that goal. The statements include many of skills exercised by good, experienced teachers and, as such, some skills are not expected of you.

How can you use such a list? The list is not a checklist of items to be ticked off as 'achieved'; the statements are not a hurdle in the race to become qualified. They can, we suggest, be used to focus discussion between you and your tutors as well as for self-monitoring. In addition, you can use the statements to:

- identify the components of a generic skill as it applies to science teaching. In the set of statements about 'Subject Knowledge', the generic skill is broken down into eight components. By using these detailed statements, you can recognise achievement, identify need and so plan development;
- provide targets for development;

- focus lesson planning. By choosing a small number of skills, you can seek to practise and develop them;
- focus the observation by your tutors;
- guide the reporting of your progress. Adopting this strategy allows the reporter to focus on agreed skills and not just on any skills that happen to interest him;
- shift the focus of your development from a low level, e.g. 'Class Management' to a higher level, e.g. to 'assessment and pupil learning'; see Assessment, Recording and Reporting (Ass1–Ass17). Development requires you to 'move on' and not be satisfied with a low level of performance;
- provide criteria for dialogue between you and your tutors;
- provide headings under which to evaluate your progress;
- provide headings under which to write your personal statement for your portfolio or Career Entry Profile.

Evaluation of personal progress can be hard work. It requires honesty on your part, trust in your tutors and teachers who observe you and confidence in their reports. You should be able to respond to critical comment in an optimistic and constructive manner and, at times, should challenge comment if you do not understand the evidence for it.

From time to time throughout this book we suggest that you check your achievements, or the responses to tasks, against the standards expected. Regular recording of progress enables you to recognise progress and simplifies your end of course requirement to write a personal profile or Career Entry Profile. Collecting evidence for your Profile should not be left until the end of the course.

GETTING STARTED

A fundamental requirement for you to start teaching science is to know some science. However charismatic a teacher you are, unless you know and understand the science you are teaching, there is little chance that your pupils will learn anything. We suggest that one of your first tasks is make an audit of personal knowledge related to the science curriculum you are expected to teach using **Task 1.3 Your personal confidence profile: science**. In this task, as set out below, the Science National Curriculum for England and Wales has been used. If you are involved in teaching a different curriculum, construct a modified table using the headings of your required curriculum.

TASK 1.3 YOUR PERSONAL CONFIDENCE PROFILE: SCIENCE

This task requires you to build up a picture of the science you feel you **can** teach now (Y), that which you **do not** feel able to teach (N) and the science about which you are **unsure** (U). Obtain a copy of the science curriculum you are expected to teach; in this example we use the Science National Curriculum for England and Wales (DFE, 1995b). Find the section Programme of Study (PoS) for Key Stage 3 (pp. 15–23) and work with the three subject areas listed in the table below. Code your responses Y, N or U as above.

Section of the PoS	Life processes and living things					Materials and their properties					Physical processes				
	Life processes and cell activity	Humans as organisms	Green plants as organisms	Variation, classification and inheritance	Living things and their environment	Classifying materials	Changing materials	Patterns of behaviour			Electricity and magnetism	Forces and motion	Light and sound	The Earth and beyond	Energy sources and transfer
KS3 PoS; Key: Y, N or U															
KS4 PoS; Key: Y, N or U															
Other comment															

Source: adapted from *Secondary PGCE Subject Handbook, Science, 1996/7*, Institute of education, University of London

Note: two sections of the Programme of Study are omitted here.

1 The area known as Experimental and Investigative Science, often referred to as Sc1.
2 A set of five over-arching ideas, referred to Sc0. Find out where these over-arching ideas are introduced in the subject area above.

Using the knowledge profile you have generated, identify the extent to which you meet the criteria under 'Subject Knowledge' in Appendix 4.

We suggest that you use the resulting profile to check your 'subject knowledge' and to identify possible targets for improving your science knowledge. One strategy is to ensure that you teach aspects of a topic of which you are uncertain. Another is to set aside time during the year to address deficiencies. The important point is to recognise gaps in your knowledge and to plan a way to plug them. You cannot remedy all deficiencies, so, armed with the audit, set modest but achievable targets for yourself at different times during your education year.

Carry out the audit again at least once in the year. Sometimes the ignorance you professed turns out to be less severe than you imagined. On the other hand, teaching does search out your understanding, and secure areas of knowledge sometimes become frail in front of perceptive pupils. We suggest you carry out an audit prior to a job interview and again when you prepare you Career Entry Profile.

SUMMARY

This chapter has drawn attention to some fundamental questions about science education, such as why should science be taught to all pupils. Although your focus in the next six to nine months is the transition from survival in the classroom to that of effective teacher, these questions do not go away but will emerge in different ways as you grow to understand more about how science is received by your pupils. When we teach science, we convey both knowledge and our position towards it. Our pupils pick this up and are influenced by it. Thus, having a view about why you are teaching science is fundamental to the enterprise.

When you start to teach in secondary school, perhaps having recently graduated in science, a common experience is the identification of the appropriate level and depth of knowledge to select for each lesson. This experience is true for many experienced teachers, although time and honest evaluation of your teaching improves that judgement. Your increased understanding of the National Curriculum assists in this process, as does a proper attention to assessment. We address assessment in Chapter 8. Understanding the relationship between teaching, learning and assessment is a crucial factor in improving your teaching and the pupils' learning.

Many teachers, especially student teachers, frequently try to teach in the manner that they were taught, especially in moments of stress. It is important to remember that behaviours change, that the lives of your pupils may be quite different from your life as a pupil. Other factors that widen the differences between your memory of school and those of your pupils include culture, economic factors as well as more obvious gender and ethnic differences. Awareness of what these differences mean in the classroom can sometimes be a shock, but an early lesson to learn is that we must teach pupils as they are and not as you would wish them to be.

Some of you reading this book may never have experienced schools in the United Kingdom. Others may have worked in the UK for some years but received their own education in another country. The same message applies: get to know your pupils as quickly as possible and teach them as they are. If you do not have experience of schools in the UK, you may wish to talk to your tutor early on in the course in order to anticipate the differences you can expect to encounter and how to respond to them. Reading how others have coped with the PGCE year is helpful (Hazell, 1996).

At some point in the course you may feel exhausted, perhaps desperate enough to feel like giving up the course. It is usually at this point that a child thanks you for an enjoyable lesson. A moment's appreciation can make everything seem worthwhile again. Pupils do have the capacity to surprise and can make the worst day seem not so bad after all. We hope too that this book may help you on a bad day.

FURTHER READING

Black, P. (1993) 'The purposes of science education' in R. Hull (ed.) *The Science Teachers' Handbook: Secondary*, Hemel Hempstead: Simon & Schuster for the Association for Science Education, pp. 6–22.
A wide ranging discussion of how the science curriculum came to be where it is and the ways in which it can be taken forward.

Dixon, B. (1989) *The Science of Science: Changing the Way we Think*, London: Cassell.
A short but packed book that covers many aspects of science and the scientific tradition. Helpful in thinking about what science can and cannot do. Chapter 9, 'Objectivity and subjectivity', is a useful place to start.

Moon, B. and Shelton Mayes, A. (1991) *Teaching and Learning in the Secondary School*, Buckingham: Open University Press.
This book is a series of many short articles that includes issues of teacher effectiveness and raising the achievement of pupils. Many of the issues addressed continue to be important and significant for your immediate future as a teacher.

Woolnough, B. (1994) *Effective Science Teaching*, Buckingham: Open University Press.
    The chapter 'Aims and unresolved tensions' discusses the aims of science education and celebrates good practice. There is a useful discussion on the contrast between 'education *in* science' and 'education *through* science'.

2 The place of science in the curriculum

INTRODUCTION

This chapter introduces you to the Science National Curriculum and provides information about its development, introduction and modification. It discusses the aims of science education and helps you to develop a framework with which to interpret the principles underlying the science curriculum. You are introduced to some factors affecting recent changes in the school curriculum and to some relationships between science and other subjects in the National Curriculum.

OBJECTIVES

By the end of this chapter you should be:

- considering how your views of the nature of science affect your teaching methods;
- informed about the recent history of developments of the science curriculum;
- able to understand the aims of science in the National Curriculum and its general principles;
- aware of the place of science in the National Curriculum;
- informed of current developments in the vocational curriculum;
- aware of links across the curriculum.

THE NATURE OF SCIENCE

Science is a highly successful human activity, a defining feature of our culture, ranking alongside the achievements of art, music and literature. A knowledge of the arts is regarded by many people as a mark of the educated person, but it is not obvious that a knowledge of science is similarly regarded.

When you start to teach science, you automatically convey to your pupils some aspects of the nature of science, such as how scientific knowledge is gained and how it is valued in relation to other knowledge. Science is characterised as a particular way of thinking about and understanding the natural world. Scientific knowledge is a product of the human urge to be curious about our environment, to explore and be able to explain the world in a rational way and to have control over the environment. The scientist tries to explain how things happen and why the world appears to be the way it is. By explaining the behaviour of events and things in the world, the scientist wishes to be able to predict future behaviour. From a basis of observation and experiment, scientists try to generate theories about the natural world that stand up to experience. Scientific theories are tentative, by contrast with the foundations for religious belief which are not tentative nor subject to testing in the same way that scientific knowledge is tested. In this sense, science and religion differ, concerned as they are with different aspects of human experience.

Science has been practised by many people throughout world history. Human beings from all cultures now and in the past have, from necessity, observed phenomena in the natural world and used them to predict future behaviour. People in earlier cultures held and used theories about their observations of the world; their survival was probably the driving force to acquire that knowledge (Dunbar, 1995, p. 47). This earlier science may not be recognisable as the highly developed, technologically based, focused activity it is now; in the Western world the Renaissance and the Industrial Revolution changed the scale and purpose of intellectual inquiry that is now science. The current achievements of science and technology are immense but rest upon the achievements of earlier cultures, notably within Greek, Chinese, Arabic and Islamic societies (see, e.g. Dixon, 1989; Horton, 1993; Huff, 1993; Reiss, 1993; Ronan, 1966; and Ronan and Needham, 1978/1981).

Scientific knowledge goes beyond the ordinary, common-sense knowledge that most people have of the world. Scientists make generalisations or create general laws, such as Le Chatelier' s Principle or Newton's Laws of Motion. Scientists conceptualise the natural and made world through theoretical models that try to explain the nature of matter and how it interacts. Scientists seek models that apply to a wide range of phenomena and then test those generalisations through experience and by experiment to check their predictive power and their reliability as descriptions of the world. Some scientific theories conflict with common-sense experience (see Figure 2.1).

Figure 2.1 Some science theories conflict with common-sense experience
Source: sketches by Janet Maxwell

Science has two aspects: the empirical aspect and the theoretical aspect. Empirical science includes collecting knowledge and developing procedures to investigate the world. Knowledge and procedures lead to further predictions that can be investigated, e.g. in order to widen the range of knowledge about the subject. The theoretical aspect comprises mental models described earlier; these lead to hypotheses that are tested by experiment.

Good theories embrace a wide range of phenomena, make the least number of assumptions in their formulation and lead to predictions that can be tested. Good theories are rich in opportunity for testing and inquiry, e.g. the particle theory of matter, the gene theory of inheritance and the theory of relativity, and may lead to discoveries of theoretical and practical importance. Theories often remain in favour, i.e. the basis for practice even when inconsistencies suggest that the theory may not be totally correct. Thus Newtonian mechanics remains the basis for much practical action, despite being superseded by the theory of relativity; the Newtonian view is a special case of the relativity applied to the macro world of falling objects and structures such as bridges. However, classical mechanics breaks down when applied to the micro world of atomic and sub-atomic particles. Thus discredited theories do not necessarily have to be discarded while they remain useful. For further discussion on the way in which science is practised see, e.g. Chalmers (1982); Dixon, (1989); Dunbar, (1995).

Some of the methods used by scientists are not exclusive to science, for example, historians also collect evidence and make hypotheses. Scientific procedures do not follow a formula, the scientific method, the use of which will guarantee sound knowledge or a solution to the problem. We suggest that you should not teach your pupils as though there is one, fixed scientific method.

Much of our scientific knowledge is reliable in the sense that it has stood up to repeated use and testing. Even some theories, which in principle are tentative and temporary and only useful while they continue to provide explanations of events, may be considered equally reliable. The Particle **Theory** of Matter is so successful that most scientists work on the assumption, quite rightly, that particles actually exist. However, you cannot see or weigh an atom, nor are we ever likely to.

It is not intended that you teach pupils about the philosophy of science; however, helping pupils to see the connections between the empirical and the theoretical aspects of science is part of your job as a science teacher. Pupils often describe as theory all the work in school science that is not practical. Such views are, perhaps, a consequence of the stereotypical view held by many people of the scientist as either engaged in some madcap experiment surrounded by tons of technology or reading large books containing inexplicable formulae and diagrams. The idea that scientists spend their time reading the works of other scientists, the better to understand their subject and to carry out their own experiments, does not seem to feature in the popular image of science, either in school or more widely. Teaching pupils to interrogate texts, journals and electronic data banks for knowledge and meaning is an important life skill as well as good science.

The science curriculum should portray science as it is, relating it to the day to day life of the pupil and revealing some of the interplay between science and society. The interplay can, for example, reveal changes in the cultural assumptions of the population. For example, since the 1960s the emergence of successful heart transplant surgery has changed the views of many people about the nature of this organ; however, for some the heart remains a special organ that should not be operated on as are other organs of the human body (Chaudhary, 1997). One aim of science education is to produce a society that understands the relation of scientific knowledge to everyday knowledge or beliefs and can evaluate the differences.

Another aim for science education is to help pupils relate technology to science. Much of modern technology is a product of science. The development of some technologies can lead to new science; for example, thermodynamics arose from the need to understand the behaviour of gases in a steam engine, whereas pure science led the way to radio and television communication, through the work of Maxwell on the theory of electromagnetism (Dixon, 1989, pp. 28 and 31). Of equal importance to science teaching is enabling pupils to understand everyday technology such as central heating or ways of overcoming eye defects through spectacles or laser technology. In this way young people become confident users of technology as adults in an ability both to understand the technology and, where appropriate, to maintain it. Such an approach may well provide enhanced motivation for pupils and improve the uptake of science post 16.

The earlier versions of the Science National Curriculum had a one-sided view of scientific enquiry, emphasising hypothesis making and testing and the fair test at the expense of other practices. Should the science curriculum reflect the range and diversity of the work of scientists? Some scientists work at the frontiers of science, e.g. the fine structure of the atom; the origin of the universe; searching for a cause and mechanism for the transfer of mad cow disease to humans; a cure for cancer and AIDS. Other scientists widen our existing knowledge, e.g. mapping the human genome; producing smaller, faster and more reliable computer 'chips' and identifying safer chemicals to act as drugs. Many scientists apply science to problems, e.g. seeking ways to clear up oil pollution; developing a fuel cell for electric cars or overcoming the rejection of organ transplants by the human body. Scientists do not always make hypotheses, they may just play a hunch! The 1995 version of the Science National Curriculum has provided room for a variety of science investigations, but the crowded syllabus remains a problem.

Other scientists work in quality control using well-defined procedures developed on the basis of secure knowledge. Such work is essential to our quality of life, e.g. forensic science; monitoring water quality; testing materials for fire proof qualities; checking fungal types in hospital laboratories. Scientists working in these situations are not usually at the frontiers of science but must maintain high standards of performance, keep up to date and be alert for anomalies. After all, the discovery of penicillin was a chance affair, the significance of which was recognised by a prepared mind (Dixon, 1973, pp. 29–30).

Not all scientists carry out experiments in the conventional sense. Astronomers cannot set up experiments, arrange the system to suit themselves or control variables. They have to imagine and predict what might be happening out in space and, at great distances, devise a way of looking for evidence. Their work is different from laboratory based science. Yet other scientists never go near a laboratory but work with pencil and paper or computer, using the research of others to develop their theories. Important theoreticians were Einstein, who developed the Theory of Relativity in 1904 (Dixon, 1989, p. 22); Chandrasekhar, who, in 1928, predicted the existence of White Dwarf stars and for which in 1983 he was awarded the Nobel prize for physics (Dunbar, 1995, p. 30); and Hawking for his work on time and space (Hawking, 1988).

As intending teachers of science, it is important for you to begin to build a repertoire of stories of science, that can be used to enliven a lesson, to depict the human side of scientific progress, to provide relevance to your subject and to portray the diversity of practice. Raising such awareness contributes to the development of your philosophy of science. Children are fascinated by stories of scientists; to enliven your teaching you could use extracts of stories in class about Marie Curie for radioactivity, Louis Pasteur for aseptic surgery, Charles Drew who worked on blood groups (Haber, 1970) or the Piltdown Man hoax (Dixon, 1989, p. 82). You should start a database of references, including newspaper sources. A list of books that may be helpful in this task is given on pp. 41–2.

Science is a human endeavour. In which ever way you break down science into its component parts for teaching and assessing purposes, it is essentially a holistic activity, involving cognitive, manipulative and attitudinal skills. The problems chosen for enquiry, the methods adopted and the values guiding the practice of science are governed by the cultural context in which it occurs. The way science is used in society expresses the values of that society or a section of it. Attitudes as well as factual knowledge are imparted to your pupils when you teach science. You should begin consciously to develop your own picture of the scientific enterprise and to formulate your own philosophy of science in order to enrich and humanise the curriculum you teach.

Through education you can help your pupils to become more human (Pring, 1995, p. 125).

TASK 2.1 WHO IS A SCIENTIST?

Read the following extract and respond to the questions below.

Dr C spends his professional time inventing gadgets. He works for a firm of consulting scientists who solve problems brought to them by small manufacturing companies who cannot support staff of their own. Most problems are practical ones, such as how to prevent mould growing on a new type of plaster board; or how to detect errors on the semi-automatic production line making mechanical toys. Dr C's work bench is littered with wire, lumps of metal, meters, glassware and odds and ends. Typically he might be found fiddling with a light sensitive photo-cell which he is mounting inside a heat resistant shield to go inside a furnace at a local iron works. It is part of new system of temperature monitoring. He has had the gadget patented and it will shortly be manufactured by an associated company on a commercial basis.

Compare the work of Dr C with the work of other scientists you know. List the ways in which Dr C might be called a scientist.

Dr C might also be called an inventor, a technologist or a technician. In which ways do these labels overlap with that of 'scientist'?

Source: Dixon, 1989, p. 34

THE AIMS AND PURPOSES OF SCIENCE EDUCATION

Politicians, science educators, scientists, industrialists, teachers and governors frequently make statements about the aims of education and, sometimes, about the aims of science teaching. The Science National Curriculum has its own aims, as should your schemes of work and lesson plans. Science teaching should reflect the aims of the school and support other areas of teaching in the school. Science education offers a means of fulfilling many of the general educational aims of the school, that is, it is an 'education *through* science' as well as '*in* science'.

The aims of schooling and the aims of science education may appear to vary from school to school, depending on the ethos of the school and the needs of pupils. However, if you examine the various statements of aims of science education set out by different bodies or organisations, many common threads are revealed. One set of aims for science education developed by the Association for Science Education (ASE) is linked to general educational aims. They suggest that, through science education, learners should:

- acquire a set of personal and social values and abilities (intellectual and physical) to guide action through a variety of experiences;
- increase personal autonomy without infringing on the rights of others;
- establish and appreciate their personal identity and self esteem within the context of positive social and ethical relationships;
- discriminate between choices realising the possible consequences of action;
- recognise the relationship between the process of learning and the outcomes of learning.

(ASE, 1992, p. 5)

The ASE identified another set of aims for science education which enable the learner to:

- appreciate science as a human activity;
- understand how science operates;
- know and understand scientific concepts and principles;
- be scientific;
- relate scientific enquiry and action to other modes of human behaviour.

(ASE, 1992, p. 6)

Schools are about teaching and learning, enabling the learner to progress. Every school should have a worked out set of aims and objectives that identify ways to progress in learning. Your school provides you with a staff handbook and a science faculty handbook. In both of these you should find the aims of the school and the aims of the science department. An example of the aims of one school is set out below in Figures 2.2 and 2.3.

Your personal aims as a science teacher develop with experience and are moulded by understanding in more detail how the aims of your science department, the aims of your school and the aims of the Science National Curriculum are connected. The first steps in understanding these connections arise when you start to identify aims and objectives in your lesson plan. Lesson planning is discussed later in Chapter 4. For further discussion on school aims see Capel, Leask and Turner, 1995, Units 7.1 and 7.2.

Following the introduction of the National Curriculum, the aims of science education have narrowed in response to Standard Assessment Tasks (SATs) at the end of Key Stage 3 and the GCSE. Increasingly schools are judged by the number of pupils who reach or exceed the expected level at KS3 or five Grade A*–Cs in GCSE. The league tables, published in the national and local press, arising from comparisons of performances in these narrow areas of teaching and learning, have focused teachers' attention on teaching what is to be assessed, often at the expense of other attributes. Teaching is being driven by summative assessment.

The aims of the Science Faculty of Swakeleys School, shown in Figure 2.3, show the range of intentions that science teaching can aspire to and reflect, in part, the aims that the ASE promote.

A comparison of Figures 2.2 and 2.3 shows how the aims of the school and the science faculty are linked throughout. For example, both the school and the faculty value each individual, they both support equal opportunities and encourage every pupil to gain a sense of achievement from the learning process. Both set of aims encourage positive attitudes, values and skills.

To create a school community on equal opportunities in which each individual is valued and where learning will thrive so that girls will gain a sense of achievement from the learning process.

To provide a challenging and stimulating environment which will enable every girl to achieve the highest level of skills, knowledge and qualifications of which she is capable.

To teach self discipline and a sense of responsibility to self and others and to foster a commitment to excellence.

To widen the horizons of all our pupils to make them aware of the rich cultural diversity of our society and to prepare them for the wide variety of roles open to women in today's world.

To foster close links with the local community and to be flexible as an institution so as to evaluate and respond to new initiations both from the inside and outside the school.

(Staff Handbook, 1996, Swakeleys School)

Figure 2.2   The aims of Swakeleys School

To enable pupils to develop an understanding of key scientific concepts and ideas.

To teach pupils to have the necessary skills to be able to carry out scientific investigations.

To widen pupils' understanding of the relationship between science and society.

To encourage positive attitudes in pupils towards other people and the environment.

To assist pupils to see science as a human activity, and to help them to appreciate the nature of science.

To give pupils access to careers in science and teaching.

(*Science Faculty Handbook*, 1996, Swakeleys School)

Figure 2.3   The aims of the Science Faculty, Swakeleys School

Clarity about the aims of science teaching in your school and how the aims relate to whole school aims can make a difference to how you approach your teaching. Task 2.2 directs you to engage with the aims of your science department in your school.

TASK 2.2 EXPLORING THE LINKS BETWEEN THE AIMS OF YOUR SCHOOL AND THE SCIENCE DEPARTMENT

1   Read through the aims of your school and list them under these headings:

- what the school provides;
- the skills the pupils are expected to gain;
- the knowledge the pupils are expected to gain;
- the attitudes and values promoted;
- what the school expects of pupils;
- what the school expects of parents.

2   Compare the aims of your school with those of Swakeleys School. Identify differences between the aims of each school? Do any differences matter?

3   List the aims of your school science department under the same headings in exercise 1.

4   Identify where the aims of your science department:

- reflect directly the aims of the school;
- loosely connect with the aims of the school;

continued . . .

- go beyond the aims of the school;
- have no connection with the aims of your school.

5   Summarise your findings on one side of A4. Give a copy of the
    report to your subject supervisor. The report may be used in
    tutorial time with your subject supervisor or with other student
    teachers in a group seminar.

THE NATIONAL CURRICULUM

Science education in England and Wales: recent background

The growth of science education in schools this century has been characterised by more and more pupils gaining access to science education
and the growth and demise of general science in relation to the separate
sciences. As the school leaving age has been raised, to 15 in 1946 and to
16 in 1971, so have the demands on curriculum developers to produce
more and relevant curricula for older pupils with a widening spread of
performance.

By the mid-1960s, the comprehensive system had been introduced
through government legislation. New demands were made on science
teaching, notably trying to develop science courses for all pupils in
schools with a comprehensive population. One way forward was the
development of integrated science curricula, which in many ways was a
return to a new form of general science. Many integrated science
courses were developed, both for able pupils and for less able pupils.
Increasingly these courses included the ways in which science was used
in society and carried a technological dimension. By the early 1980s,
broad balanced science courses of an integrated nature were well established in many state schools. At the same time, concern was expressed
again about the unevenness of provision for pupils. Issues of equity
were becoming urgent, for example the way in which many girls were
being denied access to the science curriculum through institutional policies and disproportionate numbers of ethnic minority pupils were not
succeeding at school. These issues, together with the effect of the second industrial revolution and the comparisons made between the performance of UK pupils and pupils in other countries, led to an intense
period of debate and blueprints for reform. For further discussion of
the development of science education, see Ingle and Jennings (1981);
Jenkins (1979); Jennings (1992).

The need for reform

In October 1976, Sir James Callaghan, the then Prime Minister, spoke on education at Ruskin College, Oxford. The speech became a landmark in shaping the education policy in the two decades that followed. In the speech, Callaghan emphasised the need to ensure greater relevance in education and to prepare future generations for life.

In 1979, a survey carried out by HM Inspectors of Schools (Department for Education and Science [DES], 1979) showed that few pupils received a broad science education in years 10 and 11 of secondary school, that is, an education that covered important aspects of biology, chemistry and physics. Indeed, 9 per cent of boys and 17 per cent of girls did not study any science in these years, while a further 50 per cent of boys and 60 per cent of girls took only one of the sciences. About 30 per cent of boys and 10 per cent of girls studied two science subjects. A further 10 per cent of boys and 5 per cent of girls followed all three science subjects, often at the expense of an overall curriculum that was broad and balanced.

There was much public criticism and discussion by many organisations concerned with education or with an interest in an effective science education. The discussion centred on possible ways forward for a science curriculum. In particular, the Association for Science Education published proposals for a framework for the science curriculum and, with DFE support, launched the Secondary Science Curriculum Review. This exercise involved many practising teachers and led to policy guidelines and imaginative curriculum materials (ASE, 1981).

By 1985, a remarkable consensus had been achieved, involving various government bodies, including the DFE, together with the Royal Society, many science teachers (the ASE) and the School Inspectorate (HMI) who in that year published the ground breaking document *Science 5–16: A Statement of Policy* (DES, 1985a). The event marked the first occasion this century in which central government laid down a policy for the teaching of science in maintained schools. Furthermore, the traditional autonomy of teachers to identify the curriculum had been removed (Jennings, 1992). The science policy statement mirrored the contents of a broad educational policy statement issued by central government and published earlier in the year (DES, 1985b). It highlighted the philosophy behind a national curriculum and was well received and laid the foundations for the National Curriculum. The DES also produced a white paper entitled *Better Schools* that identified measures to raise standards at all levels of ability (DES, 1985c) and emphasised the government's intention to obtain the best return for its investment in education and the increased accountability by schools. The consequences of those decisions are still being worked out.

THE ERA, THE NATIONAL CURRICULUM AND THE SCIENCE CURRICULUM

In 1988, the proposals of the Secretary of State for Education and Science and the Secretary of State for Wales were announced through the publication of *Science in the National Curriculum* (DES, 1988b). This document contained Attainment Targets and Programmes of Study in science, having a statutory status under the Education Act 1988. The Act introduced a continuous curriculum for all pupils aged 5–16. For the first time this century, legislation gave pupils an entitlement to science as part of their general education.

Aims of the Science National Curriculum

Teachers within a science faculty in state maintained schools have to use the National Curriculum as a framework for teaching science. The aims of the science curriculum within the National Curriculum are based on several principles related to the policy document *Science 5–16* (DES, 1985a); see Figure 2.4.

The Science National Curriculum introduces your pupils to basic scientific concepts and it is your task to relate the concepts to the pupils' interests and daily experiences. The curriculum should help your pupils to understand the world about them by encouraging mental and physical interaction with it. The learning experiences of your pupils should stimulate their curiosity and appeal to both boys and girls and to pupils from all cultural backgrounds.

The way in which the curriculum is expressed in schools is the responsibility of the science faculty. The Science National Curriculum attempts to show progression of ideas described in part through the Programme of Study and the Attainment Targets; see below. In this sense it reflects a spiral curriculum. In 1960, Bruner expressed the idea that scientific ideas and generalisations might be taught at different levels of generality and abstraction to pupils of different ages (or development) (Bruner, 1960). He gives the example of young children playing on a see-saw. At first they have only an elementary grasp of the laws of leverage; gradually they come to see how by change of weight and position the balance is upset. Later such children are able to explain the system using practical knowledge. Still later, they are able to explain the system using a

Science (is) for all (pupils).
The curriculum should have:

- breadth, content drawn from a range of sciences;
- balance, as between the various science disciplines;
- relevance, to the present and future lives of pupils.

Pupils should have access to the curriculum and be taught according to their age and abilities, i.e. schools should provide:

- differentiation (differentiated teaching methods);
- equal opportunities (access to the curriculum).

Pupils are entitled to expect:

- continuity (between phases of schooling);
- progression (in their learning).

There should be:

- links across the whole school curriculum;
- flexibility in, and varied methods of, teaching and learning.

Figure 2.4   Features of the Science National Curriculum
Source: based on DES, 1985a

mathematical model. The development of scientific knowledge and understanding in young people requires, first, an attempt to understand the general laws through which one might see order and system in an otherwise chaotic world of experience; second, the development of the necessary enquiry skills and the habit of testing the generalisations against experience; and third, a grasp of the models that have proved important in our capacity to make sense of the world.

There is a case, therefore, to identify key ideas to be studied by all pupils in order to understand the physical and living world and to express those ideas at different levels of sophistication in the spiral curriculum. Examples of key ideas include energy, electricity, particles, structure of materials, cells and cell processes and diversity. This is the challenge to science teaching that it has not as yet solved, particularly if you, as a scientist, try to remain faithful to the scientific explanation of events.

Your science lessons should increase pupils' knowledge and understanding of science and, at the same time, encourage them to develop positive attitudes to themselves and each other. The attitudes to be promoted include:

- co-operation with others;
- creativity and inventiveness;
- critical reflection;
- curiosity;
- open-mindedness;
- perseverance;
- respect for evidence;
- sensitivity to the living and non living environment;
- willingness to tolerate uncertainty.

(DES, 1988b, p. 9)

The ideas listed above identify the ideals expressed by generations of science teachers. They are goals to which you should aspire. Ideals are not easy to apply and sustain every day in the varied and busy contexts of classrooms. In the same way that you need a philosophy of science to help you to justify the way you teach science, so too you need ideals representing the hopes you have for your pupils and towards which you work. Without such purposes, teaching could become merely a technical task of curriculum translation and delivery.

TASK 2.3 SCIENCE EDUCATION AND THE AIMS OF THE NATIONAL CURRICULUM

The Education Reform Act of 1988 described the statutory duties of a teacher in this way: 'The curriculum of a maintained school must promote the spiritual, moral, cultural, mental and physical development of pupils and of society; and prepare pupils for the opportunities, responsibilities and experiences of adult life.' (ERA, 1988)

In which ways do the aims and objectives for science teaching of your science department link with these aims of the ERA? Take a unit of work from a Key Stage and look for specific references to the broad aims of the National Curriculum described above.

Structure of the Science National Curriculum

A key feature of the National Curriculum is 'continuity and progression'. The curriculum spans the primary and secondary phase of schooling, and connections between the two phases are critically important for the pupil as she passes through compulsory schooling. Each phase of schooling has two Key Stages. The Key Stages relate to the ages of pupils, as shown in Table 2.1.

Table 2.1   National Curriculum: ages and Key Stages

Phase	Key Stage	Age/year
Primary/Infant	1	5–7
Primary/Junior	2	8–10
Secondary	3	11–14
Secondary	4	15–16

The primary phase of schooling spans ages 5–11 and the secondary phase starts at 11+ years. For further details about the National Curriculum see Capel, Leask and Turner (1995, Unit 7.3).

The content of the Science National Curriculum allows for progression in both the range and depth of content. There are several features of the science curriculum that reveal this progression. These features are the Programmes of Study (PoS); the Standard Assessment Tasks (SATs); the Attainment Targets (ATs) with associated level descriptions; and the Non-Statutory Orders.

The secondary school science curriculum is covered by Key Stages 3 and 4 of the National Curriculum. Each Key Stage has a PoS which defines the principles and broad content of the curriculum and is the basis for school curriculum planning. The broad principles are sometimes referred to as Sc0, which is followed by more detailed description of what is to be taught to pupils in each of four areas. These are:

- Experimental and investigative science – Sc1
- Life and living processes – Sc2
- Materials and their properties – Sc3
- Physical processes – Sc4

Earth science is contained in Sc3 and 'the Earth's place in the universe' is in Sc4.

At KS4 there is a double science and a single science curriculum, each with a Programme of Study. Double science uses roughly twice the curriculum time as single science. The single science course is expected to be as rigorous as the double science course but with less content and is intended for a minority of pupils who may have good reason to spend time on other subjects.

In some schools, at the end of Key Stage 3, pupils have to choose from single and double science as a course to study during Key Stage 4. Such a choice can clearly disadvantage some pupils who, for whatever reason, choose wrongly at 14 years of age. Task 2.4 invites you to inquire more closely into this aspect of the National Curriculum in your own school. In 1994, the percentage of the year 11 cohort entering for Double Award science was about 77 per cent, for the Single Award, 12 per cent and the remaining pupils spread evenly between biology, chemistry and physics (OFSTED, 1995, pp. 27–39); see also Chapter 9.

TASK 2.4 SINGLE SCIENCE, DOUBLE SCIENCE AND THE SEPARATE SCIENCES: WHO DOES WHICH, AND WHY?

The ERA gave all pupils an entitlement to a science education from 5–16. Under that legislation it is possible to provide pupils with a choice of three separate science subjects, a single science or a double science course. What effect has this choice had on the post-16 opportunities for pupils? See also Chapter 9 for further discussion.

For Year 10 science classes (Key Stage 4) in your school find out

- the different types of science courses available;
- how pupils are directed into each type of course and which pupils end up where (you could consider the following factors when identifying pupils: their performance [achievement], gender, ethnicity and behaviour);
- what science qualification rules govern entry to A level science and similar courses in your school or the local sixth form college?

Compare your findings with those of other student teachers in other schools. The findings could be made the basis of a tutorial in college. See OFSTED, 1995, p. 27.

Do all pupils have equal access to science education or science dependent careers?

Pupils are assessed by **Standard Assessment Tasks** at the end of Key Stage 3 and by the GCSE at the end of Key Stage 4. The reporting of pupil assessment at KS3 uses **level descriptions** associated with four ATs; see DFE, 1995b, pp. 50–57. The four ATs focus on the four subject areas of the science curriculum, described above.

Each of the four ATs attempts to describe progression through that subject area of the science curriculum. At the end of Key Stages, teachers are required to identify the appropriate level description for their pupils in each of the four ATs. One of the more difficult tasks for secondary science teachers is to define pupil performance and actions at Key

Stage 3 by a level description. Many school science departments now keep a portfolio of examples of pupil work which maps pupils' work on to the level descriptions. In addition, pupils transferring from primary school to secondary school at the end of Key Stage 2 will bring with them statements of achievement including level descriptions.

Assessment by external examinations is supplemented by teacher based assessment. Teachers are expected to contribute to the assessment of pupil achievement in public examinations by up to 20 per cent of the marks. See also Chapter 9. In addition, teachers report to parents, at least annually. For both of these purposes teachers can report attainment by using level descriptions. Legally teachers have to report to parents using level descriptions at the end of a Key Stage.

There are eight 'level descriptions' plus an additional level of 'exceptional performance'. Level 1 is the lowest level; level 8 is beyond the range of most 14-year-old pupils. Since the review of the National Curriculum (Dearing, 1994), eight levels were recommended instead of the original ten. The reporting of pupil attainment at Key Stage 4 continues to be through the GCSE *grade* system.

Progress through the levels is slow, about one level per two years of schooling, and pupil development is not easy to demonstrate to pupils or parents. The spread of levels found in an age cohort emphasises the range of performance shown by pupils. In 1996, at the end KS3 tests (SATs), 26 per cent of the Year 9 cohort gained a level 4 award, 35 per cent level 5 and 17 per cent level 6. That is two-thirds of pupils are working at levels 4 and 5 (SCAA, 1996). A range of three levels can represent an age range of six years. These factors serve to emphasise the importance of differentiation in your teaching methods and identifying individual pupil progress in order to sustain motivation.

Finally, attention should be drawn to the performance of the notional average pupil at the end of Key Stage 4. As a student teacher, you need to adjust to the fact that the average performance of pupils at Key Stage 4, expressed in GCSE grades, is below that of a grade C, the lowest benchmark used by OFSTED for a 'good pass'. By the age of 16 years the range of performance of pupils in a comprehensive school can be very wide.

The statutory order for the science curriculum represents a limited definition and description of science education. Further details of the development of the Science National Curriculum can be found in Jennings (1992). The Dearing moratorium on change in the National Curriculum means that a much needed period of review and thought is taking place over the five years from 1995. The process of review has

TASK 2.5 GETTING TO KNOW YOUR NATIONAL CURRICULUM

1   Obtain a copy of the Science National Curriculum (DFE, 1995b). Using the section 'Contents', page iii, make sure you know:

- the structure of the curriculum as laid out;
- the meaning of terms Key Stage, Programme of Study, Attainment Targets and Level Descriptions.

2   Read first the section 'Level descriptions' on p. 49 of *Science in the National Curriculum* (DFE, 1995b). Then choose one **Attainment Target** (see DFE, 1995b, pp. 50–7) and find a **Level Description** for the achievement of the majority of pupils at the end of Key Stage 3. Link this description to the appropriate **subject matter to be taught** at Key Stage 3 using the PoS (DFE, 1995b, pp. 14–23).

3   Your first teaching experience involves you in teaching Key Stage 3. Select a subject area related to your own specialist subject, e.g. if you are a chemist choose 'Materials and their properties'. Now select a topic from the subject area, e.g. 'classifying material' (DFE, 1995b, p. 19) and identify the types of classification to be taught at KS3. Compare the type of classification required at KS3 for this topic with that required for the same topic at KS2 and KS4.

Describe the progression in ideas and understanding of 'classifying material' required at the three Key Stages. Where in the curriculum does classification become theoretical (based on a model of matter) instead of operational (based on directly observable properties)?

started, see, for example, Millar (1996) and Macaskill and Ogborn (1996). You should keep abreast of these developments through, for example, the publications of the Association for Science Education.

Science and the vocational curriculum – an introduction

The need for more vocational courses was recognised when the National Curriculum was designed in 1988. The National Council for Vocational Qualifications (NCVQ) was established in 1986 and provided a national framework to replace other vocational qualifications awarded by The Royal Society of Arts, the City and Guilds, the Business and Technology Education Council and other Industrial Training Boards.

The report *Learning to Succeed* highlighted a study that compared the vocational qualifications of young people in France, Germany and Britain (National Commission for Education, 1993, p. 275). The study showed that in 1978 in Germany, no fewer than two-thirds of the labour force held a certificate for a recognised craft qualification compared to one-third of the British labour force at a similar level. It showed that the gap has widened since 1978 and that in France in the 1980s, unlike Britain, vocational qualifications were on the increase.

However, changes have taken place in Britain in the 1990s. A government white paper *Education and Training for the 21st Century* (DFE/ED, 1991) established the need for more vocational courses and introduced the National Vocational Qualification (NVQ) and the General National Vocational Qualification (GNVQ). The NVQs are designed for people in work or undergoing work related training.

The GNVQ provides an institutional based qualification intermediate between the General Certificate in Education Advanced level qualification (GCE A level) and the NVQ. The GNVQ was offered at three levels: Foundation, Intermediate and Advanced. The Foundation level is broadly equivalent to two GCSEs at grades D–G and the Intermediate level is equivalent to four to five Grade A*–C GCSEs. The GNVQ Advanced level qualification is said to be equal to two GCE A levels. The courses on offer included business, health and social care, manufacturing, travel and tourism, catering, engineering and science. Both Intermediate and Advanced GNVQs became available nationally in 1994. (For further discussion of the general issues concerning post-16 education, qualifications and training, see Lucas, 1996.)

The GNVQ Foundation science course was piloted in 1994–95 (Solomon, 1996). In secondary schools, the National Curriculum science courses at Key Stage 4 are assessed by the GCSE which restricts the introduction of GNVQ science courses for pupils under 16. In 1996, new vocational courses called 'part one GNVQ' were designed for 14–16-year-old pupils and piloted in schools (Major, 1997). Some resource materials for students and teachers following GNVQ science courses have been published (Nuffield Science in Practice, 1994a and 1994b).

Many schools have made effective links with industry by means of schemes such as 'Neighbourhood Engineers' (Engineering Council, 1992) as well as through work experience programmes. These links provide pre-vocational experience and stimulate learning. Science lessons are more interesting if built on pupils' experiences outside school and may give pupils a perspective of the work of scientists. You should know by the end of your education year the vocational courses offered to pupils in your school as well as those more widely available. You should also be aware of the industrial links and the work experience schemes in your school. Opportunities to widen your knowledge of these vocational features of your school may arise in your second school placement.

Science and the cross-curricular themes

The 1988 Education Reform Act gives responsibility to schools to provide a broad and balanced curriculum that:

- promotes the spiritual, moral, cultural, mental and physical developments of pupils at school and in society; and
- prepares such pupils for the opportunities, responsibilities and experiences of adult life.

The National Curriculum is largely a curriculum of academic subjects. The drive to provide courses in the academic subjects that comprise the National Curriculum did not pay much attention to these aims, neither was it clear how a subject based National Curriculum achieved those aims (O'Hear and White, 1991). The National Curriculum Council (NCC), set up after the ERA 1988, was charged with the responsibility of helping schools to broaden their curriculum to include these key aims of the National Curriculum. The NCC identified a framework of ideas into which these aims were to be fitted in the 20 per cent of time remaining after the statutory curriculum had been constructed. There were three elements in this framework, identified as themes, skills and dimensions.

The **themes** were to help prepare pupils to take an active and informed part in adult life. The themes were:

- Economic and industrial understanding;
- Careers education and guidance;
- Health education;
- Education for citizenship;
- Environmental education.

The **skills** were viewed as cross-curricular elements, permeating the whole curriculum:

- Communication;
- Numeracy;
- Study skills;
- Problem solving;

- Personal and social development;
- Information Technology.

Finally, **dimensions** were identified with aspects of personal and social development that include positive attitudes towards cultural diversity, gender equality and people with disability. The promotion of equal opportunities was expected to permeate the curriculum and was seen as the responsibility of all teachers.

Following the publication of the Science National Curriculum, there have been five changes and versions of the science curriculum (Jennings, 1992; Woolnough, 1994). Schools and subject staff have had little time to consider, much less introduce and develop, the themes, skills and dimensions identified above. However, many schools have a timetabled personal and social development curriculum (PSE). Information Technology has received high priority in the last decade, both in schools and from central government, but its use is still limited. It is interesting to notice that the skills identified by the NCC are similar to the core skills central to the GNVQ courses.

Many themes find a place in the science curriculum, and four themes are discussed in Chapter 11.

SUMMARY

The Science National Curriculum defines the minimum content that pupils aged 5–16 should be taught in England and Wales. As a statutory requirement for maintained schools, but not independent schools, it gives an entitlement to pupils of a broad balanced science education covering content and processes of science. Transforming the Science National Curriculum into a teaching scheme remains a major challenge to science teachers. The multiple changes that occurred to the National Curriculum have stopped with a period of stability in the curriculum until 2000, by which time evidence will have accumulated about the strengths and weaknesses of the current curriculum and its interpretation. We have noted earlier that discussions are already underway about science for the year 2000 and beyond.

An important task for you during your training year is to know and understand the Science National Curriculum, the way it is assessed and how to improve and develop your own scientific knowledge to meet the teaching demands. Knowing your way about the science curriculum is an important competence for you to master by the end of your training year. For further help, refer to the list of standards required of newly qualified teachers (Appendices 1–3) and identify the level of your development with the help of Appendix 4.

For further guidance on the teaching of the Science National Curriculum see *Science: Non-Statutory Guidance* (National Curriculum Council, 1992c).

FURTHER READING

DFE (1995b) *Science in the National Curriculum*, London: HMSO.
Every school science department has a copy and you may be issued with a copy by your college tutor. It is important that you read this document in order to understand the legal requirements placed on schools. The non-statutory guidance gives further support (NCC, 1992c).

Dixon, B. (1989) *The Science of Science: Changing the Way we Think*, London: Cassell.
A brief review of the way science progresses, the work that scientists do and the effect of science on our lives. An excellent resource and reader for teachers and pupils.

Dunbar, R. (1995) *The Trouble with Science*, London: Faber & Faber.
A readable and informative book about the way in which science is carried out in many parts of the world. A well illustrated introduction to the philosophy of science.

Macaskill, C. and Ogborn, J. (1996) 'Science and technology' in *School Science Review*, 77, 281, pp. 55–61.
The paper discusses the current science curriculum and considers ways forward to develop a new curriculum that incorporates technology.

SCIENCE, SCIENTISTS AND SOCIETY: READERS FOR SCIENCE TEACHERS

Nature of science

Chalmers, A.F. (1982) *What is This Thing Called Science?* (2nd edn), Milton Keynes: Open University Press.

Dawkins, R. (1991) *The Blind Watchmaker*, London: Penguin Books.

Dixon, B. (1973) *What is Science For?*, London: Collins.

Dunbar, R. (1995) *The Trouble With Science*, London: Faber & Faber.

Gould, S.J. (1989) *Wonderful Life: The Burgess Shale and the Nature of History*, London: Hutchinson Radius.

Huff, T. (1993) *The Rise of Early Modern Science*, Cambridge: Cambridge University Press.

Wolpert, L. (1992) *The Unnatural Nature of Science*, London: Faber & Faber.

Science and society

Chant, C. (1989) *Science, Technology and Everyday Life, 1870–1950*, London: Routledge.

Horton, R. (1993) *Patterns of Thought in Africa and the West: Essays on Magic, Religion and Science*, Cambridge: Cambridge University Press.

Reiss, M. (1993) *Science Education for a Pluralist Society*, Buckingham: Open University Press.

Solomon, J. (1993) *Teaching Science, Society and Technology*, Buckingham: Open University Press.

Stories about science and scientists

Carey, J. (ed.) (1995) *The Faber Book of Science*, London: Faber & Faber; paperback edn.

Goldberg, J. (1989) *Anatomy of a Scientific Discovery* (1st edn), London: Bantam Books.

Goodfield, J. (1982) *An Imagined World: A Story of Scientific Discovery*, London: Penguin Books.

Hawking, S. (1988) *A Brief History of Time*, London: Bantam.

Jones, S. (1996) *In the Blood*, London: Harper Collins.

Medawar, P. (1974) 'Lucky Jim', in P.B. Medawar (ed.) *The Hope of Progress*, London: Wildwood House.

Ronan, C. and Needham, T. (1978/1981) *The Shorter Science and Civilisation in China*, Cambridge: Cambridge University Press.

Sagan, C. (1977) *The Dragons of Eden*, London: Hodder & Stoughton.

3 Pupil learning

INTRODUCTION

This chapter considers the development of pupils' ability to understand science. Chapter 2 addressed the nature of science and focused on the empirical and theoretical aspects of science. In order to learn and understand ideas in science, pupils have to know some facts and have had experiences. For example, pupils need to have seen a rainbow, know the sorts of conditions in which a rainbow is formed and be able to describe it before they can begin to appreciate an explanation in terms of refraction and dispersion of light.

Pupils have understandings of many everyday phenomena; their own understanding allows them to function satisfactorily in the everyday world. A common explanation for electric circuits is that the current flows from the positive to the negative end of a battery and gets used up on the way, e.g. by lighting a lamp. When the battery is used up it has no more electricity in it and you either buy a new one or recharge the battery. Pupils, naturally, assume current is energy; and so the concept of constant current at the beginning and end of a circuit makes no common sense. In your classroom, pupils' explanations often compete with the scientific explanation. But equally, of course, your pupils may bring to school accepted ideas of science. You need to be aware of your pupils' knowledge before you start teaching. Ways to improve learning and encourage thinking are discussed.

OBJECTIVES

By the end of this chapter you should:

- be aware of the need for pupils to have first-hand experience of phenomena;
- know that pupils bring their own explanations of science to school;

- be aware of the literature about pupils' explanations for phenomena;
- know the importance of listening to pupils' explanations and ideas about the world;
- be aware that pupils can be helped to explain phenomena and to be able to think for themselves.

THE IMPORTANCE OF WIDENING EXPERIENCES

A first requirement of learning and understanding anything is to know some facts about the subject. A second requirement is that pupils must have experiences in the subject; these experiences are often facts but go beyond the written word to the act of seeing, feeling, measuring, hearing, etc. Knowledge and awareness of phenomena are of great importance in practical tasks, such as when a pupil is asked to design an investigation. It is not possible for pupils to design a bridge out of plastic, card, wood and glue if at first they do not have practical experience of the properties of these materials.

Your work as a science teacher requires you to give pupils hands-on experience. Some pupils have rich experiences from home or primary school whereas other pupils have a more restricted background. You cannot assume that all your pupils bring to school the same experiential knowledge.

A common topic in the science curriculum is the solar system; pupils are required to explain some common events on Earth in terms of a model of the solar system which includes ideas such as:

- the movement of the Earth about the Sun in an elliptical path;
- the rotation of the Earth on its own imaginary axis;
- the inclination of that axis to an imaginary plane, the plane of the Earth's orbit about the Sun.

The ideas in this model (see Figure 3.1) are not easy for pupils to understand. In order to explain the seasons, pupils have to explain the motion of the Sun as viewed from the Earth, in terms of the behaviour of the Earth. Unless pupils have seen and measured certain phenomena related to the seasons, then explanations of them using the three ideas listed above will not be accepted, much less understood. Phenomena pupils should know about include the variation during a year of

- average daytime temperatures;
- the length of daylight;

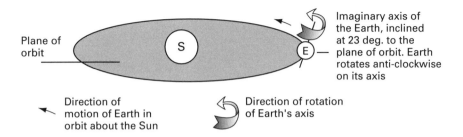

Plane of orbit

S

E —

Imaginary axis of the Earth, inclined at 23 deg. to the plane of orbit. Earth rotates anti-clockwise on its axis

Direction of motion of Earth in orbit about the Sun

Direction of rotation of Earth's axis

Figure 3.1 Diagrammatic representation of the Earth–Sun system

- the angle of elevation of the Sun at noon;
- the direction from which the Sun rises and sets.

In order to use the model, pupils need to imagine relative motion of the three bodies in three dimensions and to imagine what you see from the surface of the Earth. It is a major step forward for pupils learning science to realise that there is a need for an explanation. There is no satisfactory explanation, at present, for gravity. Many pupils just accepted events as 'that is what happens' and curiosity is stifled. A barrier to learning science is the often mentioned description of science as 'doing experiments and finding things out'. The notion of generating explanations, instead of descriptions, as part of science is appreciated less and sometimes dismissed as 'only theory'. Science teaching needs to incorporate the empirical and the theoretical if it is to succeed in portraying science as it is.

Learning science requires pupils to use language, including drawings and diagrams. Pupils need to write, talk, listen and draw. In addition, they need to use numbers and other mathematical tools. Together these skills and tools are the only ways in which pupils can convey to us what they know and understand. Pupils can demonstrate understanding by carrying out a task, e.g. performing a distillation, but language is needed in order to share that understanding. Many pupils are held back by their inability to use language to express ideas and think. Handling abstract ideas requires thinking in words and pictures 'and imagining things which go beyond the real', e.g. electron clouds, chemical bonds, ecological niche. Language is central to learning and enables understanding to be shared and differences explored. Helping pupils to learn science requires positive attention to the use of language; see Chapter 7.

Pupils need opportunities to talk and write about their science and to share their understanding with others. A major advantage of practical activities is the opportunity given for pupils to talk to each other about their work. The more they can be encouraged to discuss their work, the more likely pupils are to develop understanding.

What do pupils know and understand of science?

Considerable research has been conducted in the last twenty years into finding out how well pupils perform science investigations and their understanding of scientific ideas. Two important research foci were the Assessment of Performance Unit (APU) and the Children's Learning in Science Project (CLISP).

Table 3.1   Categories of science performance

These categories were used by the APU to develop criteria against which to measure the performance of pupils

1 Use of graphical and symbolic representation	Reading information from graphs, tables and charts. Representing information as graphs, tables and charts.
2 Use of apparatus and measuring instruments	Using measuring instruments. Estimating physical quantities. Following instruction for practical work.
3 Observation	Making observations. Interpreting observations.

4 Interpretation	a. Interpreting presented information. b. Applying: biology concepts
	             chemistry concepts
	             physics concepts

5 Planning of investigations	Planning parts of investigations. Planning entire investigations.
6 Performance of investigations	Performing entire investigations.

Source: Black, 1990, p. 17

The APU was set up by the DES in 1974 to inquire into standards of practical performance by pupils in school science. The Science Team has produced much information about ways in which pupils approach, carry out and analyse scientific investigations and has provided a set of criteria by which to analyse pupils' performance; see Table 3.1.

The APU team was responsible for drawing attention to the importance of processes in practical work in school science. The work of the
APU formed the basis on which the first National Curriculum Science
Attainment Targets were constructed, focusing on practical investigations in school science and has emerged as 'Experimental and investigative science'. The APU has provided hard evidence about the ways in
which pupils' work in science could be assessed (Black, 1990). Their work
is summarised in four reports that focus on the performance of 11, 13 and
15-year-old pupils (Archenhold *et al.*, 1988; Johnson, 1988; Russell *et al.*,
1988; Schofield *et al.*, 1988).

The APU work focused on assessment; however, what emerged from
the investigations is important evidence about learning and the ways in
which pupils could demonstrate what they can do and know. One task
used by the APU is given in Figure 3.2.

This question is one of a set of similar questions set to 13- and 15-year-
old pupils. The success rate varied between the questions despite their
similarity. Amongst 15 year olds 49 per cent were able to express the cor-

---

Records are kept of the total amount of energy a country uses each year,
from oil, coal etc. From this the average amount used by each person in
that country can be worked out. The table below shows the percentage
of the population working in agriculture and the amount of energy used
per person each year for six different countries.

Country	% of population working in agriculture	Amount of energy used per person (units of energy per year)
Ceylon	50	0.8
Cuba	42	5.1
France	26	19.5
Italy	31	8.4
USA	12	66.0
W Germany	23	26.8

Q   Describe what the table shows about the way the percentage of people working in agriculture relates to the amount of energy used per person in a country.

Figure 3.2   Investigation to test 'interpreting presented information',
Category 4a
Source: Black (1990, p. 20)

rect relationship, although only 14 per cent were able to make explicit use of the units. Set in the open-ended way, the marking depends on the way in which the criteria are interpreted. The question is made easier or harder by the way in which the data is presented, e.g. if the data is presented in numerical order instead of alphabetically by country. An opportunity to try out this task is given in Task 3.1.

TASK 3.1 WHAT EFFECT DOES PRESENTATION MAKE ON THE WAY IN WHICH PUPILS RESPOND TO A QUESTION?

Make a second version of the table in Figure 3.2, with the data presented in descending order of '% population working in agriculture'. Use the two versions of the question to explore the effect of presentation on the way in which your pupils can interpret information.

Identify satisfactory responses and draw up a common marking scheme for both questions. A satisfactory answer might be 'The *higher* the amount of *energy used per person* the *smaller* the *percentage of the population* are working in agriculture.'

The data are an example of an inverse relationship. Do pupils find this type of relationship difficult to identify and express? Do the responses to the task reveal anything about this feature of the problem?

The task gives you insights into alternative ways in which questions can be presented to your pupils and their different responses. If necessary, re-write the question to help your pupils make a better response.

Measurement is an important skill necessary to carrying out investigations. This skill is identified under Category 2 of the APU checklist (Table 3.1). Extensive studies by the APU in a number of experimental situations has shown that, whereas pupils were able to perform a measurement as an isolated task, many pupils were unable to apply that knowledge in a practical investigation. Pupils would not see the necessity for careful measurement but instead applied qualitative methods, even when an appropriate measuring instrument was available (Harlen, 1986, pp. 4–6, 9–12). Measurement involves more than the skill of 'reading the instrument' and includes a knowledge and understanding of:

- when to measure;
- what to measure;
- how to measure.

It is common at KS3 to see pupils measuring the property of a variety of disconnected objects in order to help them use the instrument, e.g. a thermometer. Such exercises frequently lack real purpose because no use is made of the readings and the pupils' ability to read the instrument correctly is not assessed. It is preferable to give your pupils a task to do that requires them to take meaningful measurements, the use of which solve a problem.

Investigations that depend on two measurements being made are more complicated for pupils to cope with and are frequently associated with difficult concepts, e.g. concentration, rate (speed) and density. Your pupils will need careful guidance if they are to be helped to design investigations for themselves. For guidance on measurement, see Froufe (1990).

The APU research showed the central importance to teaching and learning of:

- the need to use a wide range of assessment methods to find out what pupils can do, in order to produce reliable test results;
- including practical situations in the assessment methods. Pupils respond differently to a practical task than to the same situation in a pencil and paper test (see Task 3.2);
- the way in which an assessment is made. The response of the pupil is affected by, for example, the context in which the problem is set, the language used or the structure of the problem;
- teacher assessment over an extended period of time. Formative assessment provides priceless evidence to help direct teaching and contributes to summative assessment (see Chapter 8).

The work of the APU has shown that teacher assessment over an extended period is a good way of assessing pupils but is costly, time consuming and requires in-service training. An APU investigation is shown in Task 3.2.

A number of activities similar to that in Task 3.2 were set by the APU. Over 70 per cent of pupils were able to set up an investigation that enabled measurement to be taken. However, fewer pupils (20–30 per cent) were able to make effective measurements. In the 'Survival' activity in Task 3.2, for example, many pupils did not realise that to compare cooling rates of two systems, temperature measurements need to be made over the same time period. Some pupils did not measure the volume of warm water accurately but relied on vague measurements, such as 'half full'.

Pupils were less successful in activities in which two variables need to be varied in a systematic way. When the task was set as a paper and pencil exercise, fewer that 30 per cent of pupils were able to plan investigations

TASK 3.2 SURVIVAL: AN APU ACTIVITY FOR 13- AND 15-YEAR-OLD PUPILS

Imagine that you are stranded on a mountain side in cold, dry, windy weather. You can choose a jacket from one of the fabrics in front of you.
This is what you have to find out:

Which fabric would keep you warmer?

You can use any of the things in front of you. Choose whatever you need to answer the question. You can:

- use a can instead of a person;
- put warm water inside it to make it more lifelike;
- make 'it' a jacket from the material;
- use a hairdryer to make an imitation wind.

Make a clear record of your results so that another person can understand what you have found out.

Equipment list: plastic sheet, blanket, kettle, scissors, pins, sellotape, rubber bands, cord, stopclock, 2 tin cans and a plastic can all of the same size, 2 more different sized tin cans, measuring cylinders, lids for cans with thermometers and an electric hairdryer.

Questions:

- Which skills or knowledge are being tested in this exercise?
- Identify the variables that need to be investigated. Which is the dependent variable?
- Identify some measurements you would expect a successful pupil to make in order to solve the problem. How would you expect the measurements to be recorded?
- Would you expect pupils to carry out trial runs? What benefit would that give a pupil?
- Suggest differences you might encounter in the plans of pupils if the activity was set as a paper and pencil exercise with no equipment in front of them?

Write answers to the questions and share them with other science students.

Source: Welford, Harlen and Schofield, 1985, pp. 29–38

that would work, in striking contrast to the 70 per cent in the laboratory situation. For a deeper discussion of pupils' responses to APU tasks about planning investigations, see Archenhold *et al.* (1988, pp. 86–94).

It is clear from this example that deciding what a pupil knows and understands is not an easy matter. The answers you get depend on the way in which you ask the question, the depth to which you probe and whether the task is 'hands on' or a written task. You cannot assume that routine science operations such as identifying and controlling variables is an easy task for many pupils. Experimenting in a systematic way needs to be taught.

The work of the APU focused on analysing in great detail the response of pupils to tasks set by teachers and testers in the laboratory situation. What the pupils know, understand and can do is determined by what the tester sees and by reading the pupils' reports.

Listening to pupils

The Children's Learning in Science Project (CLISP) undertook interviews with pupils and listened to what they said about scientific events and phenomena. Pupils were asked to write or draw their ideas, or to respond to written material. Often pupils were provided with objects, material and equipment to manipulate while they were explaining. The interviewer would be involved in the discussion in ways that sought to uncover meaning or to confirm views expressed by pupils.

The CLISP research was carried out over several years and has been replicated in many parts of the world. An extensive literature is now available on pupils' knowledge and understanding of a range of science topics, and you should be aware of it; see, for example, Driver, Squires, Rushworth and Wood-Robinson (1994); Driver, Leach, Millar and Scott (1996); Osborne and Freyburg (1985). The last book in the list is a good place for you to start.

Studies have shown that common features of explanation for a given phenomenon exist among pupils in many parts of the world. Many pupils' understandings are firmly held and make sense to the pupils. Arising from this work has been the suggestion that pupils, and others, construct their own meaning from their experiences. That is, meaning is not told and learned but put together by the pupil in the light of their experience with the world. This view of learning has been called 'constructivism', and pupils' alternative understandings of science are referred to as 'alternative frameworks'. Unsurprisingly, personal construction of knowledge leans heavily on the pupils' use of language, through discussion, explaining, writing, listening and thinking. In the short period in which pupils are in school and studying science, it is unlikely that pupils can construct their own meaning unaided.

Pupils' understanding of science: some examples

Plant nutrition

Considerable research has been conducted into pupils' understanding of how plants get their food. An interview in 1994 with a graduate student from a prestigious technological university, shown on prime time UK television, showed that many graduates have a hazy notion of photosynthesis. Many of these technology graduates, like school pupils, do not believe that wood is, essentially, made out of air and water by a process in a green leaf.

The most common and persistent view held by pupils about plant nutrition is that plants get their food from the environment, mainly from the soil, and that plants feed through their roots. Studies in two countries showed that

- 70 per cent of a cohort of American 11-year-old pupils (N=229);
- 50 per cent of a cohort of Scottish 13-year-old pupils (N=344);
- 33 per cent of a cohort Scottish 14–16-year-old pupils (N=627)

believed that plants feed in the same way as animals. In the UK, a study of hundreds of 15-year-old pupils showed that only 8 per cent knew that plants made their food from materials from the environment (Bell and Brook, 1984). Further studies have shown that some pupils believe that plants have multiple sources of food.

In many of these studies, these views are held in the face of persistent teaching of the correct science. However, the views expressed by pupils make common sense. The condition of the soil is a prime factor in discussions of food yields, and gardeners talk of 'feeding the plants' by adding fertilisers. Farmers put manure or manufactured fertiliser on the soil to improve plant growth, or employ crop rotation methods to enhance yields, so it is not surprising that teaching photosynthesis is not very successful (see Driver, Squires, Rushworth and Wood-Robinson, 1994, pp. 30–5).

Current electricity

Extensive work has been carried out into pupils' understanding of current electricity (Shipstone, 1988). The circuits commonly used in school include dry cells, lamps and bits of wire – an arrangement quite unlike that in domestic circuits. Domestic circuits are often hidden or appear as one wire going directly to the device.

Faced with an electric circuit and asked to discuss the relative size of the current at different points, the relative brightness of lamps or the necessity for a complete circuit in order for lamps to light, many pupils propose non-scientific explanations. In circuits similar to that shown in Figure 3.3, pupils describe the current as being used up as it goes round the circuit, from A to D.

There is an intuitive feeling that the current should be different in different parts of the circuit and smaller at D than at A. Even when ammeters are placed at these points and readings taken, the evidence of a constant current is often assumed to be wrong (Figure 3.4).

Studies involving pupils in many countries have revealed the extent of confusion. Research has shown that four models are used commonly by pupils to explain the passage of an electric circuit through a circuit; see Figure 3.5. These models are:

- the one-pole model in which only one wire is needed. The current is used up by the lamp. Often the second wire is considered to play no part or is a safety device;

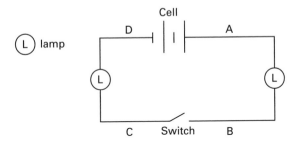

Figure 3.3   A series circuit commonly discussed in school science

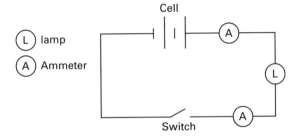

Figure 3.4   The ammeter test

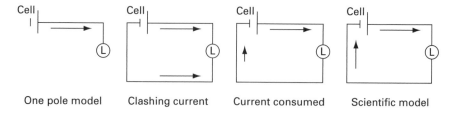

One pole model   Clashing current   Current consumed   Scientific model

Figure 3.5   Common models of an electric circuit given by pupils and students. The size of the arrow reflects the relative size of the current

- the clashing current model. The light generated at the lamp arises from the clash of opposing currents;
- the current-consumed model, in which current is gradually used up as it goes round the circuit. Current is used up by a device in the circuit, e.g. a lamp;
- the scientific model. The current is the same at all points in the series circuit. Energy is transferred from the current to the lamps.

Many pupils understand cells to be sources of electricity and not as devices for maintaining a potential difference across the circuit. It is understandable, then, that pupils use an 'emptying out from cells' model of electricity because this fits with the experience of filling them up again, by recharging them, or replacing old cells with 'full' cells. The non-scientific or 'alternative' models of explanation are held to strongly by both pupils and some older students, even when they can successfully carry out calculations and set up complicated circuits beyond Key Stage 3 or 4. In one study of pupils in comprehensive schools in the UK, the scientific model of current was used by under 10 per cent of 12-year-old pupils, by 40 per cent of those aged 15 years, while 60 per cent of pupils aged 17 years adopted the correct model. The oldest students had studied electricity in their A level work.

A feature of the research is the tenacity with which pupils adhere to the non-scientific model of current, despite teaching and experimental evidence to the contrary (Driver, Squires, Rushworth and Wood-Robinson, 1994, pp. 120–1). This research evidence supports the views held by some scientists that some explanations offered by science contradict common-sense experience.

The importance of knowing about pupils' views and explanations of science are an important step in improving teaching. There is a growing body of knowledge about common features of pupils' alternative explanations; examples of this literature are given in the text and in the Further

Reading section. Another way to gain first-hand experience of how pupils explain common phenomena is to interview some pupils about their understanding of science; an example is given in Task 3.3 which probes pupils' understanding of light.

Light

Many secondary age pupils may believe that light behaves in one or more of the following ways:

- light from near sources does not travel. It takes no time to light up a room. Light from great distances does take time, e.g. the Sun's light travelling to the Earth.
- light travels further in the day than at night;
- light does not exist unless it is intense and produces perceptible effects. Paper does not reflect light; our eyes do not receive light.
- light is not conserved, it can disappear without interaction with matter. Light can be intensified, as when using a magnifying glass.

Children use only a few models of light with which to interpret a range of phenomena. Their use of the scientific model is rare (Driver, Guesne and Tiberghien, 1988, pp. 10–32). The models pupils use include:

- an all pervading sea of light in which you are immersed;
- light travels from the source and from the eye separately to the object;
- light travels to the object from the light source; there is no connection to the eye;
- the scientific model in which light travels from the source to the object and is then reflected into the eye.

The models used often by pupils should be contrasted with the features of the scientific model of light, which includes these features:

- Light is all around us; light from the Sun is dispersed by the atmosphere.
- On the moon the sky is black because there is no atmosphere.
- Light travels from a source until it is reflected or absorbed.
- Light travels in time.
- Light travels in all directions from a source.
- Light travels in straight lines.
- Seeing occurs when light enters the eye.
- An object can be seen when light from the object enters the eye.
- Shadows are seen in the same way but they reflect less light.

TASK 3.3 WHAT DO PUPILS KNOW AND UNDERSTAND ABOUT LIGHT?

Interview a number of children, in pairs, of different age or ability about their understanding of particular effects of light. Interview at least three pairs each for about 20 minutes. Record what they say, using a tape recorder plus brief hand-written notes. Tell pupils why you are talking to them; that the activity is not a test and will not be marked or contribute to their grades. You should get permission first from the class teacher and be prepared to share what you find with her. You should clarify your own understanding of light before you start. See p. 55.

Sample questions:

1   Where is there light in this room? This could be followed up with one or more subsidiary questions:

- is light and daylight the same thing?
- how can you see outside when it is cloudy?
- how can you see in a room when the Sun is not shining into it?

2   Throw a shadow of an object on to a piece of card with a torch. Ask 'How is a shadow formed?' Additional questions include:

- is there any light in the shadow?
- is it different light (to the torch light)?
- how can you see a shadow? Draw a sketch to help your answer.

3   How far does light travel? Show pupils sketches of situations in which light is being made and ask 'How far does light travel?'

Light from a candle

Watching a film

continued . . .

> You can make other examples of similar situations, such as walking in the sunshine (or moon shine) or searching in the dark with a torch.
>
> 4 Ask pupils to interpret how they see something, e.g. see a tree while standing on the school field. Ask pupils to draw a sketch of how your eye sees something, showing the direction in which light travels.
>
> *Source*: adapted from Osborne and Freyburg (1985, pp. 8–9)

FINDING OUT MORE ABOUT PUPILS' IDEAS AND EXPLANATIONS

In Task 3.3, pupils were invited to respond to an imagined situation or to pictures. There are a number of other strategies you can use. For example:

- **Explaining**: give pupils a set of pictures each related to the same concept. Invite pupils, alone or in pairs, to write their own explanation of the phenomenon.
- **Imagining**: ask a pupil to pretend she is on the Moon. If she drops a stone from her hand, what would happen to it? Ask her to explain her answer.
- **Responding**: give a short demonstration of a phenomenon and invite pupils to describe, and then explain, what they see. For example, the expansion of a solid (see Figure 3.6).
- **Designing**: invite pupils to design a way to investigate a problem, e.g. how to get the dye from a red cabbage leaf; or which of two toy cars travels furthest down a wooden ramp.
- **Present a case orally**: ask a group of pupils to present evidence for the hole in the ozone layer.

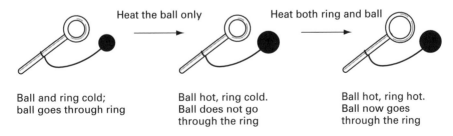

Figure 3.6 Demonstrating the expansion of a solid ball and ring

- **Present a case by poster**: invite pupils to devise a poster to explain how plants get their food.
- **Classify information**: sort picture cards into two or more sets using given criteria, for example living things into 'animals' and 'not animals'; or materials into 'natural' and 'manufactured'.
- **Write sentences**: responding to trigger words. For example, ask pupils to write a sentence for each set of words:

  magnet, north, pole, south;
  attract, like, poles, repel;
  bar, field, force, lines, magnet.

- **Predict**: which type of sugar will dissolve the quickest in water, granulated sugar or cube sugar. Pupils are asked to explain their prediction and then to test their idea.

Each strategy needs an appropriate context and some activities can be set for homework. By marking their work before the next lesson, you can plan your next teaching. Some activities must be done in class; the timing needs to be thought through carefully if the results of the activity are to direct further teaching.

The strategies enable you to set appropriate work for different groups of pupils, i.e. to differentiate your teaching. Further active learning strategies appear in Capel, Leask and Turner (1995, Table 5.2.1).

HELPING PUPILS TO LEARN

The research described above has provided insights into how well pupils understand the world about them *and* that scientific explanations and pupils' common-sense understanding can sometimes conflict. Learning to adopt the arguments and reasoning of science is not easy. If pupils are to adopt the explanations given to them in their science lessons, they need to be persuaded that the new understandings offer an advantage over their existing explanations. On occasions, however, the new knowledge appears to contradict common sense. Scientific explanations are often valued by scientists because they fit into a wider theory – an argument not always appreciated by young learners. However, if pupils can be engaged in such a way that part of the challenge is to link their own knowledge and understanding with new learning, then some progress in understanding can be made. The example of rusting and chemical change below shows a way forward.

Rusting

As part of a section of work on chemical change, a teacher gave each pupil a clean, shiny nail and instructed them to take the nail home and 'put it in a place where you think it would go rusty'. Pupils were asked to write down answers to the following questions:

- where did you put the nail?
- what is it about the place that made you put it there?
- why do you think that will make the nail go rusty?
- what do you think rust is?

The pupils returned the nails after two weeks and the teacher set up a display in the laboratory. The display provided much information about his pupils' thinking about rusting. Most pupils said that water is needed for rusting. In addition, some pupils said that

- rusting needs air;
- cold was important;
- acid would help;
- salt would help rusting;
- rust was like a mould.

Many pupils did not see rusting as a chemical change, which was the focus of the unit.

Arising from this homework, the teacher then arranged for pupils to test their ideas about the role of water, salt, cold, etc. in the rusting of iron. The teacher focused the work of some pupils on the role of air, the purpose of which in rusting many pupils did not appreciate. As a result of these further investigations, the factors essential for rusting were established. Even so, a number of pupils argued that the rust was 'underneath the surface' of the nail and had simply 'come out' when the conditions were right. You should consider how you would respond to that question. Finally, the teacher returned the pupils' attention to the display and discussed rusting in chemical change terms and compared the extent of rusting to the conditions used. (Adapted from Driver, Squires, Rushworth and Wood-Robinson, 1994, pp. 11–12.)

The study above shows a number of interesting factors about teaching, which include:

- the focus by the teacher on pupils' starting points;
- the imaginative use of homework to gain information about pupils' prior knowledge and understanding;
- the use of a display technique to open up discussion;

- the use of discussion, as opposed to just telling;
- the use of practical work to solve a real problem.

Coming to understand an idea requires effort on the part of the learner. It is probably the reason why pupils prefer practical work to non-practical work, to take notes rather than to make their own and, sometimes, to be told what to learn rather than to discuss and evaluate ideas and evidence. The research described has produced a number of important teaching strategies. In order to learn and understand science (as in any subject), each pupil has to engage mentally with the topic and make the knowledge his own, and not just knowledge that someone else has told him.

You can help your pupils' learning by paying attention to:

Prior knowledge – find out what the pupils already know about the topic before teaching them. Prior knowledge includes:

- what has been taught before;
- the science taught in primary school;
- the experiences pupils have of the topic;
- what pupils of this age usually know of the topic (see above);
- evidence from brainstorming with your class.

Understanding – what are the common features of pupils' understanding and misconceptions of the topic? You can find this information by:

- reading summaries of the research literature;
- knowing the prior experience of pupils;
- planning to find out what pupils know before you teach the topic;
- evidence from brainstorming with your class.

In due course you can build a picture of the common understandings of the views of pupils at different stages of development.

Linking the topic to previous work – most topics have links with work taught previously or have significance in everyday life. Try to:

- identify direct links to other units in the curriculum;
- connect the topic to relevant events or phenomena outside school;
- identify ways in which understanding the topic interests your pupils.

Personal scientific understanding – ensure that you know:

- the science of your lesson – if in doubt refer to a text book or ask a colleague;
- the ideas and concepts that make up the unit of work. Consult your school's scheme of work;

- how your school equipment works. Do not assume all equipment is the same.

The difficulty of the concept – experience suggests that some topics are more difficult for pupils to grasp than others. The ability of pupils to grasp an idea depends on a number of factors, which include:

- the *relevance* of the topic and their experience of it: contrast decay of food with radioactivity;
- the *prior knowledge* necessary to understand the concept: has it been taught or otherwise introduced to pupils?
- does the idea *integrate* with previous knowledge or challenge it? A moderate degree of challenge, or dissonance, can motivate, but if the credibility gap is too large, then it is likely that pupils will 'switch off';
- the *nature of the intellectual demand*: does the topic require pupils to handle abstract ideas, e.g. heat, energy, electrons, cell respiration? Abstract thinking often requires pupils to use their imagination and to go beyond what is seen in front of them. In some investigations, pupils have to identify variables that may affect a phenomenon, to plan ways of investigating one of them while controlling the others. The ability to do this represents a high intellectual demand. Older pupils are better at these tasks than younger ones, but not all 16–year-old pupils are competent (Adey and Shayer, 1994, pp. 18–21).
- the *mathematical demand of the concept*: does the topic require the use of ratio and proportion or the construction or interpretation of line graphs? These particular mathematical concepts are often barriers to understanding scientific ideas, e.g. rate, density, molar quantities or interpreting data from investigations, e.g. identifying the ratio of phenotypes in a genetics investigation or a graph constructed from readings obtained with a ticker timer. You should check with science or mathematics colleagues what concepts and skills are taught to your pupils before your lesson. In some circumstances, pupils may need to be taught an algorithm for the purposes of the activity and hope that use and teaching will lead to understanding. Only a minority of pupils of school leaving age are able to work with ratio beyond doubling and halving. For further discussion, see Adey and Shayer (1994, pp. 136–8).

Ways to encourage and teach thinking – Teach thinking skills just as you do other skills. Give pupils opportunities to practise thinking and encourage them, otherwise some pupils will not develop to their full potential. Attitudes are important, and learning needs to be seen as worthwhile, even fun. Encourage your pupils to persist, and reward them by praising and recognising their achievements.

An experiment in promoting thinking

The Cognitive Acceleration in Science Project (CASE) set out to promote thinking in science by intervention in the normal routines of class teaching. By improving the capacity of pupils to think, and through exposure to higher order thinking skills by carefully planned teaching, a greater number of pupils were expected to gain access to the more difficult aspects of science hinted at above. The project worked with a number of trial schools in the UK. The results showed that many pupils who had been exposed to the intervention programme scored higher on tests of cognitive development than pupils who had not been exposed. The same pupils scored better GCSE results three years later than the control groups. More startlingly, there was some evidence that these same pupils scored better in GCSE English and mathematics than the control groups. There was evidence for a long-term effect of the intervention process, and the skills learned were apparently sustained and capable of implementation in curriculum areas other than science (Adey, Shayer and Yates, 1989a, pp. 240–8). The CASE materials are available and used by a number of schools to support the teaching of the National Curriculum (see Adey, Shayer and Yates, 1989b).

TASK 3.4 PUPIL LEARNING AND TEACHING SKILLS

Identify the relevant standards that relate to the understanding of pupil learning and identify the ways in which you can develop the appropriate teaching skills. Use Appendix 4, especially 'Subject Application' and 'Pupils' Learning' to help you.

SUMMARY

Scientists seek to describe and explain phenomena; these explanations are often in conflict with pupils' (and adults') own explanations. Teaching science requires you to be aware of pupils' own explanations and to use those explanations as a basis for developing pupils' understanding of the currently accepted scientific explanations. Your explanations need to be based on experience and evidence and thus to provide pupils with both practical experience of phenomena and the opportunity to discuss their own ideas and those of scientists. This process is not easy but is a challenge worth taking up. On the other hand, mere telling of explanation out of context of the pupils' own lives or without experience rarely works.

A good deal of this chapter has depended upon research findings into science teaching; it illustrates the importance of being aware of the products of research and looking for ways to use it in your day to day teaching. The Further Reading guide provides another step in that direction.

FURTHER READING

Adey, P., Shayer, M. and Yates, C. (1989b) *Thinking Science: The Curriculum Materials of the CASE Project*, London: Thomas Nelson & Sons.
Describes, with practical details, how activities may be used in science lessons together with conventional curriculum materials to promote thinking in science.

Black, P. (1990) 'APU Science – the past and the future', *School Science Review*, 72, 258, pp. 13–28.
A summary of the achievements of the APU and ways in which the research has or has not affected the way in which science is taught.

Driver, R., Squires, A., Rushworth, P. and Wood-Robinson, V. (1994) *Making Sense of Secondary Science*, London: Routledge.
A collection of the research into children's understandings of most topics in the science curriculum. A valuable reference and source of wider reading.

Osborne, R. and Freyburg, R. (1985) *Learning in Science*, Auckland: Heinemann Educational Books.
An important book which addresses issues of teaching and learning for pupils aged 11–15 years. A rich source of examples of pupils' perceptions from many sciences and a valuable source of teaching strategies.

4 Planning for teaching

INTRODUCTION

In Chapter 2, we discussed the aims and purposes of the science curriculum. We hope you now have a deeper knowledge and understanding of what you would like to achieve through your teaching of science and of what you would like your pupils to learn. In this chapter we consider how you can realise your aims through the development of teaching strategies and learning objectives. Other chapters in this book contribute to lesson planning, notably Chapter 6 and Chapter 8. Further guidance on lesson planning and schemes of work are in Capel, Leask and Turner, 1995, Unit 2.2.

OBJECTIVES

By the end of this chapter you should be able to:

- identify some personal characteristics that direct your teaching style;
- relate Schemes of Work to lesson planning;
- consider factors that affect the planning of lessons;
- plan a lesson;
- understand and apply the regulations of the Health and Safety at Work Act as they apply to school;
- carry out a risk assessment;
- identify the role of homework in planning;
- begin to include differentiation in your planning.

YOUR TEACHING SKILLS

All of us have participated in a variety of learning experiences and some have been more exciting than others. You probably have a favourite teacher, or can recall a particular vivid talk, lecture or demonstration.

What was it about the experience that was riveting, stimulating and exciting for you? What were the characteristics of the teacher who made a positive impact on you?

TASK 4.1 CAPTURING THE IMAGINATION

This task is in two parts.

1   On your own, or before a joint session with other student science teachers, recall an educational experience that you enjoyed or that stimulated you. Describe it in brief detail and try to identify the strategy or technique used by the teacher that captured your imagination.

With other student teachers (or your tutor) share the examples you have identified and identify any strategies they used. Discuss the qualities of the teachers or lecturers who have made these learning experiences interesting. List the positive qualities exhibited by those teachers.

2   Consider now other teachers whom you thought were less effective. Did

- they display negative qualities?
- the absence of the good qualities discourage you?
- some other feature of their teaching approach 'turn you off'?

How can you capture the imaginative qualities of the inspiring teachers and avoid the negative effects of others?

Task 4.1 helped you to list positive features of a stimulating teaching style, elements of which you could employ in your lessons. A list of positive features of a good teacher is given below. If you display all these virtues then perhaps you should not be reading this book; however, you can aspire to them! Use the following list to address Task 4.2. Successful teachers do not necessarily have all these qualities. Successful teachers:

- avoid confrontation
- are caring
- are calm
- are competent
- are confident
- behave consistently
- expect high standards
- are entertaining
- show enthusiasm
- show firm, fair discipline
- give clear instruction
- give energy and time to their pupils
- have moments of inspiration

- are lively persons
- show patience
- are rigorous in their preparation
- use praise and reward
- are sympathetic to others

- use humour
- use positive body language
- are supportive of pupils with learning difficulties
- are friendly with pupils

Source: adapted from Frost, 1995, pp. 10–12 and Woolnough, 1994, pp. 37–8

TASK 4.2 ANALYSING THE QUALITIES DISPLAYED BY TEACHERS

Some qualities of good teachers are:

- to do with the nature and temperament of the person;
- to do with their commitment to young people and the profession of teaching;
- acquired through need, training and practice.

List the qualities from the list above under two headings:

1   intrinsic qualities that you either have or do not have;
2   acquired qualities that you can develop or learn to display.

   Discuss and identify the qualities in the list above under these headings. In what ways do you expect your school experience to help you develop and acquire some of these qualities?

Your **personal qualities** determine your classroom behaviour and influence your teaching style. You need to look in charge (even if you feel otherwise). It is important that you show confidence through the way you present yourself; positive body language is a factor in personal presentation. Positive body language includes where you stand in the room (not behind the teacher's desk all the time) and your ability to circulate so as to make contact with as many pupils as possible; avoid defensive gestures, such as folding your arms in front of you for long periods; maintain eye contact with as many pupils as possible by looking at pupils when you speak and scanning the room so as to include all the class. And know the pupils' names.

   Your voice is a factor in the way you present yourself. Know what you are going to say and practise delivering it in a clear voice. Try to be calm and, as you gain confidence, modulate your voice, varying the pitch and tone. Practise speaking into a mirror and in an empty classroom; ask your tutor, or another student teacher, to listen to you.

The key to confidence is preparation: knowing exactly what you intend to say, write and do and, above all, knowing what the pupils are going to do. If pupils think you are organised, then you are half way there. A first step in becoming organised is to see how other teachers and support staff organise their time and lessons.

OBSERVING TEACHING AND LEARNING

Support staff

Science teaching depends heavily on good support from various technical support services. Science laboratories are different from other classrooms, and pupils arrive expecting to experience a different sort of learning activity from most other lessons. Although most school science laboratories have similar basic equipment, their layouts differ and are managed in different ways. Familiarise yourself with the layout of your science laboratories, the services, where equipment is kept, how it is ordered and cleared away and the health and safety procedures. Spend a day shadowing a laboratory technician. You gain valuable insights into how to request equipment by being on the receiving end; see Task 4.3.

TASK 4.3 A DAY IN THE LIFE OF THE TECHNICAL STAFF

Arrange to spend a day working with the technical support staff, starting work when they do and finishing at their time. You should become familiar with:

- routines for ordering equipment;
- the amount of time needed to prepare practical sessions;
- the limitations on what can and cannot be expected from support staff and resources;
- the role of the technical staff in providing safety checks on equipment and maintaining safe practice;
- the location and content of relevant risk assessment information, e.g. HazCards.
- the location of first aid and the accident record books;
- the procedure for accident emergency and the role of the support staff;
- the general location and extent of equipment, resources and material available in the department;
- the way in which technical staff support lessons in the laboratory;

continued . . .

- the way in which equipment and resources are set out prior to a lesson;
- how equipment is cleaned and returned at the end of lessons.

Help the technical staff complete a requisition for a science teacher.

Collect copies of relevant documents helpful to preparing lessons, e.g. risk assessment forms. Talk with the senior technician or your tutor about your experience. Prepare a list of questions in advance of the meeting.

Working in other teachers' classrooms

Before your period of practical teaching, you are given time in school to watch experienced teachers, to see the classes you intend to teach and to find out information about the school and the science faculty. Make the most of this time to prepare yourself for practical teaching by observing **with purpose** other teachers at work. Many students half way through their teaching practice indicate that they wished they had made more of their periods of observation. You should build in regular periods of observation throughout your practical experience.

You observe experienced teachers, in part, to recognise your own qualities and to obtain ideas that might work for you. By watching other teachers' use of different strategies, you learn how to start developing your own skills. Your tutors provide ideas for many observation tasks to help you develop your own style of teaching and to reflect on good practice. Begin by observing the ways in which science teachers:

- start and end lessons;
- manage time in a lesson;
- simultaneously manage pupils and teaching resources in a laboratory.

You should progress to observing science teachers and, where appropriate, other subject teachers when they:

- demonstrate phenomena or equipment
- develop discussion with a class
- are involved in field work
- use IT
- use DARTS activities
- explain concepts or how things work
- set investigations or pose problems
- use media or multi-media resources

- ask questions to elicit pupils' understanding or knowledge
- brainstorm ideas with a class
- differentiate work for pupils
- use a computer for interfacing
- use drama
- use open or closed questions
- use role play and simulations
- use the Overhead Projector

The skills listed above contribute to the competences or standards *you* should achieve by the end of your course. See Appendix 4.

Try to observe teachers exercising one or two skills or strategies; do not look for too many things at once. Focused in this way, your observation has purpose and, at times, means that you do not have to spend the whole period in the classroom. Be clear about what you are trying to find out; if necessary, write a list of questions before you approach the teacher for permission to observe. Two examples of observation tasks are described in detail below. Ideas for further classroom observation are described in Capel, Leask and Turner (1995, Unit 2.1) and King (1996).

Seek permission of the class teacher to watch her lesson and discuss when and where you can observe the class. Agree the focus of the observation task and make clear what you intend to do with your observations; ask permission to record your observations. Remember that although you are carrying out an observation of the classroom, your role is not to be critical of the class teacher. However, you often need to ask questions about her practice for clarification.

Ask the class teacher where you should sit and agree with her the extent to which you talk with pupils, or support practical work. Prepare an answer for pupils who question your presence in the lesson.

TASK 4.4 OBSERVING EXPERIENCED SCIENCE TEACHERS MANAGING CLASSES

Observe a science lesson in which you concentrate on the teacher's management. Use the framework in Table 4.1 for your observations.

After the lesson, arrange to talk with the class teacher and make a list of questions you want to ask. Identify those practices you can adopt in your teaching.

After observing several teachers, you will be able to compare teaching styles (method and personality) and describe the styles and strategies used. Teachers use a range of strategies to implement their aims,

Table 4.1 Observation recording chart: see Task 4.4

Management skills	*Your observations*
1 **Starting the lesson:**	
● bringing in the class	
● settling registration	
● opening up the topic	
How was the start of the topic signalled to pupils?	
2 **Equipment:**	
● position	
● distribution	
● working order	
3 **During main phase of lesson:**	
● teacher's movement about lab.	
● scanning and alertness to whole class	
● gain attention	
● signal change of activity	
4 **End:**	
● timing	
● signal end of main task	
● clear up/collect equipment	
● draw lesson together	
● set homework	
● dismiss class	
Other notes: keep a record on the back of the pro forma of other points to discuss with the class teacher.	

varying them for different groups of children. A teacher may use more than one strategy in a lesson. For further discussion on teaching styles see Capel, Leask and Turner (1995, Unit 5.3) and Frost (1996, pp. 10–28).

Teachers asking questions

Teachers are always asking questions, probing for information or under-standing, testing powers of observation, looking for insights into events and so on. What sort of questions do teachers ask pupils? How are ques-tions asked and what do teachers expect in reply? See Task 4.5 and below.

TASK 4.5 TYPES OF QUESTIONS TEACHERS ASK PUPILS

Arrange to observe a class teacher working with a whole class. Record the number of times the chosen event occurs, using a simple tally system, e.g. ||||...

1 Open or closed questions

Question type	*Score each question*	*Total*
Closed – one that pupils recognise as having only one answer.		
Open – one that pupils recognise can have many acceptable answers.		

Describe the balance of questions used in your observation period. Relate your findings to the topic and context of the lesson.

2 Type of thinking required – the demand on the pupil

Question type	*Score each question*	*Total*
Recall: pupils have to remember knowledge or procedure, e.g. a for-mula, a name of a part or sub-stance.		
Make observations: pupils describe what they see, e.g. a blue precipitate, a spark jumping from a metal dome to a sphere.		
Apply reasoning: this part of the leaf goes black. What does that indicate?		
Hypothesise: if I use calcium car-bonate instead of sodium carbonate with the acid, what might happen?		

continued . . .

Compare the number of different types of question used by the teacher in this lesson and discuss your findings with the class teacher.

3   Effect on the pupils

How did pupils respond to the questions? Did the pupils show any feelings, for example enthusiasm, switch off, frustration, renewed interest?

Effect	Score each question	Total
Pupil encouraged		
Pupil discouraged		
No effect apparent		

Discuss your data with the class teacher and relate her assessment of the class response to your data. Did some type of questions produce positive effects?

Source: adapted from *Secondary PGCE Subject Handbook, Science*, 1996/7, Institute of Education, University of London

In Task 4.5 you are asked to accumulate data about the questions asked, the type of learning that is encouraged and the effect of the questioning on pupils. In part 2 of Task 4.5, the cognitive demand on pupils through teacher questioning is addressed. The task has several parts but ideally should be investigated in the same lesson. You could combine Part 3 with either Part 1 or Part 2 on separate occasions.

In Chapter 8, 'Assessment', we address the ways in which higher cognitive skills are assessed by both teachers and examination boards. The opportunities pupils have to develop such skills depend on the way in which those skills are addressed in day to day teaching. The **objectives** you set for your lessons should include higher level skills; see below.

LESSON PLANNING AND SCHEMES OF WORK

A key to good teaching is lesson planning. The lesson plan is the product of planning and should summarise your thinking. It need not be a long document but is a record of your proposed lesson. Lesson plans must be kept throughout your school experience and be available for inspection by tutors and examiners.

To plan a lesson you need:

- a knowledge of your pupils, e.g. pupil grouping, range of abilities, presence of statemented pupils, ethnic mix;
- to know what pupils were taught in the last lesson, or what they were taught previously about the topic;
- your Scheme of Work;
- the National Curriculum (especially if your Scheme of Work is not annotated with respect to it);
- a text book to help brush up your factual knowledge;
- risk assessment information.

Schemes of Work

A Scheme of Work (SoW) sets out the long-term plans for pupil learning across a Key Stage. A SoW shows how modules are fitted into the three terms, year by year, and is derived from a published syllabus or directly from the Science National Curriculum. Most schemes of work are built up from topics and map out a teaching route. Many text books show routes through the National Curriculum. A science department or faculty may adapt a published resource to reflect the aims of the school and to provide autonomy. Your teaching practice school should have a SoW.

A SoW ensures that teaching builds on previous learning to ensure continuity. SoWs are designed to ensure that the knowledge, skills, understanding and attitudes of the pupils are developed in a planned way and help to ensure progression in learning. A checklist for looking at SoWs is shown below. Many SoWs identify sources of photocopiable work sheets for use with units of work. A SoW may include:

- aims and objectives;
- assessment schemes including prepared tests;
- homework schedule and suggestions;
- resources to be used;
- safety requirements;
- ways to address equal opportunities in science;
- outline lesson plans;
- criteria for identifying pupil performance with level descriptors;
- how the nature of science is revealed in the teaching;
- differentiation;
- ways in which to teach Sc1;
- how cross-curricular themes, skills and attitudes are incorporated into the teaching.

A SoW shows the aims of the course overall and the aims of the topic or unit of work. The lessons that make up a unit of work may be identified in your SoW. However, it will be your responsibility as a qualified teacher to prepare lessons in accordance with the SoW and in response to the needs of your pupils. Lesson plans need both aims and learning objectives for your pupils.

TASK 4.6 REVIEW YOUR SCHOOL'S SCHEME OF WORK

Obtain a copy of your Scheme of Work and use the checklist above to review the document. Find out:

1   whether you need other documents when you plan a lesson using the SoW;
2   how the content relates to the Science National Curriculum;
3   how resources needed for a Unit of Work are identified.

Select a topic that you intend to teach and check that you can use the SoW to construct lesson plans. Make a list of queries to discuss with your tutor.

Planning a sequence of work

Your lesson plans are part of a sequence of work. At first the sequence is laid down for you by the SoW; in due course you need to develop a sequence of lessons throughout a topic in order to respond to your classes or by rewriting a unit of work. You may be asked to do this as part of course requirements or, as sometimes happens, the head of science invites you to contribute to rewriting a topic.

Constructing a scheme of work is a skilled task, requiring knowledge of the pupils for whom it is intended, familiarity with the content of the topic, and awareness of the way in which the earlier version of the topic was constructed, taught and received by pupils. We suggest that this is a task that should be taken on not in isolation but as part of a team. You should not be expected to construct a Scheme of Work on your own in your training year, except as part of a developmental exercise, e.g. within coursework requirements or as a *draft* for departmental discussion and development. For further discussion of ways in which to approach this task, see Parkinson (1994, pp. 76–8).

Planning lessons

Lesson planning is something that is personal but is responsive to the events of previous lessons, the needs of the pupils and demands of the

Scheme of Work. At this stage of your development you need to plan lessons in accordance with the requirements of your school. Your school and your IHE have guidelines on the way in which to plan your lessons, and you should follow their advice. One approach is for you, together with your college tutor and school tutor, to examine different lesson plan frameworks and to decide on one for you to use throughout your practice. An example of a lesson plan is given in Figures 4.1 and 4.2, and we discuss aspects of those plans later in the chapter.

A lesson plan is a summary of your planning. It normally does not contain notes on the science; these are kept separate from the main plan and many student teachers, quite rightly, need such support. Work sheets are additional items.

Design your lesson plan so that you can concentrate on the pupils and activities for the lesson. A plan is a useful check on lesson progress and continuity. The plan should be clear and concise, with estimated timings. Timings are an important aspect of planning and developing your ability to pace the lesson. Make space at the end of the plan for your evaluation of the lesson and ideas for improvement.

You are **observed** by the class teacher, your school science tutor and IHE tutor throughout your practice; they need a copy of your current lesson plan and access to your **teaching file**. The teaching file contains a record of your work, including lesson plans for all the classes you teach, together with supporting notes, and it provides evidence of your progress. Evaluations of your own teaching are an essential part of your record. Your lesson plans and supporting documentation help you to build up a set of background notes about each topic that can be adapted for future use.

Before you teach your lesson, show your lesson plans in advance to the teacher whose class you will be taking. Agree with her a time when this should happen. **The class teacher is responsible for the class and must be informed of what you intend to teach.** Be prepared to accept advice from the class teacher and draw a balance between innovation and acknowledging the teacher's experience with a particular group of children. Accept criticism of your lesson plan as constructive support.

Advice from your class teacher or other qualified science teacher about **safety must be adhered to**. If you are doubtful about any practice, ensure that you check that advice with your head of science. See the section below on risk assessment.

In due course, your needs may not be met by the first lesson planning pro forma you use. With the support and agreement of your tutors, modify it to suit your stage of development. Experienced teachers have very brief lesson plans, usually completed in a diary or teacher planner as a record of what each class has achieved. This procedure ensures that all classes have completed the common Scheme of Work. All teachers need detailed lesson plans to show to visiting Inspectors, e.g. during an OFSTED inspection.

Lesson plans

The elements of a lesson plan are shown in Figures 4.1 and 4.2. The plan is in two parts: the first part summarises essential aspects of the planning process, whereas the second part (Figure 4.2) helps you to keep track of events during the lesson. There is extensive discussion about lesson planning in Capel, Leask and Turner (1995, Unit 2.3), which we suggest you read.

We elaborate below some key features of a lesson plan and refer to the headings in Figures 4.1 and 4.2. The content and broad purpose of a lesson is determined for you by your school's Scheme of Work. The class teacher helps you to interpret that document, especially in the early lessons. Your task is to translate the general statements in the SoW into a detailed lesson plan.

The **aims** of a lesson reflect the content or general purpose and serve to focus you on the knowledge, process and skills of the lesson. The aims of a lesson might be to:

- introduce pupils to the Periodic Table;
- help pupils identify the variables affecting transpiration in a leaf and to plan an investigation to determine the effect of one of them;
- practise drawing and interpreting graphs using data from the way in which elastic bands extend and contract under changing loads.

On occasions, more than one aim is important in your lesson.

Objectives derive from aims. In our model, we use behavioural objectives that translate aims into observable pupil behaviour, that is, what pupils can do as a result of your teaching. Objectives focus on the assessment of learning by enabling you to identify knowledge, understanding or skills through the evidence of pupils' work. What pupils do, say or write, etc. is evidence of their learning. Objectives are written using 'active verbs'. For example, pupils should be able to '*explain* a phase of the Moon using a diagram of the Sun, Moon and Earth system'.

Name			Date	
Year and group	Period	Room	Class Teacher	

Topic

Reference to *Scheme of Work*; *GCSE syllabus*; *National Curriculum*

Aims	1
	2

Learning objectives for pupils	By the end of the lesson pupils will be able to: 1
	2

Differentiation
opportunities

Apparatus, books,
audio–visual aids and
equipment
needed

Risk assessment	
Item	Action taken

Figure 4.1 A lesson plan: information

Start – *settling, register, giving out books, reviewing . . .*

Middle – *development, main activity, supporting pupils, change of activity*

End – *signalling end of main activity, clearing up, cleaning, return of equipment, reviewing, consolidating, clarifying learning, setting homework, dismissing*

Anticipated timing

Time in minutes	Teacher activity	Pupil activity
0–5		

Homework – *task to be set, handing in date, etc.*	
Evaluation – *identify successful management, learning, enjoyment and the evidence. Refer to objectives. Areas for development.* **Knowledge/skills developed** **New targets**	

Figure 4.2   A lesson plan: continuity and timing

Useful verbs include:

construct	describe	explain
give	make	list
identify	predict	recognise
recall	present	solve
suggest	state	

Verbs help you to focus on pupil performance and outcome and how you recognise it; see Task 4.7.

The **timing** of any lesson is important. Attention to timing allows you to identify the time available for each phase of the lesson and to identify tasks for the pupils that fit into teaching periods. You should direct your attention to:

- the three phases of a lesson (start, middle and end in Figure 4.2);
- activities you set for pupils;
- administration, such as registration, giving out books, setting homework, clearing up, etc.

TASK 4.7 WRITING LESSON AIMS AND OBJECTIVES

Part 1 Consider a lesson you have taught or have observed. State the aim(s) of the lesson.

Using active verbs, write two or three objectives for the lesson. The following example may help you.

Aim   To introduce pupils to electrical conductors and insulators.

Objectives   Pupils should be able to:
- construct a circuit to test materials for electrical conduction;
- tell you how they know if a material is an insulator or not;
- give examples of *materials* that are conductors or insulators;
- predict the property of a new material.

Part 2 Comment and rewrite, where appropriate, the aims and objectives for each lesson set out below. These aims and objectives are taken from draft lesson plans and show aims and objectives conflated or objectives omitted. If necessary, assume an identity for the class by relating the task to a class you know.

continued . . .

Year 7	Mixed ability
Topic	Electricity; currents in circuits.
Aims/objectives	To teach about current in parallel circuits and how current is measured in circuits with ammeters. Introduce parallel circuits.
Year 10	Top set
Topic	Circulatory system.
Aims/objectives	Pupils to understand why a circulatory system is needed, and the structure and function of the heart.
Year 11	Pupils preparing for GCSE, most of whom are expected to gain C–E grades
Topic	Plant reproduction.
Aims/objectives	Know that plants and animals reproduce sexually and asexually. Realise that sexual/asexual reproduction have both pros and cons.

Plan how to **start, develop and finish** a lesson – see Figure 4.2. Do not rely on making it up as you go along. Teachers do have to think on their feet, but many 'spontaneous' responses are well rehearsed. If necessary, write down notes about:

- what you intend to **write** on the board or OHP (headings, date, diagrams, tables, instructions, homework);
- what you plan to **say**, e.g. to start the lesson; the sort of question you intend asking to elicit pupils' prior knowledge of a topic; the key points for a summary of the lesson;
- **homework** details;
- administrative or other **information** you must tell the class.

You need to **select activities** that respond to the SoW but are within the capacity of your class, both in terms of ability and behaviour and the physical constraints of the laboratory. Advice about suitable activities is often found in the SoW or the recommended text book(s) for the course. You should, in addition, build a library of references and resources to which you can turn. However, you need to check that the activity is suitable for your purposes, i.e. meets the aims and objectives you have identified for your pupils.

A key part of the planning procedure is to identify **resources**. Ensure that you know the ordering procedure for your school and comply with it. Resources should respond to your purposes. In some schools, resources are identified and allocated to certain topics or lessons as part of the SoW; this is often helpful. On the other hand, if the resource does not lend itself to the development of your learning objectives, then it is of little use. Resources need to respond to purpose and not direct the aims and objectives of a lesson.

Nevertheless, you are likely to be faced with situations such as 'this is the only piece of equipment on electrolysis we have', and you need to work out how to use it to suit your ends.

Lesson evaluation

You should **evaluate** the lessons you teach; make evaluation a regular part of your learning. Evaluation involves analysing what went well and what went poorly and looking for explanations. Both analyses lead to improvement in your teaching and provide evidence of your development; see Appendix 4.

When evaluating your lesson, attend to all the phases of the lesson but do not try to evaluate everything you do in a lesson. Prioritise your evaluation and address and analyse key situations or events. When teachers watch your lesson, discuss with them in advance the focus of the observation. Include the teacher's evaluation in your teaching file. Meet with your tutor on a regular basis, e.g. once a week, and discuss your lesson evaluations as part of your review of progress in your teaching and development.

It is important that you address the successful aspects of lessons and identify what you are doing well. It is easy to be critical and to focus on the poorer aspects of your teaching. Try to identify the factors that contribute to success, for example:

- pupils found the lesson content interesting;
- the task set could be achieved by most pupils;
- the language was at the appropriate level;
- the pace was adequate, pupils had little time for 'off-task' activity;
- the pupils learned something and how you knew that; and what they learned conformed to your objectives;
- the amount of teacher talk was about right;
- the pupils moved around the laboratory in an orderly manner.

The converse of one of these factors can be a cause or symptom of poor lessons. Try to avoid making comments in your evaluation that say 'it went well' or 'the pupils enjoyed it' or 'the experiment worked', all of which may be true but alone yield little insight into the lesson. Look for reasons and causes that you can do something about.

Early evaluations focus on class management, discipline and your personal feelings of coping with new situations. This is normal. As you progress, move to evaluate pupils' learning and identify ways in which the pupils learn. This step requires you to assess learning and to seek evidence for it. Assessment demands that you focus on your objectives. Objectives are important for assessing learning and the quality of your teaching. Attention to learning enables you to begin differentiating your work; see Chapter 6.

Use your evaluations and those of tutors and teachers to improve future lessons and to inform your lesson planning. Lesson planning is a key skill that you should address throughout your career; see Appendix 4. You are entitled to receive written comments on your progress by your tutor and regular **written** feedback from the class teacher. Oral feedback is helpful but transient; review earlier written comment and advice and look for evidence of progress. Discuss with your tutor how and when you should expect to receive written feedback on your teaching.

Differentiation

> Differentiation is a planned process of intervention in the classroom learning of the pupils. It takes into account prior learning and the characteristics of the individual.
>
> (Capel, Leask and Turner, 1995, p. 121)

The Science National Curriculum is designed to be a broad and balanced course, but is taught in a differentiated manner to meet individual needs. Teachers need to develop special skills to ensure that effective differentiation in learning takes place. It is difficult for student teachers on their first teaching practice to focus on differentiated learning, as there are other tasks of prior importance. By the second practice period, you should have established routines of class management and control, strategies for teaching and learning, and an awareness of safe practices in a laboratory. By then you build opportunities for assessment into your lesson plans and can respond to the needs of pupils. Differentiation is discussed in Chapter 6.

Risk assessment

Under the Health and Safety at Work Act 1974, it is the duty of an employer to have an up-to-date written statement of the health and safety policy and the arrangements for implementing it. You may be given a copy of this policy and asked to sign to show that you have read and understood it before beginning your practical teaching.

The Control of Substances Hazardous to Health (COSHH) regulations (Health and Safety Commission, 1989) require employees to carry out risk assessments. This means that before a teacher and pupils handle substances considered as hazardous to health, i.e. those classified as toxic, corrosive, harmful or irritant and micro-organisms, their use in the classroom or laboratory must be assessed for safe use. You need to consider the ways in which a substance can cause harm when being handled for a particular purpose before deciding what precautions are needed (see Task 4.8).

Your department keeps a file that contains the COSHH regulations and other safety documents, including *Safety in Science Laboratories* (DFEE, 1996); *Safety in the School Laboratory* (ASE, 1988) and the CLEAPSS *HazCards* (CLEAPSS, 1981). Make sure you know where the file is kept and have read the documents listed there.

The class teacher is responsible for the safety of classes taken by a student teacher and must therefore be present in a laboratory throughout the lesson. Student teachers cannot carry out practical activities unless a qualified science teacher is present. **Show your lesson plans to the class teacher to check your risk assessments well in advance of your lesson**; see Task 4.8.

Make sure you know the rules of pupil behaviour in a laboratory and the procedures for dealing with accidents. Read the chapter 'Safety in secondary science laboratories' in the *Science Teacher's Handbook: Secondary* (Hull, 1993). Keep up to date on safety matters by reading *Education in Science*, the bulletin of the Association for Science Education.

Risk assessment includes a consideration of the **behaviour of the class**. Build risk assessments into your lesson plans and record on your lesson plan the steps you have taken (see Table 4.1). Ask your tutor and laboratory technicians for advice.

TASK 4.8 MAKING RISK ASSESSMENTS

Listed below are several activities frequently given as class practical in science lessons. Consider each activity in turn and decide:

1   the potential hazards in each activity;
2   the action needed (by you as a teacher and/or by pupils) to make the activity acceptably safe (routines, precautions);
3   the advice or instruction to give your pupils.

continued . . .

Finally, make a risk assessment for each activity. Where chemicals are involved, check the appropriate HazCard in your department and decide how the risk may be contained in the lesson.

Activities:

Stretching   Investigate the stretching, and measure the breaking force, of materials used to hold things together: rubber bands, steel wire, string. Pupils are provided with stands, clamps and G-clamps, ruler, blocks and supports, a pulley and lots of weights (masses).

Heating things   Observe the changes that take place when different substances are heated in air and then allowed to cool. Pupils are provided with test tubes, Bunsen burners, stands, etc.; also small quantities of substances: ice, wood chips, copper wire, magnesium ribbon, steel paper clips, powdered sulphur, copper sulphate, expanded polystyrene.

Inoculating agar plates   Pupils are asked to find out whether washing your hands removes all the 'germs' (bacteria). Prepared agar plates are used and pupils are asked to touch the surfaces with washed and unwashed fingers, then to close the plates and leave them in an incubator for a few days at 27°C. In the next lesson they inspect the plates and draw what they see.

Homework

Homework set purposefully and marked regularly has a positive impact on pupil achievement. Homework set casually gives a message to pupils that homework is not important. 'A poor homework policy and/or practice makes its contribution to enlarging the achievement gap between advantaged and disadvantaged pupils' (Hargreaves, quoted in Stern, 1995, p. 48). Hargreaves claimed that, over five years of secondary education, appropriate homework can add the equivalent of at least one additional year of full-time education.

Most schools have a homework policy. Many schools give pupils a homework timetable specifying the number of subjects and time allocation per evening per year group; your school may provide pupils with a homework notebook. Check the way in which homework is set in your school and the role of parents in monitoring its completion.

Homework is part of your lesson planning. It should meet the needs of different pupils and allow all pupils opportunities to succeed. Homework can:

- consolidate learning;
- extend understanding;
- promote study skills;
- be differentiated;
- provide opportunities for quiet study and promote interest and intrinsic motivation;
- involve the home and parents in pupil development.

The purpose of homework must be clear to the pupil. Homework should:

- have instructions about what to do;
- say whom to hand it to, when and where;
- be clear about the form of record expected;
- give advice about what a completed task looks like;
- say how it will be made use of in the next lesson;
- give criteria for assessment;
- if relevant, link assessment to National Curriculum levels.

Make a collection of homework tasks that might motivate pupils and promote study skills. Include written tasks, worksheets, reading and collecting information, revision, preparing or carrying out investigations, drawing, designing and making activities, games, word searches, crossword puzzles, preparing a presentation, analysing data, evaluating evidence. For further ideas about homework see Capel, Leask and Turner (1995, pp. 236–40) and Capel, Leask and Turner (1997, pp. 80–2).

SUMMARY

In this chapter we have discussed aspects of lesson planning and the factors that influence it. Becoming a teacher requires you to identify personal qualities, to learn skills and adopt new attitudes. Taken together, these attributes produce your style and professional competence. In an article discussing why people choose to be science teachers, Black claimed that:

> Learning to teach involves a new way of being yourself
>
> (Black, 1987, p. 1)

Throughout your period of practical teaching, you build your confidence and teaching skills and begin to learn about the ways in which you teach effectively. This state of affairs arises from thinking about your teaching, what many writers call the 'reflective practitioner' model of teaching.

Lesson planning followed by evaluation of your teaching is part of that model. Just as your teaching is informed by formative assessment of your pupils, so your development is informed and guided by the feedback from pupils, colleagues and your own analysis of your performance. Use Appendix 4 to help evaluate your progress.

Accepting advice and support helps you to think about how to become more effective in the classroom, e.g. to communicate more clearly, to create better learning tasks, to embrace more teaching strategies, to hone your teaching skills and to develop your own teaching style. The apparent ease by which many experienced teachers command and interest their pupils shows not only experience but careful planning, commitment and the ability to learn from experience.

FURTHER READING

Frost, J. (1995) *Teaching Science*, London: Woburn Press.
  Full of ideas to develop your teaching strategies, skills and ways to develop your individual style.

Hull, R. (ed.) (1993) *The Science Teacher's Handbook: Secondary*, Hatfield: The Association for Science Education.
  Contains advice about lesson planning and developing schemes of work. The chapter on safety in the laboratory should be read by all intending science teachers.

Monk, M. and Dillon, J. (1995) *Learning to Teach Science: Activities for Student Teachers and Mentors*, London: The Falmer Press.
  Packed with practical activities for enquiring into ways in which science is taught and learned.

Parkinson, J. (1994) *The Effective Teaching of Secondary Science*, Harlow: Longmans.
  Useful and more extensive discussions on aspects of planning lessons.

Woolnough, B. (1994) *Effective Science Teaching*, Buckingham: Open University Press.
  Shows ways in which school science can be made more exciting, stimulating and relevant to young people.

5 Developing your teaching

INTRODUCTION

In Chapter 3 we discussed the knowledge and understanding about science that pupils bring to the classroom and in Chapter 4 the factors to be considered in constructing lesson plans and using Schemes of Work. We turn now in greater depth to managing aspects of practical activities with the diversity of pupils in your classes.

Each pupil in your class is different and has a unique background. Contributing to these differences are economic factors, the skills and professions of their parents and their employment status, and the value and belief systems to which the family subscribes. Differences can be as great within an indigenous population as it is between that population and ethnic minority groups. It is not adequate to describe differences in terms of ethnicity, gender and class because within each category there remain large differences between pupils. Many 'ethnic minority pupils' are third generation born in the UK. You need to know the individual pupil.

Pupils bring to school a variety of experiences deriving from parental interests, their hobbies and interests and the impact of the media and Information Technology. Some pupils have experience of living in another country and many more of overseas travel. At the same time there are children who, for many reasons, have a more narrow experience, for which the school must try to compensate. The response of pupils to your teaching and the ethos of the school depends on the background of the pupils.

As well as social and behavioural differences, you find striking differences in the intellectual development of your pupils. All these differences have to be addressed in planning lessons and promoting learning. During your school experience, one of your tasks is to get to know the extent to which your pupils differ both intellectually and in other ways. Throughout this chapter we start to address issues of language as a controlling factor in the pace of pupil learning; the place of language in teaching and learning science is considered further in Chapter 7. It is important, therefore, that you know about your pupils' language skills, their ability to write, read and comprehend and their confidence to work on their own. Some pupils may be slow learners, or have special needs, such as learning difficulties of a particular sort, or have English as their second language.

The working atmosphere of your classroom is the best indicator of your development as a teacher; the planning of your lessons should be geared towards encouraging an atmosphere in which pupils enjoy learning. Your pupils learn best when they themselves engage actively with the ideas and materials you present them. Most pupils enjoy learning in this way, and the effect on their attitude to learning can be long lasting. The most potent motivation is self-motivation, which is encouraged when teachers employ a wide range of teaching strategies and situations, relate school learning to out of school learning and encourage pupils. Learning takes place when there is clear sense of purpose, an understanding by pupils of what is expected and an atmosphere of calm and co-operation.

OBJECTIVES

By the end of this chapter you should:

- be aware of ways to motivate your pupils;
- be aware of some issues of classroom and laboratory management;
- know some management strategies involved in conducting investigations with pupils and begin to practise some;
- be aware of the need to identify the variety of backgrounds, skills and needs of your pupils;
- be developing routines of classroom management that are sensitive to diversity and promote a learning environment;
- be becoming sensitive to the central role of language in teaching and learning.

MOTIVATING PUPILS

In the introduction we drew attention to some important factors affecting the motivation of pupils. This included self-motivation, when pupils learn and become involved because they are interested in the task and want to succeed.

Many pressures act against self-motivation. A common pressure is peer pressure. A few popular pupils who reject school learning set a trend for many other pupils that is difficult for the teacher to alter. Other factors have been mentioned that are related to the environment in which pupils grow up. The attitude of parents to school is a vital factor, and for those pupils with unsupportive parents or guardians, the teacher must work hard to overcome apathy or antipathy to school. However, there are strategies that can be tried. We address a number of these strategies in *Learning to Teach in the Secondary School*, Unit 3.2 (Capel, Leask and Turner, 1995); we amplify those ideas here in a science teaching context. Initially, we make some general points.

Pupils are motivated in number of ways, as are adults. These ways include:

- success – gaining good marks in a test;
- achievement – completing a piece of work that has been difficult or time consuming;
- achievement – recognising that you have made progress, or mastered some learning;
- fear – response to threat of punishment or displeasure from teacher or parent;
- bribe – if you pass your GCSE we will buy you a mountain bike.

Short term gain is possible by all of these techniques, but understanding, which arises from commitment, emerges only when the learner is involved and has a stake in the outcome.

In *Learning to Teach in the Secondary School*, we used the terms 'intrinsic' and 'extrinsic motivation' (Capel, Leask and Turner, 1995, pp. 95–6). Intrinsic motivation describes those situations in which the pupil develops their own motivation; extrinsic motivation concerns those occasions when external factors provide the motivation. What the teacher does has a profound effect on intrinsic motivation.

One motivating factor is **success**. When a pupil completes a piece of work, she feels pride in that achievement which is the greater when the work is challenging but not beyond her. This situation clearly requires the work to be differentiated. Class work cannot be set for each individual child, but it is possible to prepare some variations on a theme, the differences between which give different support to, or make different demands on, groups of pupils. The level of independence granted to pupils is itself a differentiated approach.

For some pupils, completing part of an investigation is success; it is not necessary that all pupils all of the time have to complete whole investigations. Pupils gain confidence to go further by achieving small successes.

Recognising success is another aspect of motivation. **Praising** pupils for their achievements encourages participation and reduces unwanted behaviour. Pupils are frequently praised for academic work, less so for good social behaviour. Praising or even acknowledging improved behaviour is important for maintaining that behaviour. Praise can be a powerful tool in promoting a good working atmosphere, but over use of praise can be self-defeating. Pupils do not want to be praised for something that is, for example, the same performance as last time, or trivial, or known to be below their potential. Try not to use the same words for the same pupil – a wider vocabulary is helpful. Tell the pupil why the piece of work is good and what you have recognised as progress.

Recognising progress is a feature of good **feedback** to pupils. Motivation is enhanced when pupils understand why a piece of work has been praised or criticised. All work can be improved and you should tell pupils, orally or in writing, of ways in which the work can be improved. Different pupils need different feedback for different reasons; in this way your **feedback is differentiated**. Feedback is given in class, by a quiet word or by marking.

A word about **punishment**. Clearly, punishment is necessary from time to time but you should recognise that punishment does not change the behaviour of many pupils. For the otherwise good pupil, an occasional punishment may have an effect, perhaps out of surprise, or shame, or because their parents found out. For many pupils, their inability to do the work, or to behave appropriately, often has roots outside the classroom. Whereas you cannot let inadequate work or behaviour go unnoticed, punishment by itself does not achieve lasting effect. A school detention book often shows that the same pupils offend time and again. Meeting the needs of such pupils requires both the strategies suggested above and more; see below.

A powerful motivating factor in science classes is **practical work**. Science teaching has an advantage over many curriculum subjects because of the importance attributed by teachers to the active participation of pupils. However, unless the place and purpose of practical work is clearly defined, practical work becomes a meaningless routine and merely an escape from teacher talk. For practical work to be meaningful and to supply motivation, pupils need to take an active part in all its aspects, from planning to evaluation.

Features of **good practical work** include:

- clear purpose to the work;
- work that is within the ability of the pupils;
- enough support to stimulate interest but not spoon-feed the pupil;
- active participation by pupils in the construction of the enquiry;
- a variety of practical tasks that meet different needs, e.g. investigations, learning techniques of procedure, learning about behaviour of materials and systems and learning to use equipment; testing material or devices to check claims or quality;
- from time to time pupils should be able to suggest, plan and carry out their own investigation;
- where possible, practical work should take the pupil outside school, through its relevance to external matters, the involvement of outside agencies or clubs and competitions.

However and whatever work is set, it must be valued, taken seriously by the teacher and, whenever appropriate, contribute to external certification.

A further motivating factor is the ability of the teacher to make use of the **knowledge and skills** that pupils bring to school. Many pupils are skilled in hobbies, or use of IT, or have read books, watched TV or surfed the Net. They already have knowledge and explanations of how the world works. Very often school science is assumed to have no connection with the outside world. Opportunities to link school science to happenings at home, to current science in the news and to developments in technology should be used. See also Chapter 6, 'Differentiation and Special Educational Needs'.

Knowing what the pupils know is part of a final important set of issues to do with knowing your pupils. Most pupils, if not all pupils, can contribute to the class and subjects under study. Many pupils have knowledge of other countries, through travel, through relatives or through domicile. In some cases, special knowledge is available of how men and women in other countries do things that can enrich the class and the lesson. There is no substitute for knowing your pupils. With knowledge comes confidence; pupils recognise teachers who recognise them as people with their own interests, skills and interests. That confidence transfers to academic work, when pupils have the confidence that their efforts are acknowledged, praised when good and constructively criticised when inadequate. We bring together these desirable skills in a teacher in the summary to this chapter. Interesting insights into how pupils feel about their school science and ways to involve pupils more are discussed in *Effective Science Teaching* (Woolnough, 1994, Chapters 2 and 3).

TASK 5.1 HOW PRAISE IS USED

Draw up an observation schedule that has categories for praise given to individuals, to groups and to the class. The schedule should allow you to distinguish praise for social behaviour from that for academic performance.

Agree with an experienced teacher to observe her class. Show her the observation schedule and discuss how you will use it after the lesson.

Find a place in the class where you can hear everything. Record the number of occasions when praise is given in the categories above and when negative comment is made. Use the completed schedule to draw up a summary of your observations and discuss the findings with the teacher.

You can follow up the observation in number of ways. You could:

- observe the same teacher in another lesson and class and compare the findings;
- ask a colleague or class teacher to observe your teaching using the same inventory.

Draw up a list of words and phrases used to praise or criticise pupils.

MANAGING EQUIPMENT AND PUPILS IN THE LABORATORY

Pupils enjoy working with equipment; as soon as they know that equipment is to be used, they try to find out what it does. One important management task for you is instructing pupils how to use equipment and the handing out and collecting in of equipment. Make sure you observe the ways in which other teachers do this and discuss with them their strategies (see Chapter 4).

Further commentary on observing lessons and ways to observe a range of practices are in Capel, Leask and Turner (1995, Unit 2.1); King (1996) and Monk and Dillon (1995, Chapter 2). For detailed discussion of observations from a variety of science lessons that relate the teacher's intention to learning outcomes, see Jennings, 'Teaching Skills' in Frost (1995, pp. 12–28).

Pupils waiting to get on with an activity often neglect to check that they know what to do with the equipment. You should ensure that:

- pupils know how to use equipment in advance of the task, e.g. give a demonstration of how to set up an electrolysis circuit and to identify that the circuit is working;
- any instructions on how to use equipment are not over-complicated but written in simple language. Written procedures need to be tried out in advance. Whenever possible, use pictures instead of words and common words instead of unusual ones. Ensure that pupils know the procedure by requiring pupils to tell you the procedure in some way; see Figure 5.1. Don't ask 'Does any one not understand?' because pupils do not admit easily to ignorance;
- the equipment is suited to the job, e.g. thermometer range covers the temperatures to be measured;
- the equipment is in working order, e.g. dry cells are charged;
- there is enough equipment and materials for your purposes and for the number of groups;
- pupils know why the equipment is being used, what it shows or measures. For example, pupils asked to investigate the transpiration of a leaf, by attaching blue cobalt chloride paper to it, often lose sight of what the test tells them when the paper changes colour;
- safety checks have been implemented before distribution, e.g. power supplies are set to the required voltage and cannot be altered; what to do with spent chemicals, etc. See also Chapter 4, which deals with safety issues.

Pupils often happily carry out an activity and, when asked what they are doing, reply 'Activity 4' or 'the worksheet, Miss' or 'testing this stuff'. The act of doing is often seen as an end in itself; many pupils are not clear why they are carrying out particular procedures or what the results of the procedures tell them. As you go round talking to pupils, it is important to check pupils' understanding, by asking, for example:

- what are you trying to find out; what is the problem?
- how is what you are doing going to answer the question?
- explain why are you doing that.

There are a number of strategies that help pupils to understand better what they are doing. The more involved pupils are in the construction of the activity, the better is their response to the task and the more involved they get. Motivation is enhanced as well as understanding. However, before pupils start an activity, engage the class in one or more of the following activities. Ask pupils to:

- design the procedures themselves;
- construct the procedure with the whole class;
- use a set of cards on which are words summarising stages in the process; ask pupils to re-order the cards;
- place in correct order a set of pictures or words displayed on an OHP (use a set of separate small transparencies, one for each stage);
- tell you the procedure during whole class discussion;
- write down their procedure from the board.

The activities that require pupils to order a set of cards is very effective with pupils with learning difficulties or limited language skills. As you get to know the class, different groups of pupils can be given different tasks. It can be an effective way of intervening with pupils who struggle with a task.

An example of ways to help pupils know a procedure is described in Figure 5.1. In the investigation described in Figure 5.1, pupils need access to different pieces of equipment and materials at various times during the lesson. How might equipment be set out to accommodate these pupils? See Task 5.2.

TASK 5.2 SETTING OUT EQUIPMENT

The class referred to in Figure 5.1 is a 2nd year mixed ability class of 30 boys and girls. They work in groups of three. Devise a way of setting out the equipment in your laboratory: see section 4 below. Check which equipment is stored in your laboratory and which will have to be introduced specially for the activity.

1 Draw a plan of the laboratory you work in showing the benches, the teacher's bench and where normal laboratory equipment is stored.

2 On the plan show:

- the normal seating arrangements;
- where the equipment for the lesson is placed at the start of the lesson.

3 Make notes about how you:

- instruct pupils to collect equipment;
- return equipment;
- clean any equipment before it is returned;
- process waste materials.

Identify ways in which pupils can be involved in these arrangements.

continued . . .

---

4   Equipment, per group: Bunsen burner, tripod and gauze; beaker, 100 cm^3; measuring cylinder, 50 cm^3; spatula; stirring rod; filter funnel; filter paper, to match funnel; stand for funnel; evaporating dish, 100 cm^3 capacity.
Equipment, for all: copper (II) oxide; dilute sulphuric acid (2M)

Share your report and notes with other student science teachers or with your science tutor. Identify the knowledge and skills you are developing by these exercises. Refer to Appendix 4.

COMMUNICATING WITH YOUR PUPILS

This section focuses on aspects of communication of importance to science teachers, and the reader is referred to Capel, Leask and Turner (1995, Unit 5.2) for a general discussion of communication in the classroom.

As well as managing your classroom routines, discipline and the use of equipment by pupils, another key area of teacher activity is communicating with your pupils. Communication includes speaking, listening and responding to pupils, asking questions and responding to the answers. You communicate with pupils through writing on the board or OHP, by means of worksheets or through your choice of written or spoken material, such as video, CD-ROM, the Net and books.

Whether your class is setted, banded or mixed ability, your pupils display a range of language skills. These skills depend to a great extent on the pupil's exposure to discourse at home, the richness of the vocabulary to which they are exposed, access to books and newspapers and the habit of reading or listening to conversation. The language of teachers is not always the same as that of their pupils. Although science has a strong technical vocabulary, some of the barriers to learning science from books and discussion lie in your use of words and phrases not habitually used by your pupils. You may need to modify your language as a first step in effective communication. For example, by using:

- 'moving' instead of 'locomotion';
- 'cut' to replace 'sever';
- 'put it in', not 'immerse';

etc. you include more pupils in the discussion.

There is a good case for extending pupils' vocabulary; however, when a new idea is introduced, there is advantage in keeping the learning of the concept in mind and not blurring the issue by using unnecessary unfamiliar words. Scientists and science teachers use words or phrases such as

The following procedure is designed to help pupils make copper (II) sulphate crystals.

Preparation of Copper Sulphate.

The picture cards are cut up and distributed, one set to each group or individual, according to the aims of the teacher.

The teacher reads out the instructions step by step, repeating each one.

The pupils, in groups or individually, sequence the picture cards as they listen.

Finally the teacher rereads the instructions quickly and gives out written instructions

After checking, groups are allowed to carry out the practical.

Instructions to be read by teacher:-

1) Heat about 25cm³ of sulphuric acid in a small beaker.
2) Add two spatulas of copper oxide.
3) Stir the mixture.
4) Decide if all the copper oxide dissolves.
5) Add two more spatulas if all the powder dissolves.
6) Stop adding powder when some copper oxide is at the bottom.
7) Filter the mixture into an evaporating dish.
8) Heat the solution in the evaporating dish until the volume is halved.
9) Cover the evaporating dish with paper.
10) Leave it until next week.

The picture cards.

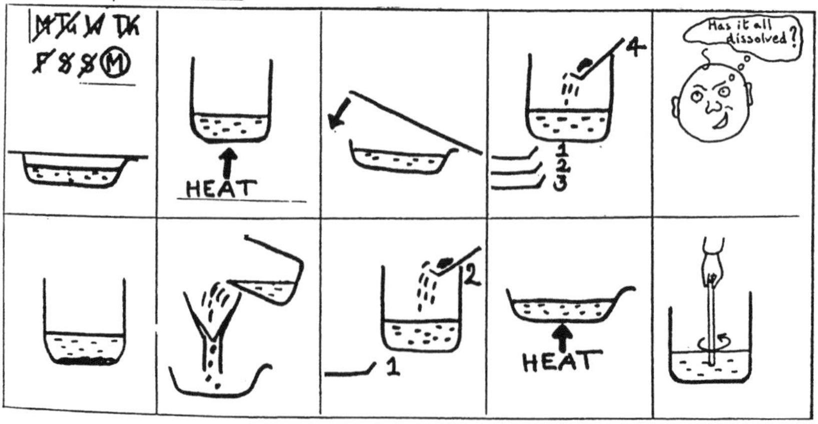

Figure 5.1 Helping pupils to understand instructions
Source: Roach, Smith and Vazquez, 1990, pp. 20-1

'tends to' and 'rank order' or 'describe the properties of'; it is not certain that pupils take from these phrases the same meaning as you do. Pupils often read the words easily but do not fully understand the meaning and are uncertain what they should do. Task 5.2 invites you to try out a comprehension exercise with your pupils.

TASK 5.3 THE LANGUAGE OF PUPILS

The following extract is from a text book for 14–16-year-old pupils entered for a double science examination. Ask your Key Stage 4 pupils to read the passage and tell you the meaning of the passage. Start with the words listed below.

Developing countries outside OPEC

> *Oil currently supplies over one half, and coal one quarter, of all commercial energy in developing countries outside OPEC. Not included in this balance are traditional household fuels of firewood, dung and crop residues whose contribution is difficult to quantify but may be at least as great as that of coal to the total energy balance.*

1 Ask your pupils to read this paragraph and explain the meaning of the words:
   currently, traditional, contribution, commercial, residues and quantify.
2 Which substances are referred to in the phrase 'as least as great as that of coal'? and do they contribute more, less or the same amount of energy to the country's energy budget as coal?
3 Rewrite the text to be suitable for your Year 10 pupils.

You should check regularly the language that you use with your pupils, particularly when pupils are engaged in following practical guidelines or working from books, video-tape, etc.

Board writing

You spend a good deal of time writing on the board. You should use clear handwriting that is joined up and not printed, because that is what pupils see in books and newspapers. An example of legible handwriting is given in Figure 5.1. Practise writing on the board to judge the appropriate size of writing for your room and seating, and keep your writing on a straight line. Go to the back of the class and check that you can read it. Ask your class teacher to comment on your writing when he observes your lessons.

Some of the work you put on the board can be planned in advance; work out how to use the board space, e.g. the headings to use, the examples to cite and where to place diagrams, tables or sketches. Use colour on the chalkboard: red and yellow are good contrasting colours. You can use a wider range of colours with the white board. Writing clearly on the white board also needs practice.

When you plan to draw a diagram in the lesson, try it out first on paper, then on the board. Make sure that you can fit the diagram in the space, that your writing is clear and the labels appropriate. Ensure that pupils know what you want them to do with the diagram.

You may wish to develop an idea with the class, or explore the pupils' understanding of a concept. You should, in advance, have some idea of how the class will respond to help you plan how to display their responses to give an orderly and coherent picture; see Chapter 3. Avoid writing down the pupils' ideas only to rub them off and replace them with your own!

The Overhead Projector (OHP)

Some science departments use OHPs as a regular feature of their teaching, whereas other departments have one in a cupboard gathering dust; you may literally need to dust it down to make use of it.

Why use an OHP? A great advantage is the capacity to prepare material in advance and to use as much as you need on the day, e.g. diagrams, tables and instructions. Second, you can use the OHP while facing your class – a priceless asset.

Transparencies can be made directly from a computer using the appropriate acetate sheet for your printer. Colour transparencies can be made with a printer or by using coloured acetate sheet, e.g. to highlight key words or pictures. Check with the reprographics office in your school and college.

There are many good commercial transparency sets and you should check your science department store and your college library. See also the *School Science Review*, the publication of the Association for Science Education in which reviews of this and similar material appear (see Appendix 5).

Transparent graph paper used on the OHP is helpful to:

- assist pupils to draw graphs and construct axes;
- show pupils how to plot points;
- show examples of graphs;

- plot data from groups of pupils;
- read off data from graphs.

Take note of the following do's and don'ts on the use of transparencies:

- the OHP is not a blackboard – a screen full of notes to copy is a turn off and likely to be illegible. It is poor teaching, too;
- font 18 point Times is a good size for most writing to ensure 'back of the room' legibility;
- make sure you know how to use the OHP before you get in the laboratory and how to adjust the screen, or the instrument, so that the display is not distorted;
- direct pupils' attention to the written material by pointing on the acetate, not on the screen; a pencil laid on the platform can be used to point to the relevant text. This strategy allows you, for a minute or two, to stand away from the OHP and move about the class;
- make sure pupils know what to do when you show a transparency. A common question is 'do we copy this, Miss?';
- if you prepare the transparency in advance, draw a border round the material to avoid the projection spilling over the edge of the screen. Check it;
- use several colours in a consistent way, e.g. to underline key words, for emphasis, contrast, etc.;
- use several transparencies to build up text, diagrams or ideas as you talk, using overlays;
- avoid revealing the whole of your transparency at once; block out regions and show them when needed;
- the OHP is a valuable way of permanently showing procedures for investigations, recording tables, safety checks, the results of investigations by pupils, etc.;
- pupils can summarise their own ideas on a transparent acetate, to lead class discussion or to report back;

Other ways in which the OHP is helpful to science teachers includes:

- displaying instruments' scales (ruler, thermometer, voltmeter) to assist pupils to read scales;
- showing chemical reactions. If the chemicals are mixed in a clear dish, e.g. petri dish, changes can be followed, e.g. colour changes, such as pH; precipitation reactions. Also small-scale electrolysis or crystal growth may be demonstrated;
- demonstrating the wave-like motion of the millipede's legs by allowing the animal to walk across the projector table (not too long, the

table is warm);
- showing the properties of polarising material on light.

and many more. The OHP can enhance the presentation of your lessons in many ways.

Worksheets

Worksheets are much used by science teachers to give information, instruction, provide a written task or act as a learning guide. There is a danger of over-use of worksheets and they can be a recipe for boredom, once described by a teacher as 'death by a thousand worksheets'. Worksheets used as support for lessons can lead to their use as a crutch for both teacher and pupil and, at worst, encourages passive learning. Worksheets are not a substitute for proper briefing of your pupils, the absence of which leads to under-use and misunderstanding by pupils. However, a dedicated worksheet can be a vital support for your lesson when linked appropriately to an activity.

Some published curriculum courses include worksheet masters and you should consult the appropriate *Teacher's Guide*. Many science departments have a stock of commercial and home-made worksheets that you should explore and exploit. Guidelines for writing worksheets are given below:

Ask yourself these questions first:

- Why do you want to use a worksheet and is the time spent making one justified?
- How does your worksheet fit in with your lesson plan and objectives?
- Does the worksheet encourage learning?

Assuming the answer to these questions is 'yes', your worksheet should:

- have a title with its purpose clearly stated;
- be written in simple, appropriate language for your pupils;
- make clear what the pupils are to do, e.g. write, read, act on, etc.;
- use the minimum amount of written material, i.e. be uncluttered;
- make use of drawings, sketches and diagrams instead of wordy descriptions; for procedural instructions consider using a flow chart instead of prose;
- ☞ have safety instructions or warnings clearly labelled, e.g. picture of safety spectacles, or a hazard sign. Use a symbol such as ☞ to focus attention;

- include instructions to the pupil as to what to do with the worksheet, e.g. staple into your notebook;
- use colour sparingly, for emphasis or to highlight key words;
- be attractive, legible and clean;
- be spell checked.

The use of double columns on a worksheet can be a way blocking off small items of work for pupils, thus encouraging engagement with the material. The availability of word processors in most departments allows you to do this. The use of a word processor allows you to:

- modify your materials quickly and easily for future use;
- introduce variations to help differentiate your teaching;
- change the basic worksheet for a special needs pupil.

In the worksheet shown in Figure 5.2, there is a minimum of wording coupled with use of diagrams that identify both the activity and the conditions. It is a written exercise, useful for pupils who have difficulty in constructing sentences. The intellectual demand on the pupils is nevertheless high, with three variables to consider: the temperature, crystal size and the use of stirring. Pupils need to be clear about the effect of each variable and to separate them in order to select the correct set of phrases. The additional questions extend able pupils.

Most worksheets can be made using your word processor, and diagrams from your scrapbook or CD-ROM etc. can be downloaded.

TASK 5.4 REDESIGNING AN INVESTIGATION

Modify the investigation described in Figure 5.2 to be suitable as instructions for a Key Stage 4 class to carry out an activity of this type. Include two extension questions that investigate the pupils' ability to use the kinetic-particle theory to explain the effect of particle size and temperature on dissolving.

SUMMARY

Your class may contain pupils of different abilities, each with a different capacity to learn and different attitudes to school. Your pupils may come from a variety of cultures and belief systems, e.g. Seventh Day Adventist, Muslim, agnostic, etc. The strength of that belief affects the way in which

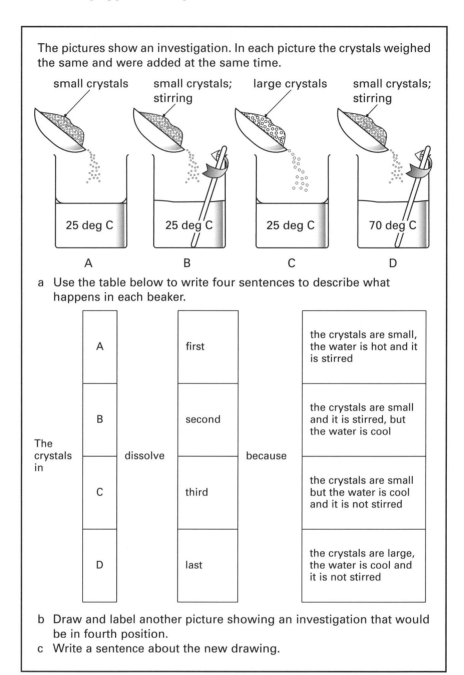

The pictures show an investigation. In each picture the crystals weighed the same and were added at the same time.

a   Use the table below to write four sentences to describe what happens in each beaker.

The crystals in		dissolve		because	
	A		first		the crystals are small, the water is hot and it is stirred
	B		second		the crystals are small and it is stirred, but the water is cool
	C		third		the crystals are small but the water is cool and it is not stirred
	D		last		the crystals are large, the water is cool and it is not stirred

b   Draw and label another picture showing an investigation that would be in fourth position.

c   Write a sentence about the new drawing.

Figure 5.2   Can we speed up dissolving?
Source: adapted from Roach, Smith and Vazquez, 1990, pp. 21–7

the pupil views science and scientific knowledge. Certain types of scientific enquiry are considered wrong in some belief systems: some people condemn experiments using animals; some pupils do not handle animal tissue because they are vegetarian; most Muslim pupils will not handle pork because it is believed to be unclean; Hindus consider the cow to be sacred. It is important to be aware of the range of practices of the pupils in your class when preparing lessons. Your school should have information about the festivals and practices of the various cultural groups represented in your school, including attitudes to sex education.

As a student teacher, the most important task is to begin to be aware of the range of views and beliefs, backgrounds, skills and attitudes that your pupils bring to your classes. Your ability to manage them and their learning depends on getting to know your pupils as well as possible. As part of your developing competence as a teacher you should:

be aware

- that you are educating pupils to live in a culturally diverse society;
- of the main features of school policy on equal opportunity, for example in relation to sex education, sexism, anti-racism and bullying;
- of the differences in response to your teaching by boys and girls across the range of cultures and backgrounds represented in your school;
- of the importance of language development in teaching and learning and the range of performance of your pupils; see also Chapter 7;
- of the main cultural groups in your school, for example by mother tongue, religious belief or cultural norms;
- and sensitive to issues of stereotyping both in your relationships with the class and between pupil and pupil.

be able to

- recall the names of all the pupils you teach;
- recognise the different cultural groups in your classes;
- develop management strategies that are sensitive to the different pupils in your classes;
- name the pupils who have English as a second language;
- name the pupils who have learning difficulties;
- name the pupils who have Special Educational Needs and know the nature of that need;
- prepare, with support, lessons that begin to take account of the diversity in your classes;
- develop ways to use the pupils' prior knowledge and understanding of science in preparing lessons for your class;

- monitor your resources for their language demand and try to ensure that your pupils have access to the curriculum;
- monitor your resources for bias and stereotyping with the support of tutors and teachers.

be willing to

- oppose bias and stereotyping in your work in schools;
- promote equal opportunities for all your pupils;
- recognise the special needs of particular pupils and be able to articulate those needs to other teachers.

The place of language in teaching and learning science is considered further in Chapter 7 and differentiation is addressed in that context. Differentiation is discussed in Chapter 6, which addresses special needs.

TASK 5.5 TEACHING SKILLS

This chapter has covered a number of teaching skills. Review this chapter by using Appendix 4 to help evaluate your own progress and development.

FURTHER READING

Frost, J. (ed.) (1995) *Teaching Science*, London: Woburn Press.
In depth discussion of the skills and strategies of teaching science. There is a wealth of practical ideas and advice and the book covers practical work as well as field work, simulations and independent learning strategies. Chapter 2, 'Teaching skills', is appropriate in the context of this chapter.

Monk, M. and Dillon, J. (1995) *Learning to Teach Science: Activities for Student Teachers and Mentors*, London: The Falmer Press.
A set of detailed activities and discussions about many aspects of learning to teach science. Chapter 2, 'Observing science teachers at work', and Chapter 4, 'Planning and managing', are useful sources of ideas for further enquiries in your school.

Thorp, S. (ed.) (1991) *Race, Equality and Science Teaching: An Active Inset Manual for Teachers and Educators*, Hatfield: The Association for Science Education.
A practical guide to working with cultural diversity in your classroom. Designed to support anti-racist teaching, the ideas represented in the manual are simply good practice that should be used by all teachers, irrespective of the cultural composition of their classes.

6 Differentiation and Special Educational Needs

INTRODUCTION

Silent, but ...

I may be silent, but
I'm thinking.
I may not talk, but
Don't mistake me for a wall.

Japanese poem by *Tsuboi Shigeji* in
Bownas and Thwaite, 1964, p. 191

The 1988 Education Reform Act (ERA, 1988) requires that pupils, regardless of race, gender, disability or geographical location, are entitled to receive a broad, balanced education and that teaching is differentiated according to their needs. Many pupils have individual needs at different points in their schooling. The term Special Educational Needs (SEN) refers to pupils who have been identified as requiring special support, which is initiated through a process called **statementing**. The section of the 1988 Education Act that addressed SEN developed from the 1981 Education Act (DES, 1981) which, in turn, was a direct response to the Warnock Report on SEN (DES, 1978b). Pupils are considered to have SEN if they have a learning difficulty that requires special educational provision.

SEN is a term that covers pupils with a wide variety of abilities. It is used to describe and include those pupils who experience severe learning difficulties, those who are physically disabled and those who are gifted, e.g. are exceptionally able intellectually or gifted musically. Pupils with severe learning difficulties are assessed through a process of statementing which identifies their individual needs and puts into place a support system. The statementing process for SEN pupils is discussed in the companion volume, *Learning to Teach in the Secondary School* (Capel, Leask and Turner, 1995, Unit 4.6). We refer you to that text for a general introduction to both pupils with SEN and the individual needs of a wider school population.

The implementation of the 1988 Education Act brought many challenges to science teachers, including the need to teach science to a wide range of ability of pupils up to 16 years. Science lessons have many features that allow pupils some access to the science curriculum, despite their learning difficulties. The 1988 Education Act made science a core subject in the National Curriculum. This has meant that all pupils are expected to learn science up to the age of 16 years, irrespective of their ability. Only a small number of pupils can be withdrawn from the National Curriculum as a result of SEN.

In addition, you need to recognise that many more pupils have individual needs that are not subject to the statementing process, including able pupils. Developing your skills to meet these demands is part of your professional development. This developmental process is, however, a life-long one.

OBJECTIVES

By the end of this chapter you should be able to:

- recognise than many pupils have individual needs;
- understand your role in working with any pupil with individual needs;
- understand the meaning of differentiation;
- plan lessons, with support, that respond to the needs of pupils;
- understand the meaning of SEN;
- recognise pupils with SEN and understand your role in working with those pupils;
- begin to identify ways in which you can work with SEN support staff in your classroom.

PUPILS WITH INDIVIDUAL NEEDS

Most of this chapter is concerned with a large range of pupils, who, while not statemented or in need of a statement of SEN, nevertheless have individual needs that must be addressed if they are to make progress. In a later section of this chapter we address the issue of pupils with SEN.

In a comprehensive school there are likely to be many pupils who have learning difficulties, including pupils who are very able. To meet their needs you, as the teacher, need to be aware of the particular learning difficulties such pupils have and seek ways to address those needs in your lesson planning. It is not the intention that you meet the needs of every pupil on an individual basis, although knowing individual needs remains necessary for lesson planning.

Postlethwaite suggests that:

> Special needs can best be met when a general concern for individual differences is uppermost in teachers' thinking.
>
> (Postlethwaite, 1993, p. 21)

This statement implies that all pupils are different. These differences are not only the way in which pupils respond to your teaching, but include the underlying causes of those differences. The causes may be learning difficulties, language limitations, cultural differences in pupils' attitudes to learning, the type of parental support, motivation or personal learning styles.

In *Learning to Teach in the Secondary School* (Capel, Leask and Turner, 1995, Unit 4.1) the case histories of a number of pupils are given. We suggest that you read that section before proceeding. The case histories include able pupils as well as pupils with learning and behaviour problems, and they give an example of how to summarise the characteristics of pupils, which can be important for lesson planning. For example, some pupils frequently disrupt the lesson by interfering with the work of other pupils. Planning how to deflect the behaviour and accommodate that pupil in your class is an important factor in your planning. The first step in dealing with a wide range of pupil performance is to know more about the individuals; see Task 6.1.

Science offers particular activities and ways of working that assist pupils with learning difficulties, and, in this sense, science has some advantages over other subjects in the curriculum. These features of science include:

- the importance of first-hand experience;
- the links between science and everyday experience;
- knowledge and skills that can be acquired through practical activity;
- many skills that are acquired in small steps; for example, that investigations include many sub-skills which can be taught separately and successfully;
- activities and phenomena that capture the imagination of pupils, enhancing motivation.

You should recognise these advantages by incorporating them in your lesson planning.

TASK 6.1 CASE STUDY OF A PUPIL IN YOUR CLASS

Identify a class that you teach that contains some pupils who have
learning difficulties. Identify one pupil with learning difficulties
about whom you would like to know more. Write a short description
of his problems in learning science, his behaviour problems or
emotional difficulties; see the case studies mentioned above.

To do this, we suggest that you:

- review his performance in the classes you teach;
- talk to his regular science teacher;
- observe one or more lessons in which he is taught another
  subject, not science;
- read his personal file, but first talk to the SEN Co-ordinator for
  permission to do this;
- talk to his class teacher (form teacher) to gain a wider perspective
  of his performance;
- look through his science notebook to assess his response to class
  work and homework.

Using the model case studies mentioned above, write a profile of
the pupil, e.g. 300 words. Ensure that you list what he can do as well
as his difficulties. You may wish to study two pupils in order to
compare their needs and abilities.

In which ways does this information help you plan your next
lesson with that class? Discuss your ideas with

1   the class science teacher;
2   your tutor;
3   other student science teachers.

Incorporate your ideas into your next lesson plan for this class.
Check the knowledge and skills expected of you and identify your
progress in this area (use Appendix 4).

The practical component of science lessons can, with careful support,
help pupils who have difficulties reading and writing to participate
actively in aspects of science lessons. The focus of much science work on
group activity allows some pupils who are weak in certain skills to be
supported by their friends. Many pupils can contribute orally to planning
tasks and hence gain insight into the whole activity. Some pupils may be
unable to carry out a complete task themselves; however, they can

contribute to the overall activity in an area in which they have some competence. In this way they exercise those skills, learn more about other skills and get an overview of the whole task.

The subject matter of science is also capable of sparking interest and enthusiasm in pupils for whom learning is a chore. The relevance of the subject can provide motivation for all pupils, including those with SEN.

As a student teacher, your early concerns in the classroom focus on classroom management, control and making sure you know the science content. As your confidence grows and your basic classroom skills develop, you need to shift your attention from class management to the needs of pupils, that is, from the routines of teaching to the complexities of learning. This shift takes place slowly. However, if you are to address the learning needs of your pupils, this shift has to be consciously supported and planned.

You should regularly review your teaching targets with your tutors and ensure that your lesson objectives focus on learning as well as management. For example, as well as ensuring that certain pupils work with other pupils who can help them, consider what you expect the pupil to be able to do or know as a result of the lesson, and how you expect to find this out. Matching the tasks you set to the skills and abilities of your pupils is a planning process that needs constant review. Addressing the needs of pupils requires you to know your pupils: being aware of how they respond to your teaching by what they do, say and write means that you will find out what they are less good at.

As well as knowing what your pupils learn from your teaching, try to find out the knowledge, skills and abilities they bring to school. This knowledge affects the way in which pupils respond to your teaching and helps to direct the way in which you differentiate the work in your lessons to meet their needs. Getting to know your pupils in this way is part of a long-term process. It involves knowing *how* to find out about your pupils as well as knowing *what* you have found out, which leads us to teaching strategies and planning for differentiation.

PLANNING FOR DIFFERENTIATION IN SCIENCE LESSONS

Differentiation has been described as:

> the process by which curricular objectives, teaching methods, resources and learning activities are planned to cater for the needs of individual pupils.
>
> (National Curriculum Council, 1992b, p. 4)

This statement includes most of the things that teachers and depart-ments do or provide. In other words, differentiation is part of the every-day work of teachers, geared to responding to the needs of individual pupils. Differentiation is not simply about providing a extension work-sheet for the faster pupils and a different worksheet for the slower pupils. You should try to:

- set objectives for pupils that are realistic; these will not necessarily be the same for all pupils;
- select your teaching methods and learning strategies to reflect your pupils' needs;
- use formative assessment, that is, use assessment to inform you about how best to structure your future teaching in order to help pupils understand what they have achieved and to set new targets; see also Chapter 8;
- choose resources appropriate to the task and the pupils' ability to use them.

The scope of differentiation described above places heavy responsibil-ities on you as a teacher. The increasing class sizes, the scale of the task of meeting the needs of many pupils and the requirement to teach the Science National Curriculum make heavy demands on teachers' time and skills. We suggest below ways in which you can met the different needs of pupils, groups of pupils and whole classes. Adopting a differentiated approach to teaching is a matter of being on the lookout for opportunities to guide, encourage and support your pupils in as many ways as possible, using whatever resources, processes and tactics seem appropriate.

Outcome vs. task: just two aspects of differentiation

One approach to differentiation is to say, 'If I set a task with the possibil-ity of different outcomes then pupils can respond in the way appropriate to them.' In other words, the pupils define the level at which they respond to the task, and their ability is reflected in the response or 'outcome'.

By contrast, if I set different tasks on a common theme, each with the possibility of different outcomes, then pupils, individually or in groups, can be allocated to different tasks chosen to suit their needs. The pupil's response is then limited by the task; the differentiation is said to be 'task' driven; see Figure 6.1.

Both methods of differentiation require that the teacher knows her pupils. In the first case, you have to judge the extent to which pupils have given the task their best shot. If left to their own devices, pupils may set-

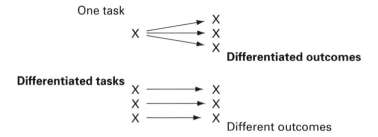

Figure 6.1   Differentiation diagram

tle for the easiest option. Your role is to push the pupil, or group of pupils, to maximise their effort on task. In addition, you have to judge what is an appropriate outcome. Differences in outcome may be recognised by the:

- extent to which all aspects of the task have been considered;
- adoption of a suitable method of enquiry;
- use of more difficult concepts in planning;
- recognition of variables and the use of appropriate controls;
- number and accuracy of readings taken;
- thoroughness and accuracy of recording data;
- presentation of data and the thoroughness of analysis;
- conclusions drawn from the activity, e.g. are the conclusions in step with the observations they have made and not beyond them?
- way in which the report is written up and the ability of pupils to express themselves in an increasingly sophisticated language;
- acceptance of limitations of the enquiry and consideration of ways to improve it.

In each of these cases you need to make a judgement about what is appropriate for that group of pupils, i.e. what is it reasonable to expect? In addition, you need to identify ways in which the task could have been tackled better by that group of pupils or by individuals.

In the case of differentiation by task, identifying different tasks around the same theme requires some ingenuity. As before, you need to know your pupils well so that the task is challenging yet within their capability. The ways in which the task can be differentiated include:

- the degree of open-endedness of the task;
- the degree of familiarity with the resources;
- whether the task is a whole investigation or a part investigation;
- the amount of information given to the pupils;

- the language in which the task is written;
- familiarity with the concepts needed;
- the amount of guidance given to pupils, for example on making measurements, recording data, drawing a graph, format for writing the report.

Both types of differentiation (task or outcome) suggest that a task is given to pupils and they get on with it. In practice, of course, you are involved throughout the execution of the task, as described below. Thus differentiation also takes place at the point of contact with the group or individual. Differentiation is not simply a case of task vs. outcome.

Your response to pupils working in class includes:

- checking that they understand what they are supposed to do;
- listening to a discussion and prompting or questioning when needed;
- helping pupils to brainstorm an idea or problem;
- asking questions about procedure or a particular measurement;
- suggesting further action when difficulties arise or motivation flags; see also Chapter 5 and Chapter 10 for discussion about motivation;
- giving pupils supporting worksheets or other written guidance appropriate to the problem in hand. The guidance might explain the science in simpler terms or simplify the language used;
- checking pupils' notebooks and noting progress;
- marking pupils' work;
- encouraging pupils by identifying success;
- setting targets for improvement;
- increasing the demand on an existing task;
- deflecting unwanted behaviour or nipping problems in the bud;
- noting unexpected events or achievements for a plenary session;
- taking the opportunity to talk 'off-task' to pupils to check their general well-being.

We suggest that you keep a notebook to record some information you glean about pupils when working in class for insertion in your more formal records.

The different ways in which you respond to your pupils' activities may affect the quality of their performance; your response to pupils is an important feature of a differentiated approach and knowing how to respond is part of the repertoire of all good teachers. Thus the dichotomy of differentiation, discussed above as a simple 'task vs. outcome' issue, hides a host of other ways in which you support your pupils. Knowing how to set such tasks depends on how well you know your pupils.

STRATEGIES FOR KNOWING MORE ABOUT YOUR PUPILS

Advanced planning

In Chapter 3, 'Pupil learning', we discussed a number of ways of finding out about pupils' understanding of science. We suggested that you conduct interviews with individual pupils or groups of pupils to find out what they know about a science topic. Clearly, such activity is part of a process of getting to know your pupils. However, it is not possible for you to talk to all the pupils in your class in this way, let alone all the classes you teach. We referred you to the literature about pupils' understanding of science that summarises pupils' views of many aspects of science; see Chapter 3.

What other ways are there to know more about your pupils? As well as knowing about their understanding of science, you need to know what motivates them, what they are interested in and so on. Their motivation and other interests come from discussions during practical activities, those few moments at the start and ending of lessons and from your involvement in extra-curricular activities. Such knowledge builds more readily in your first post and is more difficult to come by during school experience within your education course.

Returning to ways in which to find out about pupils' knowledge of science, one way is to set the class a task or test. Before you write a test, consider what **you** expect to learn from it and what it is reasonable to expect from your pupils. You should consider:

- what you **expect pupils to know as a basis for your next lesson**;
- whether the pupils have been taught the topic before;
- for new pupils in Year 7, whether the topic was taught in primary school;
- what pupils might know about the science topic from everyday life;
- the relevant section of the Programme of Study in the Science National Curriculum.

These ideas should help you to frame a **short test**, the results of which can help you to plan a first lesson. A similar idea can be used to monitor your teaching part way through a unit of work; see below. A variation on this theme is for you **set a homework** that elicits the same ideas. If the homework is set in advance and read before the lesson, your lesson planning can take account of the pupils' responses to the homework.

Another way is to open up a **discussion** with the class at the beginning of a lesson or, if it can be arranged, at the end of a previous lesson. For example, your series of lessons on 'Acids, bases and pH' starts with a discussion that endeavours to elicit pupils' knowledge and understanding of acids. The ideas are put on the board as your pupils mention them, for example as **a concept map or spider diagram** (see Unit 5.2 in Capel, Leask and Turner, 1995). You then finish with a summary of what many pupils understand about acids. In addition, the discussion tells you about pupils' misconceptions concerning acids.

An alternative strategy to a discussion is to ask your pupils to work in **small groups** and to make three lists, one showing substances 'that are acids', a second list saying 'where they find acids' and a third list of 'what acids do'. The groups come together after 10–15 minutes to draw up a common list, summarised as a table on the board.

An interesting way to elicit understanding from pupils is to set up a **demonstration** that invites pupils to explain a phenomenon. The phenomenon is chosen to reveal understandings about ideas and concepts that you wish to teach. One such example is given in Figure 6.2.

Class: Year 7, mixed ability class, a 35 minute lesson.
Topic: Change of state.
Demonstration: collapsing cans.

1   Place about 10 cm^3 of water in a can with a small hole, e.g. a used drinks can, and clamp it. Heat the water to boiling and then plunge the can upside down into a glass trough of cold water. The top of the can should be completely submerged in the water.

Ask pupils to describe what happens to the can. List on the board the features of the agreed description.

Invite pupils to explain why the can collapses so dramatically and noisily. Explanations offered by pupils include:
● hot air and steam explode;
● metal has been affected by the heat;
● steam condenses and causes the sides of the can to be sucked in.

2   Repeat the activity with a different can (e.g. clean 5 litre oil can), this time removing the air with a vacuum pump. Ask pupils to explain why this can collapses. Show that the can is re-inflated by reversing the pumping action.

Some pupils suggest that the pump sucks the can in; very few explain the collapse as due to differences in air pressure. The 're-inflation' of the can suggests pressure as something to do with the phenomenon. A feeling for pupils' awareness of air pressure can be gleaned from pupils' responses to the two short demonstrations and used as a basis for planning the next lesson.

Many teachers prefer to use the second activity alone to show the effect of air pressure, because the explanation involving the can of water is more complicated. However, pupils can carry out the first activity for themselves, with suitable safety precautions.

Figure 6.2   Air pressure
Source: Science Faculty, Swakeleys School

Finding out about pupils' understanding: a whole lesson approach

A first lesson can be planned to find out pupils' understanding of a topic and, at the same time, build in support and extension work. A good example of this approach concerns situations where you expect pupils to have particular knowledge and know certain ideas because they were taught in a previous term or year. In the example below, a Year 9 class were taught electricity and magnetism in their Year 7 class and are extending their knowledge in Year 9. The lesson described below elicited recall and understanding of previously taught topics. The elicitation phase was followed by consolidation and extension work, adjusted to meet the needs of different groups of pupils.

Read the lesson in Task 6.2 and respond to the questions that follow. The lesson is substantially as taught by a student teacher in her PGCE year. The aims, objectives and estimated timings are those of the student teacher taken from her lesson plan. The school is LEA controlled, situated in urban London and is popular and over-subscribed by parents. The school is not selective by ability. The pupils represent a wide range of ethnicity, ability, needs and behaviours.

TASK 6.2 ANALYSIS OF A LESSON FOR DIFFERENTIATION

Read the lesson description in Part A and then address the tasks in Part B.

Part A
Topic: Magnets: introduction to magnetism.
Time: 1 hour.
Class: Year 9 class, 24 pupils in mixed ability group. The class has a statemented pupil who is visually impaired and supported by a SEN teacher.

Previous taught knowledge Magnetism had been introduced in Year 7, with attention to the rules of magnetic attraction and repulsion and an introduction to the field associated with a bar magnet, using iron filings.

Aim To review and consolidate the properties of a bar magnet.
Objectives By the end of the lesson pupils should be able to:

● state that like poles of a bar magnet repel each other and that unlike poles attract;

continued ...

- demonstrate the properties of attraction and repulsion;
- identify the field around a bar magnet;
- explain the pattern of iron filings developed when two bar magnets are placed end to end and relate that to the field of a magnet.

Timing/minute

0–15 Pupils were asked to write three sentences about magnets using three groups of trigger words written on the board

magnet	like	magnet
north	unlike	field
south	attract	poles
poles	repel	lines
	poles	force

10–15 The teacher assessed the progress and performance of pupils by their response to the written task. As pupils completed the written task, small groups of pupils were directed to a station in a circus of activities. The task selected for pupils depended on the extent to which pupils could recall earlier learning and could write about it.

15–45 Group work on activities that were supported by a text book (*Bath Science KS3*). The circus of activities included:

- reviewing the polarity of bar magnets and revising the rules of attraction and repulsion;
- plotting, drawing and explaining the pattern of iron filings around a bar magnet including a) a single bar magnet; b) 2 bar magnets placed N–N and S–S and c) 2 bar magnets with poles placed N–S;
- plotting, drawing and explaining the pattern of movement of the North seeking pole of a compass needle placed at various points near a bar magnet;
- using iron filings to explore the field pattern generated by a wire carrying an electric current.

45–50 Clearing up and checking in equipment; pupils resumed seats.

50–60 Teacher conducted review of learning by asking pupils to re-write their sentences. The sentences produced now by the pupils were written on the board and discussed. The sentences were used to ensure that most had access to the

continued . . .

first two objectives of the lesson. Pupils were expected to write these sentences in their note books as a summary. Pupils' note books were collected by the teacher and the class was dismissed.

Part B

1 Check your understanding of the science involved in this lesson.

2 Answer the following questions:

- Identify ways in which differentiation was illustrated in this lesson. Consider in turn the a) teaching method(s); b) selection of tasks; c) demands made on pupils.
- Was differentiation achieved by outcome or task?
- Identify ways in which the lesson could be improved.
- Identify ways in which this lesson might be developed in the subsequent two or three lessons. Suggest an aim for the next lesson and write two objectives for it.

3 Identify the demands on the student teacher for each of the following areas of teaching skills:

- the factors to be considered when planning the lesson;
- the factors to be considered when preparing for the lesson;
- managing the resources during the lesson;
- managing the learning by pupils during the lesson;
- monitoring the progress of pupils.

Differentiation and a unit of work

Formative assessment is important for diagnosing pupil progress. (See Chapter 8 for further discussion on assessment.) It is common practice for units of work to be taught and then the pupils assessed at the end of the topic. The results of such assessments can frequently be predicted on the basis of past practice. Often not much new is learned about pupils and some pupils make little progress. If assessment is carried out part-way through a unit of work, appropriate action can be taken to help your pupils, through extension, consolidation and support activities for their learning. One possible model for structuring the teaching of a unit is shown in Figure 6.3.

Differentiation is achieved at a point within the unit of work to allow targeted support and guidance to be given to groups of pupils. This strategy can, for some pupils, minimise a sense of failure. Some pupils do not go beyond the key concepts, i.e. some content is not covered but

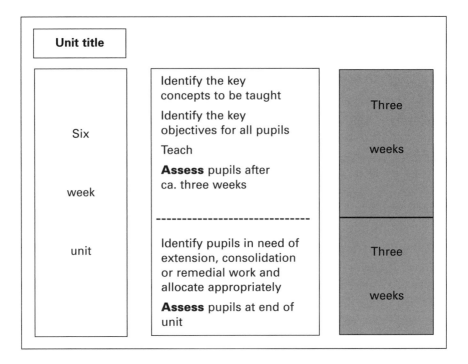

Figure 6.3   Structuring a unit of work for differentiation

the approach allows those pupils the opportunity to master key ideas. This strategy, described in Figure 6.3, needs careful planning of resources and your willingness to respond to pupil performance. The model assumes a six week unit. At some point part-way through the unit, pupils are assessed. In the example in Figure 6.3, assessment occurs after three weeks.

The strategy by which the whole unit of work is taught to all pupils and then followed by an end of unit test leads, for some pupils, to little knowledge, less understanding and a confirmation of their inadequacy; see Postlethwaite (1993, p. 89).

SPECIAL EDUCATIONAL NEEDS

The National Curriculum Council (NCC, 1992a, p. 1) groups pupils with SEN into four main categories, as follows:

1   pupils with severe learning difficulties;
2   pupils with other learning difficulties, including behavioural, emotional and specific difficulties;

3 pupils with physical or sensory impairment;
4 exceptionally able pupils.

During your school experience, you may encounter some pupils in these categories. Pupils with severe learning difficulties are likely to have been recognised and may be, for example, in mainstream classes, or in a special school, or spend part of their time working in a special unit. All pupils, including those with SEN, can benefit from science teaching. The National Curriculum Council recommends that:

> although pupils with severe learning difficulties may not understand the more complex concepts underlying scientific activities they must not be denied the opportunity of scientific experience.
>
> (NCC, 1989, Section 5)

TASK 6.3 SEN PUPILS IN SCIENCE CLASSES

Talk to your science tutor about:

- the ways in which science teachers recognise pupils with severe learning difficulties before they are statemented;
- the steps that need to be taken when concerns arise about an individual pupil;
- the extent to which the class science teacher is involved in the statementing process;
- the departmental policy on working with statemented pupils;
- SEN pupils in your classes and how they are supported.

Discuss your findings with your tutor and other student teachers.

It is essential that you become aware of the behaviours that may be displayed by pupils considered to have such learning and other difficulties so that you can seek support for their learning needs. At the same time, you should identify the skills that your SEN pupils have so that you can take them into account when planning lessons.

Pupils with SEN often have one or more of the following characteristics. They:

- absorb little from conventional teaching at any one time;
- take longer to master particular skills;
- need to repeat new learning before they are able to retain knowledge;

- need more practice than other pupils before they can generalise from a learning experience;
- find it difficult to put events into a logical sequence;
- lack the confidence to work independently;
- have a long background of experiencing failure;
- may develop behavioural and/or emotional problems as a consequence of repeated failure.

(Hull, 1993, p. 209)

Pupils who are exceptionally able may show some of these characteristics, especially behavioural problems if their abilities are not recognised and their needs not met; see the next section in this chapter.

We suggest that you identify a statemented pupil and find out more about her; see Task 6.4.

During your school experience and practical teaching, you need to be alert to the presence of statemented pupils in your class and how the class teacher is working with the support teacher and the SEN Department. In particular, discuss with the class teacher what steps you should take now in your lesson planning to support those pupils.

TASK 6.4 GETTING TO KNOW A STATEMENTED PUPIL

Identify a pupil with a statement of need in one of the classes you teach and ask the class teacher for permission to observe the class in which she is taught. If a support teacher is to be present, talk to him as well about your intentions and purposes. Remember that you are trying to find out more about the abilities of the pupil and what they can or cannot do, not to pass judgement on the school's provision for SEN.

Identify the ways in which teachers support the pupil through:

- individual attention;
- provision of written materials;
- the use of other pupils;
- a support teacher;
- use of technology, e.g. personal computer;
- any other strategies.

If appropriate, talk to the pupil about the work she is doing, or listen in when the support teacher is helping. Identify the ways in which the pupil is succeeding in this lesson.

continued . . .

> Talk to the SEN Co-ordinator (SENCO) about the background of this pupil. Identify the progress the pupil is making in learning and her ability to profit from science teaching.
>
> Write a short report on the capabilities of the pupil and types of difficulties she experiences. Show the report to your tutor. Discuss ways in which you should respond to the presence of statemented pupils in your classes, now and in your first post.

For further discussion of SEN provision please see Units 4.1 and 4.6 in Capel, Leask and Turner (1995); or Dee and Emerson (1995). The non-statutory guidance for the Science National Curriculum describes the role of science teachers supporting statemented pupils in classes (National Curriculum Council, 1989, 1992a and 1992b).

ABLE PUPILS

Sarah is a 13-year-old pupil studying science. In class she had experimentally seen that, by reversing the magnetic field in a motor effect experiment, the direction of the force was reversed. Sarah was able to predict, on her own initiative, that reversing the current in a similar motor effect experiment must reverse the force. This shows, her teacher suggests, that Sarah recognised that reversing the current is the topological equivalent of reversing the field. The insight displayed by Sarah is impressive; equally impressive is the fact that Sarah looked for and found the connection herself. Her teacher was left with the uncomfortable feeling that much science taught to Sarah in the immediate future would be unchallenging (adapted from Postlethwaite, 1993, pp. 22–3).

This able pupil has Special Educational Needs. Most schools would subscribe to a view that

> every pupil should be encouraged to develop her potential in every aspect of school life. Pupils should have access to an education appropriate to their level of ability which meets their needs as able pupils.
>
> (SEN policy document, 1996, Swakeleys School)

The National Curriculum recognises the performance of the above-average pupil by the inclusion of a level called 'Exceptional Performance' above Level 8 at KS3. At the end of KS4, the GCSE Boards now award pupils an A* grade for work of exceptional performance above Grade A.

Your science department should have criteria by which to recognise able pupils. It is the responsibility of all teaching staff, including heads of year and the form teacher, to be alert to the presence of able pupils. As with all pupils with individual needs, knowing your pupils is a first step; see Task 6.5.

TASK 6.5 ABLE PUPILS

Talk to your science tutor about the ways in which able pupils are recognised and supported in your school. Interrogate the SEN policy document for information about recognition and support of able pupils.

Identify any able pupils in your school or science classes and look for ways in which they display their enhanced abilities and the nature and extent of the support they receive, both in and outside school.

For further discussion of ways to support able pupils, see Postlethwaite (1993, pp. 79–80) and Denton and Postlethwaite (1985). The Case Project, which addresses ways in which pupils' cognitive development can be enhanced, is discussed in Chapter 3. The chapters 'Student research projects' and 'Stimulus science activities' in *Effective Science Teaching* (Woolnough, 1994) contain many ideas for working with able pupils.

SUMMARY

In this chapter we have looked for ways in which you can support pupils with SEN by working with the support teacher in your classes. You should know the procedure by which pupils are statemented. Your role in relation to teaching these pupils, at this stage of your development, is to get to know the statementing process, the nature of their SEN and how such pupils are supported. In addition, we have drawn attention to a wider group of pupils with individual needs and identified strategies for working with them. In particular, the importance of knowing the strengths and needs of your pupils and being aware of their knowledge and understanding of science has been stressed.

A differentiated approach to science teaching is needed for many pupils in your class and we have illustrated some ways in which that can be achieved. There is no one way to implement a differentiated approach to teaching. An important feature of good teaching is to know what your pupils can do and to set appropriate work to extend them. Assessment is necessary in order to know what pupils can do, say, write and understand in order to help you plan your teaching; see Chapter 8. Other ways to support pupils can be found in Chapters 3, 5, 7 and, in relation to language, in Chapter 7. For further practical support in your teaching see Postlethwaite (1993), Versey *et al.* (undated) and Hill (undated).

Finally, review this chapter by checking the main ideas against the knowledge, skills and attitudes required of an NQT; see Appendices 1–4. This process should help to identify your progress and further needs.

FURTHER READING

Dee, L. with Emmerson, P. (1995) *Special Educational Needs in the Secondary School*, Occasional Papers in Teacher Education and Training (OPTET), London: Initial Teacher Education, Institute of Education, University of London.
An introductory paper for student teachers that clarifies the meaning of SEN and identifies the legislative framework in which statementing operates. The paper also identifies the statementing procedures and the role of support services. The document includes activities for student teachers and their tutors.

Lambert, D. and Gough, L. (1994) *Differentiated Learning*, Occasional Papers in Teacher Education and Training (OPTET), London: Initial Teacher Education, Institute of Education, University of London.
A short introductory paper for student teachers that introduces student teachers and their tutors to fundamental issues in teaching and learning in mixed ability classes.

Postlethwaite, K. (1993) *Differentiated Science Teaching*, Buckingham: Open University Press.
A substantial discussion about the differences between pupils and the ways in which science teachers can respond to them. Extensive sections on teaching tactics and teaching strategies, together with practical guidance.

Versey, J., Fairbrother, R., Parkin, T., Bourne, J., Dye, A. and Watkinson, A. (undated) *Managing Differentiated Learning and Assessment in the National Curriculum (Science)*, Hatfield: Association for Science Education. Appeared 1995.
Written by teachers and teacher educators, the booklet contains useful advice about teaching and learning science and ways in which to respond

to pupil differences. It contains examples of ways of working with pupils from KS1 to KS4; case studies of pupils are discussed and their needs linked to sample activities. Chapter 5 provides some guidance on working with pupils with severe learning difficulties.

7 The role of language in teaching and learning science

INTRODUCTION

Science teaching actively encourages pupils to carry out investigations and to become familiar with the behaviour of matter and objects through direct handling of materials and apparatus. The work is most commonly carried out in small groups, not just for economy but because group work provides opportunities for talk, speculation and reflection, the recording of information and the basis for the production of concise writing. Engagement in practical activities encourages these skills and provokes reading for information and enjoyment. The following principles concerning language and learning in science were developed by the Association for Science Education:

- talk is the basis of all language development;
- talking through ideas enables a learner to clarify ideas and develop thinking;
- the development of critical awareness requires a person to be thinking and to use their thinking skills;
- equality is based on autonomy, which has stemmed from the ability to use language and develop critical awareness;
- language and its effect on learning are essential to equality.

(Thorp, 1991, p. 98).

The ways in which language can be developed alongside the promotion of science learning are considered in this chapter.

OBJECTIVES

By the end of this chapter you should:

- be aware of some issues involved in promoting language development in science;

- know the importance of language development for promoting thinking skills;
- be able to discuss learning activities in terms of passive and active participation of pupils;
- know some strategies for helping pupils to improve their literacy skills, in reading, writing, listening and talking;
- be prepared to encourage pupils to become active learners and to take some responsibility for their own learning.

THE NATIONAL CURRICULUM

The revised Science National Curriculum, which came into effect in August 1995, requires that:

> pupils be taught to express themselves in both speech and writing and to develop their reading skills. They should be taught to use grammatically correct sentences and to punctuate accurately in order to communicate effectively.
>
> (DFE, 1995b, p. 1)

This simple directive reinforces an old truism that all teachers are teachers of language. For your pupils to develop these skills, they need opportunities to practise them. Copying notes from the board or from worksheets does little to encourage these skills (OFSTED, 1995, par. 26). Pupils need help to read text books for information and encouraged to read for pleasure.

The use of text books in science lessons appears to be limited, and reading as a classroom activity remains rare. Reporting on the inspection of secondary school science departments, the inspectorate noted that:

> little use is made in the majority of schools of IT in science teaching and textbooks are frequently poorly used. Small group activities, other than for practical work, are very uncommon. In some schools, the overuse of worksheets leads to a decline in concentration and persistence, often undermining the pupils' confidence to take responsibility for their own work.
>
> (OFSTED, 1995, par. 22)

The most common activity in science lessons is investigations, but the use of the library as an integral part of investigation is minimal. The dominance of 'doing' over 'reading and thinking' appears to be a feature of contemporary school science.

The Schools Council carried out a survey of the kinds of reading that teachers set (Lunzer and Gardner, in Carre, 1981, pp. 79–80). The survey found that science teachers frequently set study reading of about twenty minutes for homework, whereas reading in class was infrequent and short; the reading material for homework was often encyclopaedias, not text books. Whereas reading was frequently challenging, it was rarely set for pleasure. On the other hand, pupils often read their notes, which was perhaps a sign that their notebooks were the source of reliable information about the topic. The researchers concluded that science teachers did not see reading as an effective way of acquiring information for most pupils of school age.

Text books are more user friendly than they used to be and have many pictures, often in colour. There has been increased attention by teachers and publishers to the reading level of text books (Sutton, 1981, p. 115). Alongside improved publishing, the dramatic increase in the availability of information through the Internet, CD-ROMs and simulations gives teachers opportunities to engage pupils in information gathering and presenting skills. These opportunities are as yet inadequately realised (OFSTED, 1995, par. 27).

The Programme of Study (PoS) for the Science National Curriculum has five overarching principles, one of which is communication and Sc2–Sc4 are written in terms of subject matter and not in terms of the five principles. The way in which 'communication' is integrated into the teaching programme is the responsibility of the science staff in school, who draw up their Scheme of Work (SoW). The SoW in your school experience school should indicate how and when appropriate communication skills are developed; see Figure 7.1.

In Figure 7.1, the italicised text shows the increased demand on pupils as they move from KS3 to KS4. It is not clear from Figure 7.1 how to interpret the difference between 'scientific terms and symbols' (KS3) and 'scientific and technical vocabulary' (KS4), and you should explore this aspect of curriculum; see Task 7.1.

TASK 7.1 COMMUNICATION SKILLS AND THE SoW IN YOUR SCHOOL

Obtain a copy of your school's SoW. Select a unit of work (e.g. force and motion) related to your science teaching specialism. Identify and record within the SoW where advice is given about the use of:

- symbols, equations and formulae appropriate to that level;

continued . . .

- the level of technical vocabulary appropriate for the unit;
- the use of SI units to express quantities;
- useful text books, videos, CD-ROMs as sources of reading, information or guidance for the teacher or pupil;
- advice about writing, reading, recording and holding discussions.

Share your findings with your science tutor and identify any action you need to take.

At each Key Stage, pupils should be given opportunities to:

Key Stage 3	Key Stage 4 double and single science
– use a wide range of scientific terms and symbols and to consider why scientific and mathematical conventions are used	– use a *wide range of scientific and technical vocabulary* and conventions and use diagrams, graphs, tables and charts to communicate information *and to develop an argument*
– use SI units	– use SI units
– present their ideas through the use of diagrams, graphs, tables and charts using appropriate scientific and mathematical conventions	– present scientific information in symbolic form or mathematical form

Figure 7.1   Communication skills to be developed in science through KS3 and KS4
Source: DFE, 1995b, pp. 14 and 25

DEVELOPING COMMUNICATION SKILLS

The English National Curriculum has four areas concerned with communication: listening, talking, reading and writing. There are numerous opportunities in the science lesson to practise these skills. Proper attention to communication skills enhances the learning of most pupils. For pupils with specific learning difficulties, then, such attention is crucial to their progress. Unless pupils talk about their science and learn, for example, how to use words in the appropriate context, then understanding is held back. Pupils need to be able to discuss the results of their investigations, both with each other and with the teacher, in order to extract meaning from data and to be able to explain their findings.

The development of ideas and understanding of new concepts takes place through new experiences, the acquisition of new words and meanings, through acquiring a deeper meaning to known words, i.e. through listening, talking, reading and writing. The rest of this chapter addresses these issues.

Listening

In a study of how time is spent by pupils in science classrooms, listening was ranked the most common activity (see Table 7.1).

When the writing tasks (Table 7.1) were analysed further, 71 per cent of them were identified as passive, including copying and answering. A large proportion of the pupil time was spent on passive activities. Listening alone accounted for 31 per cent of time in Year 10 classes. The amount of reading carried out in the classroom was small, about the same as the non-involved category. If so much time is spent in the teacher talking to pupils, then listening skills need to be promoted and pupils encouraged to be active listeners.

Listening can be a state of dozing; the listener is not mentally active but merely quiet. Alternatively, listeners can be hearing the words but not

Table 7.1 Time spent on different activities by Year 7 and Year 10 pupils as percentage of total science time

Activity	Year group	% of time	Passive role	Active role
Practical work	7	23		✔
	10	11		✔
Observing	7	7	✔	
	10	8	✔	
Reading	7	9		✔
	10	10		✔
Writing	7	11	✔	
	10	20	✔	
Listening	7	26	✔	
	10	31	✔	
non-involved	7	8	✔	
	10	10	✔	
discussion	7	13		✔
	10	10		✔

Source: adapted from Davies and Greene, 1984, pp. 22–3

actively connecting them to a task in hand or to be done. Some pupils regard teacher talk as the 'boring bit before we do the practical work'. In order to make the best use of the short time period of a lesson, pupils need to be mentally active in their reception of teacher talk.

TASK 7.2 HOW MUCH TIME DO PUPILS SPEND IN LISTENING, WRITING AND PRACTICAL WORK?

Identify a class and teacher who will let you observe her lesson and discuss the purpose of the observation, the data you plan to collect and what you intend to do with the information. Alternatively, ask another student teacher in the school to observe your teaching.

Investigate the time spent by pupils listening to the teacher, writing in their books, writing answers to questions from the board, book or worksheet and carrying out an investigation. Construct an observation sheet to help you keep track of events; see Figure 7.2.

When you talk to pupils in class they need a task to engage them actively that requires them to do something as a result of teacher talk. Sometimes teacher talk is part of a lively discussion in which the teacher engages the whole class, and we encourage this process. On other occasions, you need to tell the class some important ideas and pupils need help when listening.

An example of active listening was given in Figure 5.1. Another way to encourage listening is to give pupils in advance a set of questions, the answers to which are expected at the end of the listening activity. A sample sequence of events is shown in Figure 7.3.

The material in Figure 7.3 can be adapted in a number of ways. For example:

- The language of the text can be made simpler, e.g. the phrase 'cells can be described as the' can be replaced by 'cells are called the . . .', and so on;
- the text can be used to identify new words, e.g. ask pupils to highlight all technical words;
- the questions can be made more searching, e.g. 'cells are made of smaller parts. List the parts that animal and plant cells have in common';
- the text is accompanied by a diagram that pupils label;
- the text can be used to explore understanding of the non-technical words and phrases, for example those in italics,

– the *basic parts out of which* . . . . Figure 7.3, par. 1

– *Essentially*, all cells have the *following parts in common* . . . . par. 2

– plant cells have *a tough layer surrounding the cell* . . . . par. 3

etc.

Observe a whole lesson using this schedule. Make notes in the boxes.
Record the main pupil activity in each 5 minute period.

Class . . . . . . Topic . . . . Number of pupils . . . . . Date . . . . . .

Time in minutes	Activity by pupils (listening, copying, writing, discussing, investigating, reading, non-engaged)	Notes (to clarify activity, e.g. reading worksheet, group planning, teacher talking)
0–05		
06–10		
11–15		
16–20		
21–25		
26–30		
31–35		
36–40		
41–45		
46–50		
51–55		
56–60		
61–65		
66–70		

From your data calculate the time spent on listening, reading, writing
and practical activity. Estimate the proportion of time in which pupils
were actively engaged, passively engaged or non-engaged.

Discuss your findings with the class teacher. Evaluate the extent to
which you can judge active and passive participation by pupils.

Figure 7.2 Observation check sheet to identify types of pupil activity

The material comprises a reading text for the teacher and an answer sheet for pupils.

Procedure

1 Pupils read through the answer sheet. Pupils can attempt to answer the questions at this stage.
2 Answer sheets are turned face down.
3 Pupils listen to text and take notes as they wish.
4 Answer sheets are turned face up and a second reading of the text undertaken. Pupils tick off answers as they go.
5 Teacher does a quick check through answers.

Text

Plant and animal cells

Cells can be described as the building blocks of life. Like the bricks that make up a wall, cells are the basic parts out of which most of all living things are made. Bricks are non-living objects, identical in shape and quite large, whereas cells are alive, vary enormously in shape and are microscopic in size.

Cells are made up of many smaller parts and some of these parts are found in plant cells and in the cells of animals. Essentially, all cells have the following parts in common: a jelly-like material called cytoplasm; a very thin skin called a membrane; and a special part that controls all the activities in the cell called the nucleus.

However, there are some very important differences between the cell of a plant and the cell of an animal. Animal cells do not have cell walls, whereas plant cells have a tough layer surrounding the cell made from cellulose. Plant cells also have tiny objects within the cytoplasm called chloroplasts.

Animal cells do not have chloroplasts. The other major difference between plant and animal cells is that in a plant cell the cytoplasm contains a large space called a vacuole which contains a liquid called cell sap. However, the cell of an animal is mostly made up of cytoplasm and does not contain any vacuoles.

Answer sheet

Listen and put a tick ✔ next to your answer

Plant and animal cells

1 Cells	a are all the same shape and size; b can vary in shape and size.
2 A cell	a is made up of two parts; b is composed of many smaller parts.
3 All cells have	a 2 common parts; b 3 common parts; c 4 common parts.
4 Plant cells and animal cells	a are the same; b are different.
5 Plant cells	a have a thick wall; b do not have a cell wall.
6 Chloroplasts are found only in	a plant cells; b animal cells.
7 Animal cells	a do not have vacuoles; b have vacuoles.

Figure 7.3 A listening task: plant and animal cells
Source: adapted from Roach, Smith and Vazquez, 1990, p. 16

TASK 7.3 DEVISE A LISTENING TASK

Choose a topic you are to teach that will involve you talking to pupils to explain an idea in science. It could accompany a demonstration. For example:

- the bending of a bi-metallic strip when it is heated;
- the formation of an insoluble solid and then a soluble complex ion when concentrated ammonia solution is added dropwise to copper (II) sulphate solution;
- testing for carbon dioxide in exhaled air from a human and its interpretation by cell respiration.

Devise a worksheet that engages the pupils in listening and thinking while you talk or demonstrate. The worksheet could be:

- a text with blanks to be completed;
- a set of questions (see Figure 7.3);
- notes describing the observations to be placed in correct order;
- a diagram with equations to be completed after your talk;
- a flow diagram to be annotated by the pupils, etc.

Discuss your intentions with your tutor or class teacher before trying it out with your class. Evaluate the success or otherwise of the task and share the outcome with other student teachers and the class teacher.

Encouraging talking

A common problem for the student teacher is to stop pupils talking! However, the issue we are addressing here is to ensure that pupil–pupil talk is on task and that the quality of the discussion is high. When pupils discuss their work, their conversation is often at a level of clarifying what they are doing, who should be responsible for what or whether they are doing what the teacher wants. Much pupil discussion, even when on task, rarely gets as far as the meaning or interpretation of their results. An important step in encouraging talk is to:

- ensure that pupil discussion is on task;
- shift the discussion from procedural matters and description to seeking patterns in and explanation for their findings.

Practical work such as investigations provide the natural place for talking. To help pupils to gain the most from their discussions, help them to focus by providing stimulus material. This material is designed to structure their thinking and relate to the context of the work.

Focusing the discussion for pupils can be done in a number of ways. For example, a common investigation is to explore the relative amounts of carbon dioxide in inhaled and exhaled air. One piece of apparatus used for this activity is shown in Figure 7.4. Pupils are told that lime water turns cloudy when carbon dioxide gas is passed into it (or asked to discuss which gas or gases in the air react with lime water). The demand on the pupils can be altered by the complexity of the task you set. Pupils can be given either the apparatus or a drawing of the apparatus, depending on the class, together with some questions to focus discussion, as below:

- Blow gently at the mouth part. Which way will the air move in the left hand tube and in the right hand tube?
- Suck gently at the mouthpiece. Which way will the air move in the left hand tube and in the right hand tube?
- Explain how the apparatus only lets air in at one tube and only lets air out of the other tube. Explain how the apparatus works.
- If inhaled air contains less carbon dioxide than exhaled air, what differences will you see in the lime water in each tube?

To use:
One person take the tube in your mouth, as marked in the diagram, and breathe in and out through your mouth until a change takes place in the lime water

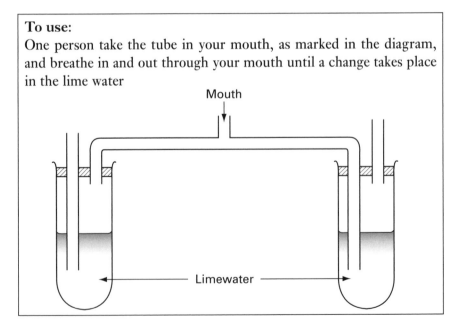

Figure 7.4   Apparatus for passing inhaled and exhaled air through lime water

- What conclusion would you draw about the amount of carbon dioxide in the inhaled and exhaled air if the lime water in both test tubes went cloudy at the same time?

Other ways in which talk can be promoted is by group discussions. A focus could be:

- Pupils could be asked to prepare a story line for a play or presentation, e.g. ways in which astronauts prepare to live in a space station for long periods, focusing on issues such as maintaining a suitable atmosphere or removing human waste products.
- Aspects of a topic can be shared out amongst groups, with each group to report on one aspect. One group is asked to assess the suitability of software. Suitable topics include:
  1 ways in which food is preserved and the sciences underpinning it;
  2 how fuel can be conserved and used more efficiently in the home;
  3 ways in which sensors (temperature, light, pressure) can be used to monitor the environment or in control technology.
- A topic could be summarised by a poster or by transparencies. Each group is given a brief to present one aspect, using word, diagram and picture. For example:
  1 the various technologies used to alleviate visual deficiency, such as long sight, short sight, astigmatism, glaucoma, cataract;
  2 ways in which blood groups are typed and how the correct blood type is selected for transfusions;
- devising questions at the end of a unit of work. The questions can be tried out on other groups. Alternatively, statements can be given to groups of pupils who are asked to devise a question to which the statement is an answer;
- marking other pupils' work – a piece of writing by one pupil could be assessed and the reasons for decisions identified and explained. Such work includes report writing, describing an investigation, explaining a phenomenon.

You will know, probably, other ways in which pupil groups can engage in active talk and develop responsibility for their own learning.

Active reading

Earlier in this chapter we noted the poor use of text books by pupils in science lessons (OFSTED, 1995, par. 22). Reading is most often used by teachers as homework, to consolidate work from the classroom, to anticipate and prepare pupils for a new topic, to prepare pupils for a test or to widen pupils' understanding. Purposeful reading requires support and guidance from the teacher. Your pupils need guidance about reading for meaning and understanding. Any reading you set for homework needs to be carefully focused.

General principles of active reading are discussed in *Learning to Teach in Secondary School* (Capel, Leask and Turner, 1997, Unit 5.2, DARTS Activities Section 4). Other useful texts include Bulman (1984); Davies and Greene (1984); Monk and Dillon (1995, Chapter 6, Section 6.3); Parkinson (1994, par. 6.2); Roach, Smith and Vazquez (1990).

Two categories of response by pupils to Directed Activities Related to Texts (DARTS) activities have been identified as reconstruction and analysis (Roach, Smith and Vazquez, 1990, p. 6). Reconstruction tasks use written resources that pupils are required to complete or transform in some way. Analysis tasks require pupils to identify and categorise material or to identify patterns in the information. Analysis activities use unmodified texts and develop independent study skills. For example, pupils can be asked to:

- gain an overview of the topic and record that in some way;
- reformulate the ideas in a new format;
- summarise a passage for a purpose, e.g. report to the class.

Pupils can be encouraged to read actively for meaning by:

- selecting reading appropriate to their age and ability that is clearly focused and of a suitable length;
- making clear why they are reading and what they are expected to get out of it;
- telling pupils what they are to do while they read, what to record and in what form;
- telling pupils how their reading is to be used in the next lesson.

Summarising text using a diagram

Pupils are given a passage to read, as in Figure 7.5, and asked to summarise the ideas by annotating a diagram, see Figure 7.6. The task requires pupils to relate what they read to a diagram, to be able to interpret the language of the text and to link two aspects of breathing, *structure (or part)* to function.

The exercise can be altered in a number of ways to make it more accessible to pupils with learning difficulties. For example, the names of structures are written on cards and the cards matched to the diagram (see Figure 7.7 'Parts'). Pupils are asked to read the text to confirm their placement. Pupils then use the text to construct their own explanation of the function of each structure and label the diagram. The above procedure can be simplified by the addition of cards that have the function of structures written on them (see also Figure 7.7). Pupils are required to match *part* cards to *function* cards and place both on the diagram (Figure 7.6). The text is used here as a reference. The text can also be used on its own to assess comprehension. See Figure 7.8 for an example of how this strategy is used.

When we breathe, air can enter the body through either the nose or the mouth. It is better to breathe through your nose because the structure of the nose allows the air to become warm, moist and filtered before it gets to the lungs.

The hairs and mucus in the nose filter the air by trapping bacteria, dirt and dust. There are also lots of blood capillaries inside the nose that help to warm the air as it passes through.

Down the windpipe   At the back of the nose and throat, the air enters the windpipe or trachea. At the top of the windpipe, there is a bulge called the voice box or larynx. This has cords in it that vibrate as air passes over them. This allows us to talk and make other sounds.

The rest of the windpipe is 12 cm long. It has C-shaped rings of cartilage. These strengthen it, so that it can stay open all the time to let the air pass from the mouth and nose to the lungs. There are also hairs to filter the air.

Into the lungs   The trachea or windpipe divides into two short tubes. Each tube is called a bronchus, which takes air into the lungs. Like the windpipe, each bronchus has hairs to filter the air, and cartilage rings for support.

Inside the lungs, the bronchus divides into many smaller tubes called bronchioles. The bronchioles take the air to all parts of the lung. At the end of each bronchiole there are many tiny air sacs. Each air sac is made up of thin membranes called alveoli which are surrounded by blood vessels. Each alveolus lets gas exchange take place. This means that the oxygen moves from the air in the alveolus into the blood. At the same time, carbon dioxide moves from the blood to the air in the alveolus.

Surrounding the lungs   The lungs are covered by a thin, shiny, slippery membrane or skin. This is called the pleural membrane and it makes a liquid so that the lungs are not damaged if they rub against the rib cage. The rib cage is made of many bones called ribs, which surround and protect the lungs and heart. Under the lungs is a large sheet of muscle called the diaphragm. This stretches across the body and helps in breathing in and out.

Figure 7.5   The breathing system
Source: Thorp, 1991, p. 96

PARTS

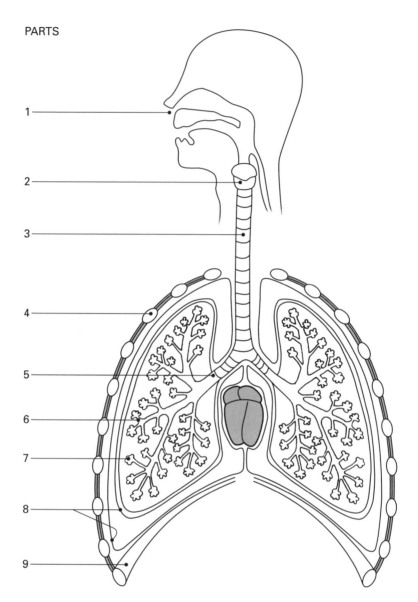

1

2

3

4

5

6

7

8

9

Figure 7.6   Organs of our breathing system

Summarising the concepts in a text

Another way to make reading active is to require pupils to construct a table that summarises the text. The amount of guidance given to the pupil allows you to alter the demand on the pupil and to set work appropriate to the ability and performance of the pupils, i.e. to differentiate.

PARTS OR STRUCTURES

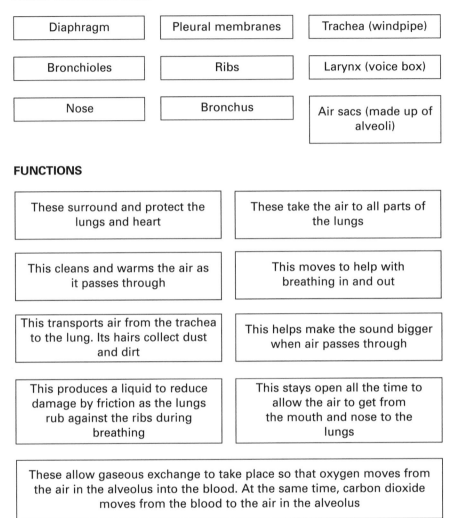

Diaphragm	Pleural membranes	Trachea (windpipe)
Bronchioles	Ribs	Larynx (voice box)
Nose	Bronchus	Air sacs (made up of alveoli)

FUNCTIONS

These surround and protect the lungs and heart	These take the air to all parts of the lungs
This cleans and warms the air as it passes through	This moves to help with breathing in and out
This transports air from the trachea to the lung. Its hairs collect dust and dirt	This helps make the sound bigger when air passes through
This produces a liquid to reduce damage by friction as the lungs rub against the ribs during breathing	This stays open all the time to allow the air to get from the mouth and nose to the lungs

These allow gaseous exchange to take place so that oxygen moves from the air in the alveolus into the blood. At the same time, carbon dioxide moves from the blood to the air in the alveolus

Figure 7.7 The breathing system: parts and their functions on card
Source: adapted from Thorp, 1991, p. 94

In the example in Figure 7.9, pupils are asked to read and then complete the spaces in a summary table. The task could be set as a means of checking how much pupils have understood from your teaching, i.e. a summative task or to prepare pupils for a lesson, i.e. a formative process. The text can be adapted to suit your pupils by altering the demand of the task.

Read the following passage and carry out the tasks written beneath it. (The text is, of course, not marked in the way shown when given to pupils.)

'When we breathe, air can enter the body either through the <u>nose</u> or the <u>mouth</u>. It is better to breathe through your nose because the structure of the <u>nose</u> allows the air to become warm, *moist and filtered* before it gets to the <u>lungs</u>.

The <u>hairs</u> and <u>mucus</u> in the nose *filter the air* by trapping bacteria, dirt and dust. There are also lots of blood **capillaries** inside the nose which help to *warm the air* as it passes through.'

(Thorp, 1991, p. 96)

Instructions to pupils:

- <u>underline</u> all those word that name a part or structure of the nose;
- *highlight* those words that describe how a part or structure works;
- highlight in another colour any words you don't understand, e.g. **capillaries**.

Figure 7.8   Reading for understanding: identifying parts and function

TASK 7.4 DEVISE A READING TASK

Prepare a reading and comprehension task for one of your classes, using the examples above to help you. If you ask pupils to mark the text, use photocopies. Further guidance on DARTS activities can be found in *Learning to Teach in the Secondary School* (Capel, Leask and Turner, 1995, Unit 5.2).

Identify a topic with a class you are teaching. Discuss with the class teacher when you intend to set the task and how you intend to mark the work. Identify ways in which the response informs your teaching.

Encouraging writing

Pupils do a lot of writing. A common criticism by HMI and OFSTED over many years is the excessive amount of passive writing that pupils are asked to do, copying notes from the board, or from worksheets or making small changes in copied notes. Some pupils are asked to write out notes in rough for transcription into best at home. Unless pupils are encouraged and helped to formulate ideas for themselves, they do not get to grips with the concepts involved. Pupils do not learn only by being told; much more is needed, such as discussion, exploration and attempts to

Read the text and then complete the table below.

You should read through the text once to get an overview of the content and then a second time, making notes of the key words to write in each box. Finally complete the table using your notes and the text for reference.

Pollution in air

Coal and oil contain a small amount of sulphur. When these substances burn, they make sulphur dioxide, a gas that then goes into the air. Sulphur dioxide dissolves in water, e.g. rain, to form 'acid rain' which gets into lakes and rivers; acid rain can destroy forests and fish. Sulphur dioxide can travel many hundreds of miles before it comes to earth as acid rain.

The exhaust fumes from cars and lorries can pollute the air, and the more traffic the greater the pollution. Old vehicles with worn out engines produce unpleasant smoke. However, all vehicles make some carbon monoxide, a poisonous gas. This gas combines with haemoglobin in the blood and prevents oxygen getting to the body, including the brain. People can get ill and die from carbon monoxide poisoning. Some cars are now fitted with 'converters' attached to the exhaust which reduce the amount of carbon monoxide in the exhaust gases.

Some cars still use petrol with lead in it. Lead improves the efficiency of the engine. However, lead in the exhaust gases of cars can be breathed in. If we take in too much lead, it affects the way in which our brain functions. It is very dangerous for young people to breathe in lead because it accumulates in the body and may cause brain damage later in life.

Ozone is a gas. The ozone layer high up in the atmosphere protects human beings from harmful ultra-violet radiation, which causes skin cancer. Some gases released into the air eventually reach the ozone layer and react with it. This reaction removes some ozone and leaves a 'hole' in the ozone layer. One gas that reacts with ozone is freon, used in aerosol cans and refrigerators. Although freon is now banned, the effects of ozone damage are still present.

Summarise the main points of this passage by completing the table below.

Name of pollutant	Source of pollutant	How does the pollutant get into the air?	What harmful effects does it have?
Lead			
			When it dissolves in rain it can destroy forests
		Exhaust gases from cars	
Freon			

Figure 7.9   Pollution in air: making a summary
Source: adapted from Roach, Smith and Vazquez, 1990, see section 'reading activities'

explain ideas for themselves. Learning is a personal, active process, supported by peers, teachers and other resources.

Pupils need to write up their investigations, and a framework for that process is important. That framework is necessary because pupils are learners, not scientists. Scientists write up research in a formal way for publication, but most papers do not represent the process of scientific enquiry (Wolpert, 1992, p. 101; Sutton, 1992, p. 87). The way in which we ask pupils to write up their investigations is not intended to relate to real science reporting or to how scientific papers are written but is meant to respond to the learning needs of pupils. You should encourage a variety of writings that respond to different tasks, e.g. writing a report for the school journal, preparing a poster, writing a poem or a story to stimulate imaginative thinking.

The day-to-day writing of pupils needs support. For many pupils it is the point at which they fail (Roach, Smith and Vazquez, 1990, p. 7); for other pupils, motivation drops often because they have difficulty expressing ideas. You know, probably, pupils who have written up the practical activity according to a format but have missed the point of the exercise. We began to address ways of supporting pupils' writing in Chapter 5. In Figure 5.2, 'Can we speed up dissolving?', a worksheet gave a structure for summarising the variables that affect the speed at which a solid dissolves in water. The worksheet supported pupils who experience difficulties in sentence construction and sorting out their ideas. We showed, too, how to adapt the resource for pupils of different abilities.

Some further strategies for supporting pupils' writing up of activities include:

- giving pupils a framework for the written report and notes on procedure. A simple framework is:

1 Title (question or problem posed);
2 Aim (what we wanted to do);
3 Method (what we did);
4 Results (what happened);
5 Conclusion (our explanation of what happened).

- giving brief notes on a set of cards of the procedure, readings and conclusions. You can provide these notes, or use those derived from another pupil, which pupils are asked to check and use to write their report.
- giving the instructions for the investigation on cards using the present tense, e.g. 'Tie cotton round one end of the small test tube'. These instructions are used to carry out the investigation. When pupils write

their report, they re-write the instructions in the past tense, ensuring that the proper time sequence is used, and freedom to modify the report in the light of their own activities. Pupils suggest ways to improve the investigation.

- eliciting the main ideas of the investigation from the class in whole class discussion with words and phrases put on the board. Pupils plan their own investigation which is checked by you and then used for the investigation and subsequent writing up.
- keeping any equipment used on show for reference.

Pupils are often asked to make notes about topics or ideas arising from discussion, reading or watching a video. Strategies for support in this type of writing include drafting sentences with gaps; the words needed to fill the gaps can be supplied, or not, according to the ability of pupils. You can choose to omit technical words, or connecting phrases (see Figure 7.10). The task can be made harder by providing excess words, or words that are similar but not quite correct, e.g. dissolve and melt.

A sample piece of text

Use some of the following words to show how the ideas in each sentence are connected.

and, because, but, if, in order to, so that, even if

1 The small intestine absorbs food easily _____ it has thin walls.

2 _____ you grind food into a powder it won't dissolve.

3 Food goes through the gullet _____ is not digested.

. . . . etc. including as many questions as you need.

Figure 7.10 Supporting writing – digestion
Source: adapted from Roach, Smith and Vazquez, 1990, p. 18

Other forms of writing help place school science in a wider context, provide motivation and stimulate the imagination. Pupils could be invited to:

- explain their hobby and the science behind it, e.g. keeping pigeons, fishing, rock climbing, model making;
- compose an advertisement setting out the advantages of a liquid crystal thermometer (or any other instrument);
- write a summary of a consumer report into, for example, liquid bleaches;
- use a cartoon to initiate discussion on a topic. Ask pupils to write a paragraph explaining the humour of the cartoon and the underlying

Discuss with other student teachers why this cartoon is amusing. Is the situation possible or have the laws of science been exaggerated? How might you use this cartoon with pupils?

Figure 7.11 A cartoon to promote discussion and writing
Source: J.F. Reay and A.D. Turner (1976) *New World Science*, Trinidad and Jamaica: Longman Caribbean

science. See Figure 7.11, which gives pupils the opportunity to discuss the change in volume of water when it freezes and its effect on a container.

- look through a daily paper for science articles, to choose one and report on it to a specified length and style;
- write to the manager of a firm for information. For example, a letter could be sent to the local water board for information about water purification, storage and distribution as part of the 'water cycle'.

Many ideas for writing can be found in Carre (1981, pp. 52–78) and Parkinson (1994, Chapter 6).

TASK 7.5 READING FOR INFORMATION

An important feature of your science teaching is to help pupils write reports of their investigations. Read the set text (reference below) and write a report (about 300 words) that summarises the writer's view of pupils' writing. Share your summary with other student teachers, or discuss the article with your tutor. Clarify ways in which you expect pupils to report their investigations. Reference Sutton, (1992, pp. 87–9).

SUMMARY

In this chapter we have addressed ways in which you can help your pupils to improve their communication skills of reading, writing, listening and talking. All teachers are responsible for the literacy and numeracy of their pupils and contribute to the development of both. Some of the ideas expressed in this chapter are designed to support pupils with learning needs. Often, the strategies devised for this purpose are useful for a wider range of pupils and make your teaching role easier. Use Appendices 1, 2 or 3 and Appendix 4 to review your development and progress in this area.

You can get help for devising support strategies from the various books referred to in this chapter, as well as from curriculum texts devised for a particular Key Stage, from staff in school, especially the Special Needs teachers or in-class support teachers. To read further into language and curriculum issues, see Burgess (1996).

We have said very little about the role of the teacher in communicating ideas to the pupils, in her role of explainer of ideas. Clearly the way in which you support your pupils in discussion, in their reading and in your response to their written work is a major input. Analysis of the ways in which teachers explain ideas is beyond the scope of this introductory text, but you can explore these ideas further in *Explaining Science in the Classroom* (Ogborn, Kress, Martins and McKillicuddy, 1996). This book arose from a research project in which science teachers were observed explaining science to pupils. The text shows ways in which teachers talk to their pupils and the kinds of strategies they use. The teachers in the department of one of us (WD) contributed to the research. Ideas for supporting pupils who have English as a second language can be found in Thorp (1991), Roach, Smith and Vazquez (1990), Levine (1990) or Smith (1997a and b).

FURTHER READING

Bulman, L. (1984) *Teaching Language and Study Skills in Secondary Science*, London: Heinemann Educational Books.
  Although dated, this is an excellent book giving the principles for supporting pupils with language difficulties and for promoting study skills for all pupils. Many examples of practical help.

Frost, J. (ed.) (1995) *Teaching Science*, London: Woburn Press.
  In-depth discussion of the skills and strategies of teaching science. There is a wealth of practical ideas and advice which covers practical work as well

as field work, simulations and independent learning strategies. Chapter 2, 'Teaching skills', is particularly appropriate.

Smith, D. (1997a) 'Materials and their properties (AT3): an activity pack for Key Stages 3 and 4 (The SPEAL Project)', London: London Borough of Islington, The Barnsbury Complex, Offord Road, London, N1 1FQ.

—— (1997b) 'Life processes (AT2): an activity pack for Key Stages 3 and 4 (The SPEAL Project), London: London Borough of Islington, The Barnsbury Complex, Offord Road, London, N1 1FQ.

Parkinson, J. (1994) *The Effective Teaching of Secondary Science*, Harlow: Longman.
A source book for science teachers, especially those starting to teach. Chapter 6 has an extensive set of practical ideas for language support in the sciences.

8 Assessment

INTRODUCTION

You are responsible for the day to day progress of your pupils and assessment is central to that process. All interactions with pupils contribute to the teacher's understanding of pupils' skills and abilities. Informal assessment takes place when marking work in class, discussing homework with pupils, joining in group conversations or supporting pupils in laboratory activity. Assessment informs teaching and learning in the classroom and is the backbone of your lesson planning.

Teachers assess pupils to tell parents, employers and examination boards something about the performance of a pupil, as in a teacher marked element of a public examination, or to report progress over the school year or to form part of a pupil's Record of Achievement (Capel, Leask and Turner, 1995, Unit 6.2). These are formal assessments.

Formal assessment is frequently summative, judgemental and important for the future of the pupil, e.g. in moving on to further education or to employment. Informal assessment is often formative and serves to guide pupils on their progress and tells you about pupils' understanding and difficulties. The importance of formative assessment as the basis for future teaching is emphasised in reports of inspection of science departments (OFSTED, 1995, pars 31–5).

Assessment is at the heart of the National Curriculum (Capel, Leask and Turner, 1995, Unit 7.3). The Task Group on Assessment and Testing set up to advise the government on the place of assessment in the National Curriculum said:

> Promoting children's learning is the principal aim of schools. Assessment lies at the heart of this process. It can provide a framework in which educational objectives can be set and pupil's progress charted and expressed.
>
> (DES, 1988a)

The Dearing Report on the National Curriculum some eight years later confirmed the importance of assessment in monitoring pupils' performance nationally and by teachers to improve teaching and learning (Dearing, 1994).

Assessment is used nationally for many purposes, from the promotion of learning to the monitoring of standards. There are two national assessment exercises: the Standard Assessment Tasks (SATs) for the core subjects at the end of Key Stages 2 and 3 and the General Certificate of Secondary Education (GCSE) at the end of Key Stage 4. The School Curriculum and Assessment Authority (SCAA, now QCA) requires these assessments to be made and they must include written examinations. The results of the examinations are used to measure the achievement of pupils; to compare pupils; to compare schools and to monitor standards nationally over time. The multi-purpose nature of this assessment exercise has proved contentious and is discussed in Capel, Leask and Turner (1995, Units 6.1 and 6.2). One concern of many teachers is that, with the pressure on teachers and schools to succeed in tests, only that which is assessed is emphasised. There is a growing tension between developing a test that is both valid and reliable[1].

The daily work of a teacher involves setting tasks, monitoring progress and assessing the pupils' work, and it is this aspect of assessment that is the main focus of this chapter. There is further discussion on assessment at Key Stage 4 in Chapter 9. The assessment and reporting of pupils' performance is a **key skill** and you should refer to your relevant national standards (Appendices 1–3) and to Appendix 4 to help monitor your development.

OBJECTIVES

By the end of this chapter you should:

- understand the principles of assessment;
- understand the roles of assessment in teaching and learning science;
- understand how practical work can be assessed;
- be able to describe how information from assessment is used;

---

1 High reliability means that most sources of variance have been removed. If pupils sit the test again, they are likely to score similar marks; or different groups of pupils sitting the same test can be compared with confidence. High validity means that the test measures what it was intended to measure. Maximum validity occurs when the test resembles the teaching and learning experiences of the pupils.

- be able to describe the assessment demands of the Science National Curriculum;
- have carried out some assessments.

PRINCIPLES OF ASSESSMENT

Assessment is the heart of teaching and learning. In what ever way the results of assessment are to be used, there are some principles that apply to most situations and inform your practice.

Assessment should:

- have a clear purpose and employ appropriate methods consistent with that purpose;
- be integral to your unit of work and lesson plans;
- reflect the aims and objectives of your unit of work;
- reveal what your pupils know, understand and can do;
- accumulate evidence as a basis for making a professional judgement;
- provide feedback for pupils, teachers and parents;
- promote a positive sense of achievement in your pupils.

Assessment has many purposes, including:

- **summative assessment** – reviewing, summarising, categorising and comparing the progress of pupils;
- **formative assessment** – finding out what pupils know, understand and can do to inform future teaching; identifying the strengths and weaknesses of pupils in order to set targets for them;
- **evaluation** – assessing the suitability of a curriculum package, or measuring the effectiveness of your teaching;
- **diagnosis** – identifying the cause of under-achievement or inappropriate behaviour so as to recommend a course of action.

Summative assessment

Assessment is most commonly understood in terms of examinations and testing – the summative mode. Results of examinations control entry to the next phase of study, profession or employment. The results of examinations are frequently used to direct pupils into single science or double science GCSE courses at the end of KS3; or into either the separate sciences or a broad science course. Entry into GCE A level is often dependent on high GCSE grades. These examples are the archetypal models of high stakes assessment, in which performance on the day of the examination is essential to success. The short tests, often used by teachers, mimic that process, especially when the marks are used to record a grade. End of unit tests are similarly summative in nature. These types of assessment are rarely used to give feedback to the pupils about their achievement, or of their strengths and weaknesses. The GCSE results are used nationally by SCAA (now QCA) to compare the performance of schools.

In a similar way, the SATs tests in the core subjects at Key Stage 3 in secondary school are used to compare both pupils and schools through the publication of the number of pupils achieving specific levels of attainment. Schools are rated according to their position above or below a national norm. The original purpose of SATs in the National Curriculum was to monitor standards nationally at the four Key Stages. This purpose does not require all pupils to be tested or schools to be compared publicly by league tables.

Formative and diagnostic assessment

By contrast with summative assessment, formative assessment focuses on teaching and learning. Formative and diagnostic assessment have common features. Diagnostic assessment focuses on identifying causes for particular behaviour, e.g. under-achievement, and seeks specific information in order to help a pupil. Formative assessment is the on-going checking of pupils' understanding and knowledge of the work in hand and is one way in which the need for diagnostic assessment is identified.

The starting point for any teaching begins with formative assessment, that is what the learner already knows, understands and can do. New learning needs to link as far as possible with previous learning; that is why in this book we have made frequent reference to getting to know as much as possible about your pupils and about what they have learned already; e.g. see Chapter 3.

As well as you gaining information about pupils, an important feature of teaching is to give feedback to your pupils about their progress. A feature of feedback is to recognise progress and give praise and encouragement, at the same time identifying ways in which your pupils can improve and develop. Sometimes feedback is oral and at other times you need to give feedback in writing. A record of your praise and target setting enables pupils to refer back to it for guidance as well as emphasising the importance you attach to it. The setting of tasks and marking of books and other written work is central to that process.

Record your comments in pupils' exercise books, etc. and maintain records of your advice. Not only does this procedure act as an *aide-mémoire* but it also builds a picture of progress and development to which you can refer. As well as keeping a mark book, maintain a confidential comment book that is readily accessible to you but at the same time is secure from the casual glance of a passing pupil.

Diagnostic assessment refers to assessment activities designed to ascertain a cause for particular difficulty or under-achievement. In many ways, the actions are similar to those used in formative assessment but are more focused. For example, some pupils have difficulty writing a report of their investigations. An assessment of writing skills, in conjunction with the English language teacher or a special needs teacher, can identify ways to support your pupil. The SENCO and other members of the SEN team in your school are helpful in diagnosing particular learning or behavioural difficulties and in suggesting ways to help you and the pupil. See Chapter 6 on Special Educational Needs.

TASK 8.1 YOUR EXPERIENCE OF ASSESSMENT IN SCIENCE

Recall a situation in your own science education, e.g. at school, in which you were assessed, the effects of which were positive, i.e. beneficial. Recall a second situation in which the outcome was negative. Compare these two events and the ways in which they affected your progress in learning. Make a brief comparative summary of these events and discuss it with other student teachers. How did your experiences fit into the four purposes of assessment listed above?

Getting to know assessment policies in your school

It is essential that you know the school assessment policy and that of the science department. These policies include a means of record keeping, the way you respond to pupils' daily work and conduct in public examinations.

Collect together documents relating to the school and science department policies on assessment. Ask your science tutor for help. Talk to the member of staff responsible for examinations and assessment for further information. The documents include the following items, often under one cover:

- school policy on assessment, including recording achievement and progress of pupils;

- school statements about marking books and homework (if not in assessment policy);
- departmental handbook;
- departmental policy on assessment;
- departmental policy on recording achievement and progress of pupils;
- Scheme of Work for science;
- guidance and information given to pupils about assessment;
- guidance for parents on the way in which pupil achievement and progress is recorded;
- guidance to parents on homework policy;
- the links made between assessment and the level statements in the Attainment Targets of the Science National Curriculum.

Now move on to Task 8.2.

TASK 8.2 USING THE ASSESSMENT POLICY IN YOUR SCIENCE DEPARTMENT

Read the documents described in the text above. Ensure that you know:

- how to set and mark work for your classes;
- how to store records of pupils' work;
- the criteria used to grade pupils' work;
- where to find guidance on the way in which investigative work in science is assessed and recorded;
- the time and duration of homework for your classes;
- how pupils and parents keep a record of homework;
- the department's and school's policy on marking for spelling, punctuation, etc.;
- how progress and achievement in science is reported to parents.

Make notes of anything that is not clear and discuss these with your science tutor. In which ways does the policy match the principles for good assessment set out on p. 149?

THE ROLE OF ASSESSMENT IN IMPROVING TEACHING AND LEARNING IN SCIENCE

Assessment is a dynamic process. The interplay between teaching and learning is effected through the regular assessment of pupils. We referred to this process as formative assessment in a previous section. The whole process is summarised in Figure 8.1.

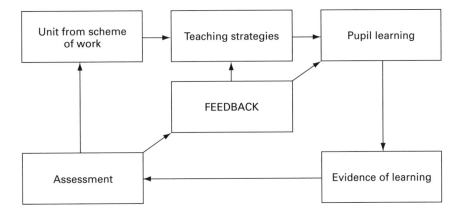

Figure 8.1   The teaching, learning and assessment cycle

The purpose of assessment is to improve pupil learning. We focus now on how to collect evidence from your teaching and pupils' activities in order to assess their learning.

Your knowledge about learning comes from a number of sources. These sources include:

- the marking of pupil exercise books;
- the response of pupils to homework; this may include marked work as well as your informal notes taken from a class discussion of a home-work;
- notes arising from other class discussions about activities you have set. These discussions include the openings of lessons and ends of lessons in which the topic is summarised and consolidated;
- your involvement with pupils during lessons when supporting their class work;
- the response to an informal test set within a unit of work;
- the end of unit test marks.

It is clear that the information you have arises from both informal situations and formal situations, the last mainly through tests. In order for informal evidence to be useful, records need to be kept, and we suggest that you keep a notebook for this, as mentioned above, for formative and diagnostic assessment.

Marking books

As well as giving you feedback about the performance of your pupils, marking pupils' work contributes to pupil motivation. The work you set your pupils must be valued and seen to be important. If you set work but do not mark it, pupils will stop putting any effort into it. The way in which you respond to their work is important. If their work is merely ticked, pupils have no idea whether it was good, poor or indifferent or whether they have even done what you asked.

TASK 8.3 GETTING TO KNOW YOUR SCHOOL'S POLICIES ON MARKING BOOKS

1   Go back through the document you used for Task 8.2 and extract the points relevant to marking exercise books. If you have any queries, talk to your tutor before carrying out this task.

2   Collect in a set of exercise books from a class you teach and for whom you have recently set work, in class or for homework. Identify the purpose of the work. It could be to:

   ● answer a question you set;
   ● write a conclusion to a pupil activity;
   ● draw a graph of readings and interpret it in some way;
   ● explain a phenomenon you demonstrated;
   ● draw a diagram and annotate it using a supporting text, etc.

3   Having identified the purpose of the work, write down three objectives, i.e. what pupils should do, write or explain. Write out an acceptable answer that would gain high marks. You should now have some features with which to identify a good answer.

4   Read through some representative pieces of work and get a feel for the response. Use only about 5–10 minutes for this activity.

5   Using the knowledge gained in 4 above and your school's marking and grading system, draw up a marking scheme that contains criteria for awarding marks.

6   Mark the books and record marks and comments in your record book. You should:

   ● note any unexpected answers to discuss with the individual or your tutor;
   ● identify the extent to which pupils achieved your objectives for the task;
   ● plan the next piece of work with this evidence in mind.

7   Identify ways in which the school's marking policy helped you to mark the books. Discuss any difficulties with your tutor.

When work is set, pupils need to know:

- the purpose of the work;
- what they need to do to fulfil the purpose;
- how marks are awarded or withheld;
- what the marks mean.

What do you look for when you mark pupils' books? You need clear objectives for the work you give pupils that link with those in your lesson plan. The pupils need to be aware of your objectives. The work and how it is marked must conform to the departmental policy on setting and marking. The departmental policy should include information about:

- frequency of marking books;
- marking for accuracy and information;
- marking for effort and progress;
- giving grades as numbers or letters and what they mean;
- how grades are linked to National Curriculum levels;
- correcting mistakes in spelling and grammar;
- how pupils are to correct errors in their work;
- writing comments on the pupils' books to encourage learning.

Homework

Homework needs similar care in setting and marking, and should clearly promote learning and enhance motivation. The way in which you set homework should conform to school and department policy.

TASK 8.4 HOMEWORK

1   Read the relevant sections of the departmental policy on assessment and make sure you know how much homework can be set to various classes and when it is set. Make a record of the marking policy for homework and if it differs from any guidelines for marking other types of work. See Task 8.3.

2   Read 'Active learning' (Capel, Leask and Turner, 1995, Unit 5.2) for ideas about setting structured activities.

Homework is of little value if the work can be done satisfactorily watching a television programme. The work you give them should fit clearly into your unit of work. Whenever possible, it should link clearly with the last lesson or the next lesson. Homework takes place without the presence of the teacher so the instructions you give must be clear and purposeful. They should include:

- what to do;
- the form of record expected (writing, drawing, tables, notes, graph);
- advice about what a completed record looks like;
- how you plan to use the work;
- the criteria for assessment;
- whom to hand it to, where and when.

If your homework is to follow these guidelines then it must be planned. Homework set off the cuff is often vague and pupils do not know what to do. A homework like 'read the section on uses of sulphur' does not produce a good response. Pupils need:

- page references;
- to know what to look for when they read;
- to know what to record;
- to know how much detail to record;
- to know how the work is assessed;
- to be aware of how you plan to use the reading in the next lesson.

A homework such as 'write up your lab notes on the pendulum investigation in your best books' can be a low level task if it means transcribing rough notes into neat notes, unless the pupil has to translate and interpret his records into new prose, etc. Homework should require the pupil to add something, not merely to copy work. Unless something is added by the pupil, then assessment is difficult and you may award marks for completeness and neatness alone.

Similarly, a homework set like this: 'read Chapter 6 on plastics and I will give you a test next time', or 'read all you can about blood typing', lack clarity and purpose and leave many pupils confused and uncertain about what they have to do.

When properly set with clear instructions, homework consolidates learning and extends understanding and is an opportunity to develop study skills. We suggest you refer to Unit 5.2, 'Active learning', in Capel, Leask and Turner (1995), which contains examples of how to structure learning activities. A well structured piece of work often produces better feedback about pupil understanding and supports assessment than one that is unstructured. The Scheme of Work for science in your school often contains examples of suitable homework tasks.

Tests

Teachers frequently set tests to monitor learning during the course of a unit, as well as setting end of unit tests. The latter are prepared tests constructed by the staff of the science department or are supplied with the curriculum package. In the case of modular courses, the examination board supply the module tests. These tests are usually summative assessments.

We consider first those tests set by the teacher as part of her teaching programme and which are designed to check learning in the middle of a unit or to keep pupils on their toes. Tests set in this way are useful because they can contribute to formative assessment. Tests can:

- make sure that material taught has been learned;
- give an opportunity for pupils to review the work;
- identify learning difficulties;
- establish key ideas necessary for further work;
- enable differentiated work to be set; see Figure 6.3.

The marks for the test are, in themselves, not as important as the feedback to you and your pupils. However, if you record the marks and they count towards a reporting and grading system for pupils, then the test needs to be constructed with particular care. It is easy to think up a set of simple questions and allocate marks on a one question–one mark basis without giving much thought to what is being tested or the importance of one item over another. Such tests can lack balance, with a preponderance of recall questions over those testing understanding and higher skills (see below).

To construct a test, the results of which are fed into a record system and used formatively to monitor pupils' progress, you should take into account the following points:

- the aims and objectives of the unit of work;
- the balance between recall, understanding and higher skills (see below);
- the way in which you allocate marks.

Your test should reflect the knowledge, understanding and skills your course (through its units of work) aims to promote. If the test is given part-way through a unit of work then you need to identify the relevant objectives to make sure you are on target with your teaching. See Task 8.5. You should refer to Figure 6.3 in which the result of a test is used to direct differentiation in a unit of work.

TASK 8.5 ANALYSING A TEST: MATCHING ITEMS TO OBJECTIVES

Find a test paper that you have constructed for one of your classes. Do not choose an end of unit test supplied by an examination board or curriculum package. Have available the marks you awarded to pupils. Tackle the task in two stages.

Stage 1 The marks

Analyse the marks you gave overall for the test and look at the spread of marks. For a set of marks out of 10, have three categories, e.g. 0–3; 4–7 and 8–10.

How many pupils fell into each of the three categories? Did the marks distinguish between pupils' performances or were the marks bunched?

Now look at individual questions. Were:

- any questions too easy?
- any questions too hard?
- one or two questions dominating the test and so skewed the marks?
- the questions differentiated?

Which of these suggestions applied and how could you improve the test?

Stage 2 The objectives

List the objectives of your teaching up to the point of the test. What do you expect pupils to recall, understand or explain?

Examine each question in turn and identify which objective it was designed to test. What does this analysis tell you about the objectives that were:

- tested;
- omitted;
- given too much or too little prominence;
- achievable by most of your pupils?

Using the findings from both analyses, describe the ways in which

1 you would improve the test and why;
2 the test informs your planning for the next lesson(s).

Tests and examinations produced commercially, such as by examination boards and writers of curriculum packages, are constructed on principles that relate to the aims of the unit and endeavour to strike a balance between knowledge, skills and attitudes. It is these aims that we consider, before turning to a discussion of end of unit tests.

Knowledge, skills and attitudes

Many curricula use an analysis of learning to construct assessment schemes that identify different types and levels of learning. The types of learning are often identified as:

- cognitive skills;
- psychomotor skills;
- attitudinal skills.

Cognitive skills are those most commonly examined and valued in our society; they are to do with thinking; see also Chapter 3. Cognitive skills are frequently structured hierarchically, as follows:

1 **recall** – the ability of pupils to remember knowledge, ideas and procedures;
2 **understanding** – the ability to explain a phenomenon or process that they have been taught, e.g. to translate an idea from one form to another, such as annotating a diagram. Deeper understanding is that exhibited by pupils who can **apply** their knowledge to a new situation. An example is to explain the expansion of a metal from a knowledge of the Particle Theory of Matter (not having been taught that application of the theory).
3. **Higher skills** – sometimes referred to as analysis, synthesis and evaluation. Higher skills are exhibited when pupils can:

- plan and carry out an investigation into the factors contributing to, for example, the rusting of iron;
- construct an explanation for global warming using a knowledge of how greenhouses maintain their temperature above the surroundings and the increase in carbon dioxide in the atmosphere;
- discuss and criticise explanations for an investigation that showed, for example that the fish population in a lake was declining;
- choose and construct an appropriate graph to illustrate a set of observations.

Psychomotor skills are concerned with the ability of pupils to handle equipment correctly and in a controlled manner, e.g. construct an electric circuit, clamp a flask on a retort stand or inoculate an agar plate. Many pupils at Year 7 have not developed these skills, often through lack of practice, and may appear clumsy. These skills are important in all subjects that require good hand–eye co-ordination. These skills can be observed only in the laboratory or during field work.

The ability of pupils to select appropriate equipment and use it, or to interpret the scale of a meter, etc. are a combination of psychomotor and cognitive skills.

Attitudinal skills are bound up with motivation and a willingness to see purpose in activities. Attitudes are probably as important as cognitive potential; unless pupils are prepared to tackle tasks and to persevere, intellectual skills are not realised. Attitudes include willingness, perseverance, interest, enthusiasm and not being daunted by failure. Attitudes are not readily measured in written examinations, hence the concern by

---

TASK 8.6 ANALYSING YOUR TEST FOR SKILL CONTENT

Look back to the test you analysed in Task 8.5 and analyse the questions for the cognitive demand they make on the pupils; see above under cognitive skills. Classify the questions into the categories as follows:

- *recall*: did the pupil just have to remember without necessarily understanding?
- *understand* an idea or process that had been taught: that is, the pupil could recall a taught idea by explaining it in his own words;
- show understanding of an idea or process by *applying* it to a new situation: i.e. not taught;
- situations in which *higher skills* are needed: as in the exemplars above.

Further questions

1   Consider the balance of your test items in relation to the different skills listed above.
2   How does the balance of skills in the test items reflect the aims and objectives of your unit of work?
3   How should the test be adjusted better to respond to your aims?
4   Would you use the marks from the test as part of your record keeping and contribute to an end of unit grade for the pupils?
5   Did any of your questions test skills not listed?

teachers about the narrowness of examinations; see the introduction to this chapter. Attitudes are often recorded in reports to parents and in Records of Achievement.

End of unit tests

These tests are often constructed by a team of writers and tested on pupils both for presentation, e.g. to minimise ambiguity, and to check the spread of marks they produce. Each question in a test is given a mark allocation so that the overall test has the marks weighted in a particular way that reflects the aims and objectives of the unit of work. You should tell pupils how marks are allocated in your tests. Read through the test to be used with your pupils and ensure that your teaching allows pupils to answer the questions.

Items in a commercial test have been tried out with pupils to test reliability, remove ambiguity and improve presentation; they are therefore more likely to be have higher reliability and higher validity than your own tests (see p. 148). Work through Task 8.7 now.

TASK 8.7 GETTING TO KNOW AN END OF UNIT TEST

Collect together information about an end of unit test that you intend to use with your class. This information is likely to include:

- a copy of the test;
- the mark scheme together with specimen answers;
- the aims and objectives of the unit;
- information about how the test and test items relate to the aims and objectives of the unit; this is sometimes referred to as the test specification;
- the administrative information about how to organise and run the examination session and procedures for collecting, storing and marking the scripts.

Ensure that you:
- know the arrangements by which your class sit the test and what you need to do about it;
- know who marks the test and your role in the marking;
- have taught the material to be tested.

Activities for you to try:
- answer the test paper yourself;

continued . . .

- identify the aspects of the Science National Curriculum this unit of work addresses;
- estimate the balance of skills tested in the paper; see Task 8.6. Check this against the test specification above;
- find out how the marks are weighted in relation to the various cognitive skills;
- list the skills and abilities that you think are important but which are not assessed by the end of unit test. Are they assessed elsewhere in the unit?

Discuss any difficulties or queries with your science tutor in school.

ASSESSMENT OF PRACTICAL WORK

The Science National Curriculum separates experimental and investigative work from the content of science for assessment purposes at all four Key Stages. The Programmes of Study describe an outline progression in practical work in order to be challenging to pupils. The broad types of practical activity that your pupils should experience include:

- **observational tasks** in which pupils are given instructions to carry out an activity and collect data. The task requires pupils to collect, record, order and interpret data;
- instructional tasks to **learn techniques and become aware of phenomena**. In addition, pupils can collect data as in observational tasks, although the emphasis is on learning techniques;
- more **open tasks** in which pupils are required to plan and carry out an **investigation or enquiry**. Skills include planning, carrying out, recording, interpreting, concluding, evaluating and reporting. Pupils need prior knowledge of content, processes and skills in order to carry out these tasks. More demanding tasks require pupils to seek and learn new techniques in order to solve the problem.

The Attainment Targets of the Science National Curriculum list eight levels of performance (plus one of exceptional performance) by which pupils may be assessed (DFE, 1995b, pp. 50–1). Practical work at Key Stage 4 is assessed through the GCSE. You should become familiar with the current model of assessment of practical work in GCSE which identifies four skill areas: planning, obtaining, analysing and evaluating evidence (POAE); see Chapter 9, 'Models for science coursework' (p. 179).

Assessing practical work is time consuming and difficult. One method is to set a common practical examination. Such a method limits what can be tested because it:

- has to be reliable across a range of situations;
- cannot test all the skills needed to perform an investigation;
- reduces practical work to a special exercise instead of being an integral part of science learning.

All laboratory based assessments raise questions about:

- maintaining standards of assessment across many schools and teachers;
- comparing the difficulty of tasks;
- making judgements *in situ*;
- keeping records,

which have led to a continuing search for ways to raise the quality of assessment of practical work (Laws, 1996).

Pupils should be assessed while carrying out investigations as part of their learning science. Pupils can be seen in many situations and skills can be checked and monitored over time. The evidence you need to collect comes from both laboratory observation and marking written work that arises from the practical work. This process depends on good record keeping, being alert to assessment opportunities and your ability to devise situations to provide assessment opportunities. Continuous assessment allows you to know what the pupil can do and what he needs to do next, and promotes progression (Chapter 3) and allows for differentiation (Chapter 6).

TASK 8.8 THE ASSESSMENT LEVELS FOR PRACTICAL WORK IN THE SCIENCE NATIONAL CURRICULUM

Read through the Programmes of Study (PoS) for 'Experimental And Investigative Science' for Key Stages 2, 3 and 4 and look for the progression on ideas and skills that pupils can achieve. Consider in detail one element in the PoS, e.g. *obtaining evidence*, and compare the different demands on a pupil moving from:

- primary school to secondary school;
- KS3 to KS4 double science.

The task may be more easily managed by taking an experimental situation, e.g. measuring the rate of water loss in a plant, etc.

continued . . .

> Record your findings by responding to these questions:
>
> 1 What sort of activities have primary pupils experienced in relation to the skill 'obtaining evidence'?
> 2 What range of skills should pupils be able to perform in relation to 'obtaining evidence' if they are between levels 5–6 at the end of KS3, entering KS4? *See* Attainment Target 1.
>
> Share your findings with other student science teachers.

Setting practical activities for assessment requires clear aims and careful translation of those aims into objectives for the lesson. Your objectives should reflect the aims of the unit of work. You should:

- avoid setting a special examination to assess skills in which the content bears no relation to the content of the topic; link the activity to the topic and so provide context for assessment;
- identify the assessment opportunities;
- limit the assessment task to a few skills rather than test all possible skills, i.e. prioritise the skills to be assessed;
- be able to collect evidence, by observation or from pupils' reports.

To know more about assessment of practical work, see Task 8.9.

Sources of investigations and activities for assessment of practical work

Most curriculum packages have examples of assessment tasks that either fit into an existing Scheme of Work or can be adapted to your needs. The SoW in your school includes ideas for assessment tasks and you should consult it. However, you need to check carefully that the objectives for the activity meet your requirements. Other sources of assessment tasks include *Science Scene* (Avison, Bailey and Hill, 1995), which links activities to the National Curriculum, and the ASE publication, *Science Through Sc1 Investigations* (Solomon, Duveen, Scott and Hall, undated), which includes many examples of pupils' work with a commentary. Developing graded investigations has been the target of research and advice on how to plan different levels of investigations can be found in the report of the OPENS Project (Jones, Simon, Black, Fairbrother and Watson, 1992). The GCSE examination boards also publish advice about activities suitable for investigation.

For further discussion concerning the place of scientific investigations in school science across Key Stages 3 and 4 and post-16 courses, see Frost (1995, pp. 60–97).

TASK 8.9 ASSESSING PRACTICAL WORK

Arrange to observe a teacher assessing practical work or, better still, ask your class teacher if you can assist in the planning and carrying out of an assessment of practical work. Collect together copies of the:

- unit of work;
- assessment task for pupils and the teacher's notes;
- equipment list;
- marking schedule,

and read through the instructions. Clarify anything not understood with the class teacher. Identify:

- the relevant sections in the Programme of Study;
- the skills and knowledge to be assessed;
- the levels pupils are expected to attain.

Answer these questions and keep a record of your findings:

Advance preparation
- In what ways were the pupils prepared for the assessment?
- What were pupils told about the activity and the assessment, e.g. which skills were being assessed?
- What instructions were given to technical staff?
- How had the teacher planned to observe and record evidence?
- What was your role in the activity?

During the activity
- What instructions were given to pupils about what was being assessed?
- Was evidence about all skills collected from pupils or just evidence about a few skills of some pupils?
- What evidence did you collect? Keep a note of how you interpreted what you saw and made judgements about the quality of the evidence.

After the activity
- Identify the skills that were easy to mark and assess and those posing a problem. Describe why some were difficult.
- How was the evidence turned into marks for records or pupils assigned to National Curriculum levels?
- Talk with the class teacher about the success of the activity. Share your observations of the process with her.

For further discussion of the assessment of practical work at Key Stage 4 see Chapter 9.

SUMMARY

This chapter has addressed the principles of assessment and their relationship to teaching and learning. A contrast has been drawn between the different purposes of summative and formative assessment. The danger of trying to use one assessment tool for many purposes is mentioned. In setting pupils work, the importance of clear objectives is emphasised because they identify the focus of assessment. At this stage of your development as a teacher, it is important to get practice in the variety of assessment methods and to discuss the implications of assessment on teaching and learning with your tutors and other student teachers. Go back to the standards list mentioned in the introduction to this chapter and check your progress and future training needs. The further reading section gives more guidance. For a critical review of the assessment of scientific investigations in the Science National Curriculum, see Laws (1996).

FURTHER READING

Avison, J., Bailey, M. and Hill, G. (1995) *Science Scene: Investigations and Assessment Book*, London: Hodder & Stoughton.
Detailed specification of a range of practical activities linked to the 1995 National Curriculum.

Dunne, D. (ed.) (1996) *The New Science 1 Book: Experimental and Investigative Science*, Northampton: Northampton County Council (The Science Centre).
An updated version of the 1993 book.

Frost, J. (ed.) (1995) *Teaching Science*, London: Woburn Press.
Chapter 4 discusses ways in which practical work is carried out and the factors to be considered in planning, execution, reporting and evaluating investigations. It includes examples of investigations and the work of pupils is discussed.

Gipps, C. and Stobbart, G. (1994) *Assessment: A Teacher's Guide to the Issues*, London: Hodder & Stoughton.
An excellent book for gaining an overview of assessment and its place in the National Curriculum and in teaching and learning.

School Curriculum and Assessment Authority (SCAA) (1995/6) *Exemplification of Standards in Science*, London: SCAA.

A useful document for relating pupils' work to levels in the National Curriculum.

Solomon, J., Duveen, J., Scott, L. and Hall, S. (undated) *Science Through SCI Investigations*, Hatfield: Association for Science Education (about 1995).
The book provides a discussion of the role of practical work in secondary science and addresses in particular the use and assessment of scientific investigations in teaching school science. The text contains an extensive range of pupils' work.

9 Public examinations

INTRODUCTION

Whilst studying this chapter, it is helpful to think back to your own experience of science examinations. Did you take all three subjects – biology, chemistry and physics – through to public examination level, as all pupils in maintained schools now do, or did you make choices between them? Which of your examinations did justice, in your own view, to the course you had taken and the study you put in? How did you prepare and revise for them? Which patterns of study were helpful and which were not? Did you experience examinations where the testing was spread out over the course, as modular patterns in schools now do? Did you do coursework projects, and in what ways were the demands of these similar to, or different from, those you make of your own pupils?

Your own experience is a valuable starting point for understanding examinations. During your periods of school experience you should look out for examination arrangements that work in a variety of ways. It is the purpose of this chapter to enable you to understand and compare them. A variety of experience is particularly useful before your first post, when you become 'locked in' to a limited set of public examination arrangements.

School examinations have experienced rapid change, alongside the curriculum changes, since the common 16+ GCSE arrangements were introduced in the later 1980s. Following the post-Dearing version of the National Curriculum, GCSE science examinations were stable for a few years (Dearing, 1994). The post-16 picture remains much less clear. Substantial further changes to GCE A and AS levels, as well as further revision of General National Vocational Qualifications (GNVQ) assessment, are scheduled for the late 1990s.

The great majority of pupils, 80 per cent nationally in maintained schools in 1994, are entered for at least two GCSEs in science (the Double Award), or for three separate subjects (OFSTED, 1995). In most schools, therefore, the results in science have a large impact, for good or ill, on the school's headline results, in particular the score for A*–C grades in five or more subjects. The publication of these figures in prospectuses and in local and national league tables remains controversial but it has focused attention sharply on the factors contributing to the improvement of pupils' examination grades. This chapter should help you to understand some factors to do with the science examinations themselves. Although significant, these factors are only one part of the larger picture to do with the quality of teaching and learning in science which shapes pupils' performance at the end of their courses.

OBJECTIVES

By the end of this chapter you should:

- be familiar with the range of public science examinations taken in schools and with their main features;
- understand tiers of entry at GCSE and know what is involved in choosing the appropriate tier;
- recognise how GCSE syllabuses differ and how they are related to the National Curriculum;
- understand the implications of examination arrangements for the curriculum in Year 10 and above;
- understand the place of coursework in science examinations and know about the ways in which your own marking needs to be moderated.

WHICH SCIENCE EXAMINATIONS ARE AVAILABLE IN SCHOOLS?

The range of public examinations and qualifications available in science subjects and taken in schools is wide. Most examinations are now taken in National Curriculum based GCSEs and in separate subject GCE A levels. However, you should be aware of the other qualifications. At some stage, alternatives to traditional A levels are likely to grow substantially. All syllabuses have to be approved by the Qualifications and Curriculum Authority (QCA); see the section below on 'GCSE and the National Curriculum' (p. 175). In the following categories, the figures given are the numbers tested nationally in 1996, to the nearest hundred (*Times Educational Supplement*, 16, 23 and 30 August, 1996):

- GCSEs covering National Curriculum science: Single Award, Double Award, and biology, chemistry and physics as separate subjects. Total entries 1,139,000.
- GCSEs in other science subjects, e.g. rural science, human physiology and health, astronomy. The numbers taking these are relatively small.
- Certificate of Achievement in National Curriculum science. This is a new qualification intended to recognise achievement below GCSE grade G at the end of Key Stage 4, and first examined in June 1998.
- GNVQ science Foundation level, equivalent to four GCSE grades D–G. This can be taken pre-16 or post-16. The take-up has been tiny so far (200).
- GNVQ science Intermediate level, equivalent to five GCSE grades A–C. Take-up of 3,700, of whom just over 50 per cent gained full awards.
- GNVQ science Advanced level, equivalent to two or (if extra units are taken) three A level passes. Take-up figures in 1996 were around 1,400 and 1,000 respectively.
- GCE A and AS levels in biology, chemistry and physics. Take-up figures for the full A levels were around 51,900, 40,500 and 32,800 respectively.
- GCE A and AS levels in other science subjects, e.g. modular science for a Single or Double Award, environmental science, geology. Total take-up was around 5,100.

TASK 9.1 THE EXAMINATION COURSES IN YOUR SCIENCE DEPARTMENT

Find out what science courses are on offer in your main teaching experience school, and make a list or table of them. Do not forget to include Year 12 (Sixth Form) one year courses, and possibly subjects taken in evening classes or a community programme. You may also find that closely related subjects are taught in other departments in the school, e.g. electronics taught within the technology area. For each examination course, list the:

- title;
- level of study and qualification to which it leads;
- Examining Board/Group or Awarding Body;
- Year group(s) studying it;
- number of pupils entered, analysed by tier of entry if possible;

continued . . .

• number of lessons (or time in hours) of study.

Amongst these examinations there may be a subject or course with which you are unfamiliar. Use the issues raised in this chapter to prepare a set of questions, and ask the member of staff responsible if you can meet with him or her to find out more about it. If possible, arrange to observe a class at work on the course.

UNDERSTANDING THE SYLLABUS

Before the GCSE, syllabuses were often quite short: a list of topics to be taught with details of the examination papers. If you have not already done so, you should now look through the entire contents of the main GCSE syllabus booklet that governs your work with Key Stage 4 classes. Try also to gather the following items together with the syllabus itself. The school may be able to lend them to you. If not, the Examining Board can supply them, though there may be a cost for some items:

• The *Guidance* (or *Support*) *Material* booklet. This contains exemplar material for coursework tasks and their assessment.
• The *Specimen Question Papers*, or (better) a set of recent past papers.
• A recent *Examiner's Report*, which refers to an earlier pattern of examination if published before 1998. Nevertheless, the nature of the comments will be helpful to you.

There are three kinds of syllabus according to their relationship to the Key Stage 4 Programmes of Study (PoS) for Sc2 to Sc4 of the post-Dearing National Curriculum (DFE, 1995b)[1]. An Examining Board does not permit pupils to be entered for more than one of these *in any one round* of examinations. The differences between them, along with grading arrangements and tiers of entry, are probably the most common queries that parents put to staff about GCSE science. Tiers are discussed in the next section. The three kinds of syllabus are:

• Single Award science syllabuses, which must include (but may go beyond) the Key Stage 4 single science PoS. They must provide access to the full range of grades A*–G, and are intended to be of

---

1 The PoS is written separately for each Key Stage and contains five sections: an introductory section (sometimes called Sc0); a section 'experimental and investigative science' (Sc1) and three content sections, Sc2, Sc3 and Sc4.

equal difficulty to the Double Award. They are, however, predominantly taken by lower achieving candidates (OFSTED, 1995).

- Double Award science syllabuses, which must include (but may go beyond) the Key Stage 4 double science PoS. They lead to a double grade on the certificate, always comprising two equal grades A*A*–GG. In most cases, additional information is provided about candidates' relative performance on individual papers testing the biology, chemistry and physics components. This is known as the 'breakdown' of the grades.

- 'Suites' of biology, chemistry and physics separate subject syllabuses, sometimes known as the Triple Award. Taken together, these must also include (and may go substantially beyond) the Key Stage 4 double science PoS. They are separately examined and lead to separate grades from A*–G. There is no statutory requirement for pupils to take all three examinations if they take any of them, even in maintained schools. The minimum statutory requirement in maintained schools is to teach all of the single science PoS.

All syllabuses have to meet a number of other national criteria laid down by QCA or its predecessor, the School Curriculum and Assessment Authority (SCAA). These criteria and discussions between the Examining Boards have led to standard patterns both for tiers of examination and for assessment of coursework that apply to cohorts of pupils examined from the summer of 1998. This standardisation has reduced the diversity of the mainstream syllabuses on offer, and has correspondingly reduced the opportunities for science teachers to take part in syllabus innovation in co-operation with other schools and the Examining Groups. Nevertheless, substantial variations between the syllabuses do remain, in the details of content, layout, examining arrangements and guidance or support for teachers. You should investigate these variations through Task 9.2 on p. 177.

Tiers of entry

The standardised pattern is two tiers of entry: Foundation tier, with access to grades G–C, and Higher tier, with access to grades D–A*. There are separate written papers for each tier, but the papers contain a proportion of common question material in the middle range of difficulty. This is one means by which examiners can check on the comparability of standards, especially at the grade C/D borderline, for the same grades awarded through taking different tiers.

There are two ways in which syllabuses have allocated their subject content to the two tiers of study. Some are devised on a **core plus extension** model. All pupils must be taught the Foundation tier material, which is therefore a core, and there are extension items for the Higher tier. Others are devised with **three layers of content**, where the easiest items are examined only at the Foundation tier, items of moderate difficulty at both tiers and the hardest items only at the Higher tier. The latter model is more complex but has the advantage of narrowing the focus for more able pupils. In practice, it avoids the need to spend time on simple approaches to concepts that should be familiar to more able pupils from Key Stage 3 studies.

You may come across the view of some teachers that with Foundation and Higher tiers we are 'back to the old CSE and O level system'. The Certificate of Secondary Education (CSE) had a top grade of 1, recognised as equivalent to grade C of GCE O level, in the same way that now the GCSE Foundation tier has an upper limit of C. The GCE O level scale extended from A to E; performance below E, like that below D in the GCSE Higher tier, was ungraded. However, the situation is in most respects very different. A GCSE syllabus is designed as a single, coherent whole. O level and CSE syllabuses were drawn up by separate examining bodies, with wide differences in content, emphasis and style of question papers. The GCSE certificate does not identify the tier of entry: a C grade is a C grade, whichever papers are taken.

Who enters for what?

In the case of some pupils it remains difficult to decide on the appropriate tier for which to enter them, just as it was hard to choose between O level and CSE. Earlier versions of the GCSE system did not all present this difficulty. For example, some science examinations consisted of common core papers taken by all candidates and optional extension papers for those aspiring to the higher grades.

On the one hand, there are over-confident pupils (or ambitious parents) who press for entry to the Higher tier when their teacher's judgement is that they will do well to reach grade C. In this circumstance there is a danger that, tackling unsuccessfully the harder questions on the Higher tier papers, they fall below the C and possibly even the D grade boundaries. On the other hand, there are easy-going pupils (and uninterested parents) who are content with the prospect of a C grade to be gained by a comfortable route, despite the teacher's recognition of their potential to do better if they apply themselves to the task.

You should find out how science staff approach the job of advising pupils and parents in these cases. If possible, attend a relevant parents' evening. Your science department may have an agreed entry policy. A lot depends on the timing and context of the information that is available during the course. For example, some syllabuses include module tests taken during the course which count as a component of the final examination, or a written paper at the end of Year 10. These have the advantage of providing externally validated feedback to pupils and parents before a final decision is taken over the tier of entry in Year 11.

The science Double Award provides a different basis for GCE A level to the three separate sciences. Many schools, mostly independent schools, teach separate sciences from Year 7 because of the importance of preparation for A level, but this is done so at the expense of other subjects, especially at Key Stage 4; see Task 2.4. Several attempts have been made to reform A levels in the past ten years, but the narrow, specialist course of study (two to three subjects) has been retained because of its high academic standard and use as the university entrance examination. The future of post-16 education remains under review (Dearing, 1996).

COMBINED, CO-ORDINATED, INTEGRATED OR MODULAR?

Science teaching to 16+ has a long history of curriculum development. Before the 1960s, single subject science courses held sway in grammar schools while general science courses were common in secondary modern schools. Several GCSE syllabuses have their origins in specific curriculum development projects that accompanied the era of comprehensive reorganisation of schools. Although some syllabuses have now lost their original links, their layout and their choice of additional content still reflect their origins.

- **Combined science** courses were the first to bring together a selection of the content from the separate sciences, to fit into a single or double O level or CSE course.
- **Integrated science**, notably the Schools Council Integrated Science Project of the 1960s (Hall, 1973), took the 'combining' a step further by arranging the content into themes that drew on more than one traditional subject area – structures, for example, or human senses. This approach has become less common especially with the recasting of the National Curriculum along traditional subject lines. Ask around, however, and you may find some science teachers who still advocate the strengths of a holistic approach to science.

- **Modular science** courses began in the 1970s with practical, everyday selections of topics aimed at lower ability pupils and supported by resources such as the Science at Work project (Rowlands and Snape, 1992). The intention was to work through self-contained modules with separate tests at the end of each. These courses were subsequently redesigned, and have become well established for the whole ability range. There are nationally defined limits to the percentage of the final marks that may be accumulated through module tests, however.

- **Co-ordinated science** courses are the most recent, dating from the 1980s, e.g. Dorling, Hunt and Monger, 1988. They aim to keep the subject areas identifiable but to make explicit links between them, and to establish a coherent approach to the central scientific ideas, such as particles and energy transfer. The Nuffield-Chelsea Curriculum Trust, Suffolk Local Education Authority and the Salters Institute have all supported the development of popular courses of this kind. The resulting GCSE syllabuses are offered by the Midland Examining Group (1996, Syllabuses A, B and C respectively).

There is now perhaps the same kind of confusing distinction between these types of course as between schools describing themselves as comprehensive, grammar, selective or non-selective. The biggest difference is whether the content is laid out by the three subject areas and examined at the end of the course, or whether it is studied in modules with module tests as well as the end of course papers. There are, however, considerable differences in style and content too.

GCSE and the National Curriculum

We referred above to the way in which GCSE syllabuses match National Curriculum requirements in respect of minimum content. However, there is more to the syllabus than that. Three issues arise, each of which has its implications for the choice of syllabus and the way in which it is translated into a department's scheme of work.

First, it is the syllabus *as a whole* that fully covers the relevant Programme of Study. The items set out for the Foundation tier may not cover parts of the PoS in detail or even at all. The Examining Boards[2] have

---

2 The old Examining Boards have been brought together into five Groups. Some Groups include the word 'Group' in their name, e.g. Midland Examining Group, while others use a different collective term, e.g. Council. We retain the use of the word 'Board' in this book to describe a body responsible for the setting and marking of examinations.

selected material they consider appropriate for low and middle ability pupils. This selection varies between syllabuses.

Second, the Examining Boards, starting from the arrangements of content that had developed historically before the National Curriculum, have in effect enhanced as well as reorganised the substance of Sc2–4. The reasoning behind this is to add some of the more interesting 'flesh' of scientific applications to the otherwise rather dry 'bones' of the National Curriculum. Syllabuses have attempted to mould the whole into a more accessible and appropriate 'body' of a curriculum for the 14–16 age group. The Dearing review slimmed down the National Curriculum content with this in mind. The nature of the additional material varies between syllabuses.

The third issue is what the syllabuses do about investigative work (Sc1) and the 'introductory requirements', sometimes known as Sc0 and discussed in Chapter 2. All syllabuses include the framework, agreed across the Examining Groups, as to how investigative work is to be **assessed**, but they do not specify the skills that are to be **taught and learnt**, which are set out in the PoS. The resources or guidance material that accompany some syllabuses may incorporate investigative skills; otherwise it is left to schools to build them into their Schemes of Work. At one extreme is explicit teaching of the skills through exercises focused on a few skills at a time, e.g. analysis of a given set of experimental data. At the other extreme is development of the skills through a sequence of whole investigations, with teacher guidance. There are arguments for and against both approaches. You should find out to what extent the department you work in has developed either or both of these approaches.

The statutory material of Sc0 presents similar issues at Key Stage 4 as at Key Stage 3 (DFE, 1995b, pp. 38–9). Some syllabuses indicate which of these requirements are already met through the subject content, and where opportunities for others, notably in respect of IT, need to be provided. Other syllabuses have little to say about Sc0. If your school is using one of the latter syllabuses, an offer by you of help to undertake cross-referencing between Sc0 and their Scheme of Work, identifying any gaps in coverage, is likely to be welcomed by the department.

MAKING SENSE OF QUESTION PAPERS

If the syllabus is the 'rule book' for a public examination, then the question papers form the 'case law'. The question papers show by example the depth of treatment expected in teaching the course, and the relative emphasis given to different parts of the syllabus. You should therefore study the question papers carefully at an early stage in your education year, especially if you are teaching examination classes. Write out your own model answers and, if possible, check them against a mark scheme. Make notes of the guidance that you need to give your pupils, especially when the time for revision comes round, in order to improve their ability to gain marks.

SCIENCE A LEVELS AND GNVQ

The structure of GCE A levels in all subjects is in the process of change in the late 1990s. The AS level is mutating from 'Advanced Supplementary', as difficult as A level but half the size in content and value, to 'Advanced Subsidiary', intended to examine the easier first half of an A level course, at an intermediate standard between GCSE and A level. The GCE A level syllabuses are being rewritten in two sections, the 'AS' section with a 40 per cent assessment weighting and the 'A2' section with a 60 per cent weighting. As with GCSEs, modular structures have become popular and there are varied styles of syllabus and patterns of examination.

The GNVQ qualifications are also under review. Science GNVQ has so far most commonly been adopted at Intermediate level as an alternative to retaking GCSE in Year 12 (first year Sixth Form); see p. 170. Students on this course carry out substantial individual projects with an emphasis on science as it is used in the workplace, for example work on analysing the composition of substances or on monitoring the performance of human physical activity. Specified ranges of content and core skills, including communication and IT, have to be covered during the course of these projects.

TASK 9.2 ANALYSING A SELECTION OF GCSE SYLLABUSES

Use the questions below to compare at least two syllabuses, with their associated guidance, offered by different Examining Groups. Your school may wish to evaluate an alternative to their present choice of syllabus, in which case your science tutor can suggest a syllabus to look into and will be interested in your findings. Alternatively, you could work on this task together with a student teacher placed in a different school. The Double Award syllabuses

continued . . .

---

are extensive. If you choose one of these syllabuses, focus on the comparisons of content in one subject area only.

This task does not attempt a complete evaluation of the syllabuses; it only compares organisation and content. The testing and examination arrangements are of equal importance, not to mention the costs of resourcing if replacement text books and teaching support materials are involved.

For some questions, you may need to refer back to explanations earlier in this chapter.

- Is the content laid out by subject specialisms or in shorter modules? Is there evidence of co-ordination, e.g. by cross-reference to other subjects or to other modules? If it is modular, how long are the modules? Are any of the modules integrated, i.e. drawing on more than one of Sc2–4?
- How is the content divided between the two tiers? Is it a core-and-extension model, or arranged in three layers? Does it enable rapid identification of what needs teaching to whom?
- Is the content cross-referenced to the appropriate National Curriculum PoS? Does any referencing include investigative skills (Sc1) and/or the introductory requirements (Sc0), or are these left to the school to build in?
- Is the Foundation content an appropriate and manageable selection for low and middle ability pupils?
- Which items are additional to the PoS? At the Higher tier especially, is the additional content for the more able pupils suitable for those who may wish to go on to A level?
- Is the syllabus one of a compatible set of Single Award, Double Award and separate subject syllabuses? Could the additional material for an extra GCSE grade be identified and taught in extra lessons rather than in separate classes?
- Is the content specified in detail or in outline? Is the depth of knowledge required made clear as well as what pupils are asked to do with their knowledge (e.g. recall facts, describe functions or explain reasons)?
- Are learning experiences or pupil activities suggested in the syllabus or in materials associated with it? Are different learning experiences suggested for Foundation and Higher work?
- What other forms of support, e.g. the syllabus content on computer disk or photocopiable masters for pupils or teachers, are available in the syllabus or its associated materials?

COURSEWORK AND MODERATION

Ways of assessing practical work have already been considered in Chapter 8. In this section we turn to how and why such assessment is counted towards your pupils' public examination results.

Some GCE A level syllabuses in science subjects introduced coursework projects as early as the 1960s. Since then, coursework has slowly gained ground, either as an alternative to formal practical examinations of the traditional type or replacing them altogether. The argument runs that if pupils should be involved in observational and experimental science on a regular basis, then coursework is an appropriate way of giving status to that part of their work and of assessing it. Practical examinations have often been seen as too far removed from day to day practical science, unduly limited in scope by the time and equipment that can be made available.

Models for science coursework

For similar reasons to those cited above for GCE A level, coursework was established as integral to science GCSEs from the outset. In the early years of the GCSE, in the mid-1980s and before the introduction of the National Curriculum, coursework assessment schemes varied in emphasis. 'Whole investigation' projects featured in only a few. Categories of skill such as 'manipulating apparatus' and 'following instructions' paid close attention to how pupils actually carried out their practical work. The inclusion of these categories made assessment points readily accessible to lower achievers. Other syllabuses assessed 'communication skills' which encouraged pupils to report their findings clearly and imaginatively. Just as the science content of the curriculum is very much a matter of debate, it is equally hard to determine which skills and processes should be taught and assessed through practical work in science.

You should become familiar during school experience with the standard pattern for GCSE coursework introduced in 1996 or its successor. You should be aware of the strengths and weaknesses of the model of investigative science implied by the four 'skill areas' of planning, obtaining, analysing and evaluating evidence (POAE). For example, does this model of practical work focus too heavily on the kind of science associated with academic research activity, at the expense of the hands-on expertise needed for systematic technical work? Are the requirements easier to meet through quantitative tasks than through the qualitative testing more commonly found in practical activities in chemistry and biology? If possible, find out about different coursework schemes in use nationally, such as the extended individual projects in the Nuffield A level physics course (Harris, 1985), or the requirement for pupils to write reports on an industrial visit in Salters A level chemistry course (University of York Science Education Group, 1994).

Coursework requirements for the GCSE have focused on assessing experimental and investigative work (Sc1) as it is defined in the National Curriculum. As one of four equally weighted Attainment Targets in a Single or Double Award course, it carries 25 per cent of the total marks, equivalent to 'half a GCSE grade' in the Double Award. In the science department in which you are working, is as much as 25 per cent of total lesson time given to this type of work over the two years? This question of priority in the use of time is potentially important for pupils' achievement. It is also hard to judge how much time is used in this way. The time spent on Sc1 includes learning and practising a host of component skills and knowledge, from the use of meters and microscopes to the subtleties of proportionality and correlation. The teaching of these is usually spread widely across different lessons. Most schools offer more opportunities for coursework than the minimum required by the Examination Board, so that pupils can improve their performance progressively.

Pupils should develop their skills in the four areas (POAE) throughout Key Stages 3 and 4 so that they know how to carry out a scientific investigation and write a report of their investigation, so as to improve their understanding of the processes and know how to maximise their marks. You can help pupils by reading carefully the guidance on the assessment of coursework issued by your Examination Board. All five GCSE Examining Groups work to a common framework of skills and an associated mark scheme. You should note the way in which practical skills are broken down for teaching and assessment purposes and know the meaning of terms as used by the Boards, such as fair test, dependent and independent variable and key factor. You should also ascertain the Board's and your school's approach to safety issues.

Examination rules and professional judgement

It is the job of your department's teaching team to end up, towards the end of Year 11, with a valid and reliable set of coursework marks to submit to the Examining Board. Look back to the beginning of Chapter 8 to remind yourself of what 'validity' and 'reliability' mean in general terms. In the context of coursework: do the pupils' marks reward good experimental and investigative work that they have done for themselves, in line with the expectations of the syllabus and mark scheme? If they do, they are valid. Is the standard of marking fair and consistent across different pieces of coursework from any one pupil, and across different teachers' marking? This is the test of reliability. Both issues are addressed by the Examining Board's rules, and both are also quite a professional challenge. The same issues are, of course, being raised nationally concerning teacher assessment at the end of Key Stages 1, 2 and 3.

Validity and 'authentication' of coursework

As with tasks of any kind, what pupils achieve in their coursework depends on what they are asked to do, how it is introduced to them and the help and support available to them whilst doing it. Choosing appropriate tasks in the first place is a challenge for teachers. If tasks are not suggested in the department's Scheme of Work, then see the guidance and exemplar material provided by the Examining Board. Most Boards provide lists of suitable tasks as well as marked examples of pupils' coursework, including examples of tasks of varying difficulty.

Your school's Examining Board probably asks teachers to report the help given to pupils. 'Help' includes advice given to the class as a whole, for example through 'helpsheets'. The teacher may also be required to make a note on pupils' scripts of help given to individuals. The Board should set out how to take such help into account in the marking of pupils' work. Such guidance is required under the *Mandatory Code of Practice for the GCSE*:

> The examining group must specify the conditions under which coursework can take place. The specified conditions must facilitate the supervision and authentication of candidates' work. Where, because of the nature of the subject, the syllabus requires Centre-based candidates to undertake some assessed coursework activities outside their school or college, the examining group must require that sufficient work takes place under direct supervision to allow the teachers concerned to authenticate each candidate's work with confidence.
>
> (SCAA/CAAW, 1995, par. 75)

This requirement may lead to decisions taken within the school, or by the Board, about where and when coursework may be done, perhaps limiting some or even all of it to the classroom. It may also provide guidance about how and when to give credit for pupils' use of text books and other resources. Task 9.3 invites you to enquire into the range of help and support that may be available to pupils.

Coursework can remain credible and educationally productive only if teachers act professionally in the way they conduct it. In general terms, the Examining Boards have encouraged teachers to provide positive opportunities for pupils to show what they can do. This means a careful balance between providing pupils with some freedom of choice and yet providing an appropriate framework within which they can succeed, and a further balance between encouraging their resourcefulness and at the same time ensuring practicality and safety. These considerations place considerable demands on teachers' skill and professionalism.

TASK 9.3 HOW CAN I HELP?

Find an opportunity to observe or teach a class tackling a coursework task for GCSE. You should ask questions about what the pupils did before the start of the coursework itself. Look at pupils' completed scripts and identify how they are marked. The following checklist is relevant to how pupils are helped along with their work:

- How do previous lessons lead into the work? Has the class done similar work before? How similar, and how recently?
- Does the teacher remind pupils of what to do in general terms, e.g. 'choose a variable' or 'draw a line graph'? Or are they taken through the specifics of the topic, e.g. told which variable to choose or what axes and scales to use?
- Are the reminders oral or in writing, e.g. a worksheet, a 'helpsheet' or a copy of the assessment points?
- Do pupils work on their own or in groups, either for the practical work only or for planning and writing up too?
- How does the teacher respond to questions from pupils? Is it treated like a practical examination or like a teaching lesson?
- Do pupils complete all the work in school, or are they allowed to take it home? Are they allowed to use family members and home computers as part of the resources available to them?
- How does the marking take account of any of these sources of help? Does the teacher annotate the script to show help given?

Compare your findings with other student teachers. You may find considerable variations in practice between schools. It has been said that: 'Marks should be given for how help is taken up, not taken away because help was given.' Do you agree, and how is this view implemented for the different kinds of help you have seen?

Reliable marking and 'moderation' of work

Moderation is the process through which marks for coursework are brought in line with a common standard, thus making them reliable. 'Internal' moderation seeks to establish a common standard within the school. 'External' moderation is intended to maintain standards across schools and nationally.

Internal moderation may be carried out in various ways. For science coursework, teachers generally aim to establish the correct standard of marking as early as possible, and at least before they mark the pieces of work that are likely to count towards the selected marks sent to the Board. Commonly, teachers together look at the Board's guidance and interpret it for their own circumstances; they may produce marking guidelines for particular coursework tasks, illustrating pupils' responses for different marks; they exchange scripts, mark them separately and then discuss them to resolve differences. The latter may be organised annually at a formal moderation meeting in the science department. Even when teachers have become familiar with applying the Board's criteria, any marks reported to pupils or their parents are provisional, since they are subject to external moderation. Feedback to pupils is valuable, especially if there is a chance in the future for them to improve their performance; however, schools and departments may set their own rules about what feedback is allowed.

TASK 9.4 INTERNAL MODERATION

This exercise asks you to compare your own judgements in marking coursework with another teacher's judgements. If possible, do this first with the regular class teacher of a class you are working with and for a task you have seen them do.

Both the regular class teacher and yourself should mark the same scripts independently, without access to the other's marks. Mark at least three pupils' work, selected from the top, middle and lower ranges of achievement in the class. The first marker annotates the script in line with the Board's guidance. Then compare the POAE marks each of you has given; discuss the reasons for any differences and note how these are resolved. See pp. 179–80 for discussion of POAE.

You may be able to follow up this exercise by attending a moderation meeting in your science department. If not, you should repeat the exercise in collaboration with another student teacher and

continued . . .

by exchanging groups of scripts from different tasks. It is considerably harder to decide on marks when you did not see the class do the practical work. This highlights the importance of knowing how the task was introduced and of annotating the pupils' work concerning the individual help given.

Each year, early in the summer term, your science department works out the marks that represent pupils' best achievement according to the Board's rules. They supply a number of sample scripts to an external moderator appointed by the Board, selected from across the range of pupil achievement and from different classes and teachers. The moderator has the right to ask for additional scripts if necessary, so the department must keep all the pupils' scripts that contribute to their final marks until after the external moderation is completed. It is not uncommon for moderators to make adjustments to the school's marks, for example if the school's marking is too generous at one end of the achievement range. The adjustments are made to all pupils' marks from the school, even though based on a small sample. It is assumed that internal moderation beforehand makes this a sensible process. External moderators write a short report on their decisions, a copy of which is returned to the school.

PREPARING PUPILS FOR THEIR PUBLIC EXAMINATIONS

Schools and science departments pay increasing attention to preparing pupils for examinations. This is a task with several aspects:

- developing pupils' study skills for revision;
- teaching 'examination techniques' for answering questions effectively;
- providing specific resources to help revise course content;
- actively supporting pupils during the revision process;
- building up their confidence and motivation (most important of all).

The preparation of pupils for public examinations at both GCSE and GCE A level is discussed in detail in Capel, Leask and Turner (1997). In addition, some science text books provide helpful advice on revision, for example Johnson (1991), or on how to tackle the various types of question in science examination papers, for example Dobson and Sunley (1996).

VALUE ADDED

Examination results should be considered alongside other 'performance indicators' by which a school is judged. Local Education Authorities

(LEAs) and government agencies, as well as schools themselves, use a variety of such indicators to monitor school performance, including also the result of SATs (see Chapter 8) and attendance statistics.

Research is underway in several centres in the UK to develop ways of measuring the relative success of schools in promoting the performance of their pupils over time. This approach is known as 'Value Added', borrowing the metaphor from the little understood taxation system of VAT. The central question is 'what has the school done to improve the performance of its pupils? (Stoll and Fink, 1996, p. 179), and the hope is that Value Added answers will provide a fairer way of comparing school performance than league tables based on data that ignores any differences in pupil intake.

Science is tested nationally through the SATs at the end of Key Stages 2 and 3 as well as at GCSE, so that alongside English and mathematics these results are being used in calculations of Value Added. Your school may have started making comparisons of this kind, perhaps to monitor performance by departments or to identify pupils who appear to be under-achieving. In addition, a number of schools use tests of cognitive ability, such as the Cognitive Assessment Tasks (CATs) produced and standardised by the National Foundation for Educational Research, to provide base-line data about pupils early on entry and to predict or compare with their eventual performance at GCSE. Enquire in your school about these developments.

SUMMARY

Examination success is a highly visible and rewarding aspect of your teaching and a source of professional satisfaction and pride. The annual set of GCSE and GCE A level results is one way in which individual teachers, subject departments and schools as a whole assess their performance, as well as an important basis on which they are judged, not least by their local communities.

As a science teacher, you need to know your way around the syllabus thoroughly, not only its subject content but also its relationship to the National Curriculum, its style, emphasis and organisation and, crucially, the pattern of assessment it uses, through question papers and coursework. You have a particular professional responsibility for the fair and responsible marking of coursework. In addition, you need to be aware of considerable variations in the provision that schools make for examination courses. For example, within one borough the time given to teaching the Double Award science GCSE courses varies between 3.5 hours and 7 hours per week. In some schools, Single and Double Award courses, and in others Double and Triple Award courses, are given the same time allocation.

There are also wide variations in the provision of material resources, including books and whether pupils have suitable text books to use at home. Such considerations may be important to you when you seek your first post.

FURTHER READING

Study carefully the guidance in the syllabus and its associated publications for the science examinations towards which the pupils are studying in your school experience school. Make sure you are familiar with the examination papers and with the rules for assessing coursework. Read the materials made available to pupils, both during the course and for revision purposes, and assess their strengths and weaknesses. Use the sections in this chapter on 'Understanding the syllabus' and 'Combined, co-ordinated, integrated or modular?' to help you.

UNIVERSITY COLLEGE OF

ST MARTIN

Science Dept
Bowerham

10 Beyond the classroom

INTRODUCTION

This chapter encourages you to use out-of-school opportunities in your science teaching. Environmental education is discussed in Chapter 11. Pupils in school often do not relate what they read, hear, see and do in the science lesson with their everyday world, so pupils often say 'What is this to do with me, what use is it?' Using the living and technological environment can give reality and purpose to science lessons, helping pupils to relate their world to science lessons and science to technology. By using the environment, pupils may develop a sense of wonder and understand why so many people, often scientists, seek to explain the behaviour of living and non-living things. At the same time, pupils become aware of the ways in which scientists contribute to the development of everyday technologies that make our lives more comfortable and safe. By understanding how science is used, pupils may be better encouraged to find out more.

The use of the resources beyond the classroom can help to bridge the gap between examination syllabuses and the way in which science is used. Taking science out-of-doors or bringing events or people from outside into the classroom creates contexts in which pupils may see relevance in their studies and be motivated to study science.

The pressure to deliver the full content of the National Curriculum and meet public examination requirements does not encourage out-of-door activities, yet the importance of these studies to pupils' understanding of science, as opposed to just knowing the science, is immense. Our purpose in writing this chapter is to encourage you to take opportunities to widen your teaching horizons whenever possible.

As a student teacher, you are not in a position to influence the practice existing in your school experience school. Many teachers, however, do use the environment in their teaching, and your support as a second teacher in the classroom during school experience makes that possibility more likely. Look for opportunities to support teachers in that work and suggest ways yourself to use the out-of-doors. Seeing opportunities and, on occasions, using them helps you to develop an attitude and expectation which carries over into your first teaching post and beyond.

OBJECTIVES

At the end of this chapter you should be:

- encouraged to widen your range of teaching strategies;
- convinced of the importance of relating science out-of-doors to the science curriculum;
- aware of opportunities for field work in the Science National Curriculum;
- able to plan and carry out some teaching in the field;
- aware of the advantages of residential field work for teaching science;
- know the safety and legal factors to be considered in involving pupils in field work.

THE NATIONAL CURRICULUM

The Programmes of Study (PoS) for the Science National Curriculum are clear in their support of bringing science out of the classroom into the wider environment. Under the broad heading of 'Application of Science' (part of Sc0), which applies at all Key Stages and across the four science areas (sometimes referred to as Sc1, Sc2, Sc3 and Sc4), the Key Stage 3 statement requires teachers to:

> a   relate scientific knowledge and understanding to familiar phenomena and to things that are used every day;
> b   consider how the applications of science, including those related to health, influence the quality of their lives;
> c   relate scientific knowledge and understanding to the care of living things and of the environment;
> d   consider the benefits and drawbacks of scientific technological developments in environmental and other contexts.
>
> (DFE, 1995b, p. 14)

A similar but more detailed of statements applies to Key Stage 4 double science (DFE, 1995b, p. 24).

The availability of multi-media resources and the wide viewing habits of young people mean that many environmental issues can be brought into the classroom and laboratory for investigation, discussion and evaluation. However, the impact of many issues is greater when pupils can experience them first hand or talk to people in their workplace. For example, pupils appreciate the nature and scale of the problems associated with water purification and supply when they are taken to see modern water treatment plants. The science makes more sense when it is seen in action; see, for example, Davies (1996, p. 6).

Experimental and investigative science (Sc1) at both KS3 and KS4 specifically requires teachers to 'recognise contexts, e.g. field work' and in Life Processes and Living things' the section called 'Living things in their environment' invites the use of field work to teach many of the ideas.

The way in which the four science areas of the National Curriculum are written suggests that field work applies only to biology. Two science areas, Sc3 and Sc4, concerned with physical science, omit much reference to placing their subject matter in a wider context. It is left to the imagination, drive and wit of teachers of physical sciences to seek wider contexts. There is a sharp contrast between the statement within the first part of each Programme of Study (Sc0) called Application of Science, cited above, and the narrow focus of the content in science areas, especially Sc3 and Sc4.

In their review of inspection findings in 1993/94, OFSTED inspectors commented favourably on the teacher's command of subject matter and noted that good lessons were marked by the use of a variety of teaching strategies. However, no mention was made in that report of the use of field work, of links with industry and technology, of visits to industrial or commercial premises, or the use of outside speakers as a significant factor in that variety (OFSTED, 1995, par. 21–6).

The dangers of approving a narrow, academic focus for the science curriculum were signalled some years ago by Dobson who, when writing about the 1992 version of the science curriculum, wrote:

> The syllabus for 11–14-year-old pupils is now larger and more difficult than two 'O levels' put together. At best they will learn superficial facts they do not understand. At worst they will switch off.
>
> (Dobson, 1992)

The 1995 revision of the Science National Curriculum gave some overall reduction in content. Since that occasion, however, the growing importance of league tables and achievement in SATs and GCSE leaves the comments of Dobson a continuing concern. The academic focus of the Science National Curriculum, i.e. on pure science, may explain, in part, the apparent narrowness in the way in which OFSTED report on teaching and learning in science. Concerns about the Science National Curriculum are echoed in the current discussions about a new science curriculum, e.g. Millar (1996). The ASE has set up a Task Group to review the school science curriculum, referred to as 'Science Education 2000' (Ramsden, 1995, p. 22). You should follow this important development through the ASE.

TASK 10.1 IDENTIFYING OUT-OF-SCHOOL OPPORTUNITIES IN THE SCIENCE NATIONAL CURRICULUM

Select a unit of work you are going to teach or an area of personal interest, e.g. structures and forces, rocks and rock cycle, etc. Identify the reference in the Science National Curriculum. Read your school's Scheme of Work and identify the opportunities it provides for field work, visits, speakers, etc. and the guidance it gives in developing such activities.

Discuss your findings with other student teachers in your school or other student science teacher in college. Do the resources suggested in your Scheme of Work to support the teaching of the topic give advice about strategies using out-of-school activities? For further guidance, interrogate the *Teacher's Guide* to the set text recommended for use with your pupils.

In Chapter 11 we discuss cross-curricular links. We consider here links that may well have cross-subject connections, but principally discuss how to make use of people, events, institutions and environments outside the school.

OPPORTUNITIES

Field work

There are many opportunities for taking pupils outside the classroom to carry out investigations, to know better the content and ideas being discussed in class or to see science and technology in action. As well as biolgical field work, there are opportunities to use the environment to support the teaching of physics, chemistry and earth sciences including astronomy and weather studies; see, for example, Sanderson (1987); Osborn (1986); Jennings (1986).

Most schools have a playground, which is a source of habitats, materials and structures; many schools have a playing field or access to open spaces, either formal or wild. Planned carefully, double period science lessons can make use of outdoors. One day field trips and longer residential trips are to be encouraged if time and financial support are available; see later in this chapter.

Sites of special interest

There are often such sites in the neighbourhood. They include field centres with special exhibitions; nature reserves; local environmental groups studying a local site of interest; a hands-on science centre; local or national museums; local industry, e.g. glass manufacturer or the local weights and measures offices. The buildings in the High Street or village are useful sites of materials, structures (bridges) and habitats; see, for example, Jennings (1986); Woolnough (1994, p. 88).

Some centres cater specially for groups of pupils and are staffed to run teaching programmes. Other centres have a special focus, such as those run by the Royal Society for the Protection of Birds. Yet other centres have permanent displays related to their special situation, e.g. the Ironbridge Museum celebrating the origin of the iron industry in England. Sites of local interest may be known to school staff, or a list may be available from your local library, the LEA science adviser, the local ASE network or ASE headquarters; see the useful addresses provided in Appendix 5.

People with knowledge or expertise

It is highly motivating for pupils to bring into school people who have special knowledge that links with your science teaching. In recent years, many schools brought successful women into school to illustrate how science and engineering can be a rewarding and successful career, which contributed to many young women gaining scientific and technical qualifications. There remains a continuing need for many pupils to meet and talk to successful men and women with whom they can identify.

Environmental safety officers can provide a useful link between health and hygiene, and micro-organisms and decay, etc. Sources of speakers include local industry, chambers of commerce and your local FE college and IHE. Many professional and learned societies provide speakers, e.g. Institute of Biology, Institute of Electrical Engineers and the Medical Research Council. Parents and governors of the school can also be a source of expertise. Build a data base of contact names and addresses; see Appendix 5.

Work experience

Many schools organise interesting work experience for their pupils. An awareness of how this is organised forms part of your general professional development, and in addition local business and industry may provide you with opportunities to make important links for specific curriculum purposes. Your pupils can also give personal insights into industrial processes by telling the class about their experiences. Talk to the work experience co-ordinator in your school experience school.

Second-hand resources

It is not always possible to get first-hand experiences. Teachers rely on resources of various kinds to substitute for first-hand experience, including books, posters, videos, CD-ROMs and simulations of various kinds. The ASE has published a set of resources, called Science and Technology in Society (SATIS), which you should explore (see also Chapter 11). The first set of publications comprised twelve books, each containing ten units. There are publications for primary, secondary and post-16 phases of education, and new material is added frequently; see McGrath (1994, p. 2).

Some field centres carry out research and have experimental data that they may make available to schools, e.g. data base of the animal population in ponds; the changing bird population over a year. Such data can be used to develop pupils' skills of analysis and report writing. If there is a centre near your school, find out whether they offer this facility.

TASK 10.2 DEVELOPING AN OUT-OF-SCHOOL ACTIVITY FOR YOUR TEACHING PROGRAMME

Task 10.1 asked you to examine opportunities for including out-of-school activities in your teaching. Select one or two topics from the unit of work you have chosen in Task 10.1 and work up some background information on ways to incorporate an out-of-school activity, as described under the headings above. The background information should include the:

● class you teach and how their characteristics may affect your choice of activity;
● lesson content and area to be covered;
● nature of the activity, e.g. visit, speaker, field work, etc.;

continued . . .

- financial costs, if any;
- venue for the activity or source of the invited speaker;
- need for other staff support, including the regular class teacher.

Check with your school tutor about school policy on the activity you suggest, in particular the protocols to be observed in relation to your department, other staff, school management and parents and in organising visits or visitors.

When you have briefed yourself, discuss your proposal with your class teacher before proceeding with the activity.

DEVELOPING FIELD WORK

Why do field work?

Field work is more difficult to organise than classroom and laboratory work. Plants and animals do not perform to order; pupils have greater freedom to talk and move about, though this enhanced freedom can have a beneficial effect on behaviour. Despite the added work and associated difficulties, there are important benefits to pupils and teachers.

The greatest benefit is motivation. Being outside allows pupils to get on with their work and at the same time enjoy more freedom of discussion. We discuss in Chapter 7 the importance of language in learning; field work encourages dialogue and enquiry. Even the time taken by pupils in off-task talk can be compensated for by the fact that many actually engage in some on-task discussion. The unexpected can occur, which can make an opportunity to capture pupils' interest. We identify some reasons doing field work below.

Field work:

- promotes enthusiasm for science and the environment;
- increases knowledge of the living things and other environmental features;
- promotes awareness of the local environment, e.g. its ecology and geology;
- encourages a lifelong interest in the environment;
- allows understanding of how data are collected in the field and the difficulties associated with that enterprise;
- promotes awareness of the issues surrounding environmental damage and protection;
- reveals the impact of humans on the environment.

Field work is necessary because:

- it is the only way for pupils to experience some phenomena, e.g. the diversity of grasses, the diversity of animals living on a bush, the motion of the stars and planets; the effects of pollution; the scale of natural events, e.g. the time scale displayed by the sedimentation patterns in the walls of a sand quarry;
- it relates abstract ideas to real life, e.g. forces to structures, as in a suspension bridge; pH and soil characteristics; evolution to fossil deposits; Round Earth theory to shadows cast by the Sun: see the activity below, 'Measuring the Earth'.

Field work provides opportunities for pupils to:

- practise whole investigations;
- identify opportunities for enquiry;
- develop process skills;
- use data-logging equipment;
- work together;
- develop positive attitudes towards the environment;
- bring material from the environment into the school for further study and discussion.

Some field activities suitable for a double period

The amount of work that can be done outside the laboratory depends on many factors. Most important is the policy of the school, or your department, about such excursions. Before considering any activity like this, find out from your tutor what policies operate in your department and across the school. You should consider the:

- length of a double period;
- size of the class and your ability to monitor and supervise safely their activity;
- number of suitable sites for outside study;
- safety factors, such as busy roads, local ponds or streams and machinery;
- presence of unpleasant plants, such as stinging nettles and hog weed, or poisonous plants, e.g. the nightshades and laburnum;
- allergic reactions of pupils. Check the incidence of hay fever amongst pupils especially in the summer months;
- role of the regular class teacher in your activity. As a teacher in training **you cannot take a group of pupils outside on your own**; the class teacher or another qualified person must be with you.

Many activities can be performed outside the laboratory in a double period. Some examples follow with brief explanatory notes. All such activities need careful planning with focused instruction that clearly identify the purpose of the activity, the data to be collected, how it is recorded and how it is followed up in class.

A quick excursion to collect data or materials

The students can process the data when they return to the laboratory. Examples include:

- measuring the length of shadows as a prelude to calculating earth size; see below 'Measuring the Earth';
- checking traps used to sample the animal population in the grounds, e.g. pitfall traps, vegetable traps, water traps, sticky surfaces and Longworth Traps;
- reading instruments in the weather station;
- sampling a plant population using quadrats, line or belt transects or point frames;
- estimating the mass of wood in a tree, from measurements of height and circumference, as preparation for work on photosynthesis;
- collecting soils from different sites for analysis;
- estimating the earthworm population on the school field.

A useful source of ideas for planning similar activities can be found in Richards, 1989; Richards, Collis and Kincaid, 1987 and Richards, 1991. For a simple biology field guide see Science and Technology, Institute of Education, London in **useful organisations to contact** at the end of this chapter.

A trail with clear but limited objectives

This is set up to give pupils experience of particular phenomena or a range of experiences. Examples of trails include:

- identifying rocks used to construct the school building or other build-ings in the vicinity of the school. The trial can be supported by a set of photographs with brief explanatory notes. Questions can be set at each station, e.g. 'Why is this material used in this setting?', 'Has the material special properties that make it useful?'; see Figure 10.1;
- identifying corrosion and erosion in buildings, walls, statues, railings and walkways; see Figure 10.2. Notes direct attention to points of interest and pupils are encouraged to sketch one or more sites.

Figure 10.1   The statue of the Duke of Bedford in Russell Square, London. The base plinth is limestone and the statue made of bronze. The main plinth is granite (granodiorite)
Photo: Janet Maxwell and Alan Barrett.

Figure 10.2   A clay brick wall damaged by water freezing
Photo: Tony Turner.

Erosion often reveals fossils, for instance in buildings constructed from limestone. Questions can be set to provoke discussion about the causes of corrosion, e.g. acid rain, traffic fumes, oxidation by air or the run-off of rain water from roofs. Erosion can be caused by wind, water, frost, and people walking;

- identifying and counting tree species. A trail could be set on the edge of a school field, in a park, wood or formal gardens, if supervised carefully. Pupils need guidance about identifying, counting and recording their data. Try out the exercise yourself in advance. The observations can be recorded as in Table 10.1;
- field centres and some LEAs publish trail guides. These can be used directly or adapted to suit your purposes;
- sites of interest in a city, e.g. see Rosen and Rosen (1994).

Table 10.1   Recording of tree species

Tree	Leaf shape		Other identification	Numbers seen
		Ash	5–8 pairs of dark green leaflets on one leaf; black buds; smooth, grey-green bark	
Ash			**Your notes**	
Beech				

An example of a trail is given in the section below under 'Radiation in the environment'.

Activities in the field: some examples

Radiation in the environment

The study of radiation and waves is remote from pupils' experience. In Table 10.2 there are suggestions of ways in which radiation can be made more relevant to pupils. The items in Table 10.2 can be stations on a trail; pupils can bring back questions to school for further study. Pupils are briefed on what they are expected to see, do and record, and space allowed on the worksheet for pupils to record questions generated on the trail.

The reference beneath Table 10.2 contains many more examples of activities that can be investigated outside in a largely urban environment across a range of physics topics. Similar activities that can be adapted for trails or excursions can be found in Borrows (1984) (chemistry); Dove (1994) (geology in churchyards); Harding (1994) (swimming pool chemistry); Smith, R. (1996) (using playground apparatus, suitable for upper primary and lower secondary pupils); Spurgin (1994) (athletics).

Measuring the Earth

Explaining the seasons requires pupils to know the way in which the Earth moves in relation to the Sun; see Chapter 3 and Figure 3.1. As part of the background information to build a picture of the seasonal changes, pupils measure the changing elevation of the Sun at different times of day and at the same time of day at different times of the year. In this way explanations for the seasonal changes of temperature at a point on the Earth can be discussed. A suitable way of finding the elevation of the Sun is by measuring the length of the shadow of a vertical stick at various times of day.

When the shadow made by the stick is shortest, i.e. noon GMT, the Sun is at its maximum elevation. There is scope for collaboration betweeen classes from different schools in the UK on different lines of longitude to compare the times when the shortest shadows are found (Richards, 1972, pp. 9–10).

The organisation of the shadow measurement is simple, although maintaining the integrity of the equipment out-of-doors for long periods on school premises is less easy; see Figure 10.3. A secure place is needed. The stick must be vertical for between–site comparisons to be useful. Pupils need to be warned about the dangers of looking directly at the Sun at any time.

This activity can be extended to schools in other countries. A measurement of the elevation of the Sun in two geographical sites at the same moment, together with the distance between the sites, can be used to estimate the circumference of the Earth. The sites should be on the same line of longitude.

By prior agreement, measurements of a shadow stick are made at the same moment and the results communicated by telephone or e-mail for

Table 10.2   Radiation in the environment

Topic	What to measure or observe	Some questions
Radio activity	Take a background reading and then a reading over granite.	What is the origin of the background radiation?
		Which minerals in granite are radioactive?
Street lighting	Where is the lamp post in relation to the kerb?	What is the purpose of the dome above the top of the lamp post?
	How high is the lamp post above the road?	Does it matter how high the lamp is, or its distance from the kerb?
		Street lamps are often coloured; how does the colour arise?
		What is the power rating of street lamps?
TV aerials or satellite dishes	In which direction do the aerials point?	Find out how to calculate the frequency of the carrier wave for the TV signal.
	Are all aerials the same size?	
	Is the spacing between the rods the same for all aerials?	Where is your local transmitter or booster station?
Traffic noise	Measure the noise level at different points along a road.	Look up in your text book an example of 'dangerous noise'.
	Compare the noise emission of different vehicles. Find out about the decibel scale of noise.	
	Compare the energy levels of two points on the decibel scale.	
Greenhouse	Describe or sketch a greenhouse.	Explain how a greenhouse gets warm and stays warm.
	Find the temperature inside and outside a greenhouse.	What is the greenhouse effect on the world climate and why are many people worried about it?
		Name a planet that is heated by the greenhouse effect.

Source: adapted from Foster (1989, pp. 18–22)

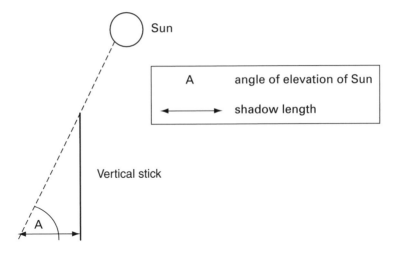

Figure 10.3   Measuring the elevation of the Sun

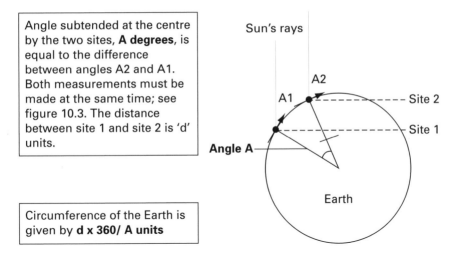

Figure 10.4   Measuring the circumference of the Earth
Source: adapted from Ogborn, Kouladis and Papadopetrakis, 1996, p. 89

immediate processing. The difference in the angle of elevation of the Sun at the two sites is numerically the same as the angle (A) subtended by the sites at the centre of the Earth; see Figure 10.4. From a map, the distance 'd' between the two sites can be calculated.

In one such recent collaboration, Patras in Greece and London were linked. In addition, in this investigation the interpretation of the measurements in terms of the Round Earth theory and the Flat Earth theory were contrasted and discussed (Ogborn, Kouladis and Papadopetrakis, 1996). Although the two sites are not on the same line of longitude, the readings were taken when the Sun, London and Patras were roughly in line (see also Hayton, 1997).

This classical method was adopted by Eratosthenes in Greece in about 200 BC. By measuring the length of the shadow at noon in Alexandria (mouth of the Nile) on the day that no shadow was cast down a well at noon in Syene (nearly due south down the Nile), Eratosthenes calculated the difference in latitude and, together with the distance between the two places and, assuming a round Earth, he calculated the circumference of the Earth (Ronan, 1966, pp. 47–8). The distance between the two sites was measured by pacing. The difference between his estimate and today's measurement is about 80 km; the circumference of the Earth is about 40,000 km.

What is this building made of?

Pupils are asked to sketch a building and to identify the different types of material used in its construction. Interesting materials are used in the construction of houses, churches or banks. Older buildings are often made of, or contain, natural stone. You need to try out the activity first yourself in order to see if it yields sufficient information; that you can safely stand a class of 25–30 pupils nearby or in the grounds of the building; and that the trail is safe.

Brief the class about the intention and purpose of the activity. In addition, identify what you are going to do with the information back in school. You may wish to have a sketch of the building available for pupils to use. However, it is instructive for pupils, if they can, to make their own sketch. Sketching an object or organism can be a powerful way of enhancing observation and generating questions for investigation.

Once outside, ask pupils to look at the building and note some objects and then to identify, if possible, the materials of which they are made. Help pupils to distinguish between object, e.g. gutter, and material, plastic. When pupils have a first list, ask them to sketch the building, identifying the main features (e.g. slate roof tiles). These features are then labelled and annotated with the name of the material and the property that makes it suitable for the job; see figure 10.5. Additional questions can include:

- are there plants growing on the building? If so, where? Mark any significant growths on your sketch;
- is lead used on the building? Is their any plant growth near the lead?
- are the windows double-glazed? How can you tell? What material is between the two panes of glass?

Chimney pots–terracotta

Chimney stack–clay bricks

Flashing–lead

Roof tiles–slate

Window surround–sandstone

Windows–wood

Sill–concrete

Door–African hardwood

Door knob–brass

Railings–cast iron

Steps–concrete topped with fired tiles

Figure 10.5   Some materials used to construct a house

On return to school, the materials identified can be listed and classified as required, e.g. made material or natural; element, compound or mixture; metal and non-metal. Opportunities now arise for further research into how some of the materials are made, e.g. cement and concrete; zinc; glass. See also Hollins (1986).

Using the local cemetery

Cemeteries are interesting sources of different rock material and sites for growth of plant material. The headstones used for many graves are often old, have been undisturbed for many years and can offer a site for sustained algae and lichen growth. Pupils can:

- identify the different materials from which headstones are made;
- list the different types of organisms that grow on the headstones: algae, moss, lichens;
- estimate whether one side of the headstone has more growth on it than the other side;

- measure the direction in which the headstone faces;
- estimate the age of the headstone.

A useful exercise for pupils is to sketch two headstones and compare them; see Figure 10.6. Lichens are useful pollution monitors (see Brooks and Hawes, 1995).

What to do

Select two gravestones that have different plant populations.

Sketch the distribution of plants on one side and label the sketch to show the different organisms. Select sides that face in the same direction.

Label the sketches to show the types of organisms and the name of material of which the headstone is made. It may be helpful to use colour to distinguish some organisms.

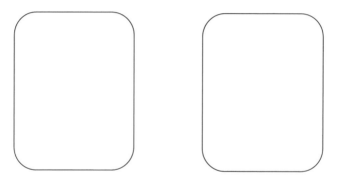

Follow-up questions:
- Give an explanation for the difference in growths.
- Devise an investigation to find out more about the pattern of plant distribution on the headstones in the cemetery. Identify the variables you need to control.

Figure 10.6 Exploring headstones

Residential field trips

Residential courses are opportunities to get to know the pupils and science staff much better. You see pupils in a new light. Activities are possible that you cannot carry out in double periods or even one day at school. There is a chance to plan and carry out substantial pieces of investigative work with your pupils.

As a student teacher you are not expected to plan and organise a residential field trip. However, you should be alert to the opportunity to join in such a venture and, if appropriate, offer to help with the planning and preparation; see Task 10.3.

A useful planning checklist for field work can be found in Parkinson (1994, pp. 101–2); and further guidance on safety out-of-doors in Vincent and Wray (1988).

TASK 10.3 PLANNING A FIELD TRIP

If the opportunity arises, join in a field trip. As part of your involvement, collect together information about the following aspects of the enterprise

Educational aims
- what are the purposes of the trip and how do they fit in with the school's Scheme of Work?
- What experiences and facilities does the field centre offer? Collect information about this and other centres.
- How are the pupils briefed and prepared for the trip?
- How is the work at the field centre followed up on return to the school?
- In what ways does the work contribute to coursework and public examinations?
- On return, evaluate the ways in which the field centre is suited to the aims of the field course.

Legal responsibilities
- Which LEA and school regulations apply to field trips?
- In what ways does the Health and Safety at Work Act direct the organisation of the trip?
- Are there special risk assessments to be carried out for pupils doing field work?
- How is insurance effected for both travel and on-site work?
- What are the responsibilities and rights of parents while their children are away on residential courses?
- How are the finances organised? Can pupils be refused a place on the trip if they cannot afford it?
- How many adults must accompany a group of pupils travelling to a centre and during the field work?

continued . . .

- What is the nature of the agreement to which parents consent when they agree to a field trip for their son or daughter and how is that consent obtained?
- If pupils are injured or fall ill during the course, what are the staff required to do?

Advance planning
- Is the course to be held at a well-equipped centre or does the school take equipment to the centre?
- Who prepares the written course materials?
- What are the domestic arrangements for eating, cleaning and sleeping? Is the course self-catering and, if so, are the pupils involved in any way?
- Pupils and their parents usually have to pay for the trip. How is the cost calculated and the money collected?
- What arrangements are made for pupils or parents to get in contact in an emergency?
- What are the transport arrangements?

Safety
- What guidelines are there about ways of working and behaving in the centre and in the field?
- What advice is given about suitable dress for field work and the English weather?
- Are there any special hazards associated with the field centre and how are these dealt with?
- See also Health and Safety at Work Act, in Legal responsibilities above.
- Are pupils briefed about the Country Code of Practice?
- The handbook on safety issued by the Institute of Biology is very useful; see p. 208.

What happens while you are away?
- How are your classes covered and taught while you are away? What arrangements do regular class teachers make?
- Do you expect to return from the trip to a backlog of marking?

SUMMARY

The way in which different schools, science departments and individuals use the environment depends very much on both attitudes and contexts. A tradition of using the out-of-doors to promote science teaching encourages its continuation, and the absence of such practice can be a barrier to innovation. Whatever the circumstances in which you find yourself, there are often opportunities to go beyond the classroom in planning your lessons. In some schools, inter-departmental field studies often take place, e.g. geography and science, and opportunities can arise in this way.

Examine the list of competences or standards as set out in your national requirements for a NQT and identify where using the environment contributes to your teaching profile. Use Appendix 4 as a checklist.

What is possible depends on the local environment, your ability to identify opportunities and the support you get. In this chapter we have made suggestions, by means of examples, of ways in which to use the out-of-doors. We hope that these ideas spark further ideas in you. That spark can be kept bright by reading, for example the ASE publications *School Science Review* and *Education in Science*. They contain articles by practising teachers and carry notices about similar activities and promotional literature about resources from commercial and non-profit making organisations.

You can widen your range of teaching strategies by referring to *Science in the Locality* (Jennings, 1986). To broaden your understanding of environmental education, see Hardie and Hale (1993) and Lakin (1995).

FURTHER READING

Hardie, J. and Hale, M. (1993) 'Science and environmental education', in R. Hull (ed.) (1993) *Science Teachers' Handbook: Secondary*, Hemel Hempstead: Simon & Schuster.
Discussion of how environmental education can be approached together with Schemes of Work. It carries a list of articles showing how some teachers have tackled science out-of-doors and gives useful addresses of supporting organisations.

Jennings, A. (1986) *Science in the Locality*, Cambridge: Cambridge University Press.
Shows how waterways, bridges, the local market, grasslands, the weather and a construction site can be used to teach science. Practical advice about how to go about excursions, together with notes about the science. The references, although dated, point to sources of further information.

Learning Through Landscapes (1994) *The School Grounds Resource Directory*, Winchester: Learning Through Landscapes.
This directory covers over 200 resources for school grounds. It is well indexed and cross-referenced.

SOURCES OF INFORMATION AND ADDRESSES

Books

DES (1989) *Safety in Outdoor Education*, London: HMSO.

Dillon, J., Watson, R. and Tosulungu, C. (1993) *Chemistry and the Environment*, London: Royal Society of Chemistry.

Institute of Biology (1990) *Safety in Biological Fieldwork*, London: Institute of Biology.

The Good Resources Guide, Chemical Industry Education Centre, Department of Chemistry, University of York, Heslington, York, YO1 5DD

Useful organisations to contact

See Appendix 5 at the end of this book for addresses

Association for Science Education

British Association for the Advancement of Science (BAAS)

British Association for Young Scientists (BAYS); see BAAS

British Interactive Group (BIG) – information about local interactive science centres

Council for Environmental Education

Institute of Biology

Institute of Physics

Neighbourhood Engineers

Royal Society

Royal Society for Chemistry

Royal Society for the Protection of Birds

Science and Technology Regional Associations (SATROs)

The Health Education Authority

Field guide

Science and Technology, Institute of Education, Bedford Way, London WC1H 0AL; tel. 0171 612 6777. Copies of a simple biology field guide may be obtained at a cost of £2.50, including p/p, from the secretary.

11 Cross-curricular issues and the science curriculum

INTRODUCTION

The view of the curriculum as one defined by the subjects of the National Curriculum is a limited one. Such a view is very different from the curriculum based on 'areas of experience', such as the scientific and the human and social dimensions, that is described in many documents published prior to the Education Reform Act in 1988, including HMI reports: 'The curriculum, whether for schools as a whole or for individual pupils has to be presented as more than a series of subjects and lessons in the timetable' (DES, 1980, p. 31).

Even when the National Curriculum was introduced in England and Wales in 1989 it was recognised by the National Curriculum Council (NCC), the government agency that was responsible for its implementation, that there were other aspects of the curriculum that needed to be incorporated into the work that was undertaken by schools. In 1990, the NCC published a series of slim, but influential, booklets that were designed to inform the development of what were termed 'cross-curricular' themes. The themes identified included four that will form the focus of this chapter:

1 Education for economic and industrial understanding (NCC, 1990a)
2 Health education (NCC, 1990b)
3 Environmental education (NCC, 1990c)
4 Education for citizenship (NCC, 1990d)

Each booklet outlined the contribution that different subjects might make to the teaching of such themes. The four themes provide a useful starting point for thinking about strategies that can be used to promote teaching in these areas. Aspects of environmental education have been considered in the previous chapter; environmental education cannot be confined to science, it encompasses other subjects such as geography and consideration of the effect of human beings on their environment. Such considerations apply also when addressing issues concerned with, for example, health education, which cannot be conceived of within narrow subject boundaries. A common feature of all four themes is that many of the issues that need to be explored are perhaps best tackled in Personal and Social Education (PSE) rather than individual subjects, although the subjects do have an important contribution to make in teaching about specific topics. However, some teachers, although knowledgeable, do not feel confident in tackling sensitive issues without guidance.

This chapter looks beyond science as a subject defined by the National Curriculum to consider how links between other subjects might be made and how the 'areas of experience' referred to above might be used to inform the teaching and learning of science. This chapter looks also at what is often called the 'hidden curriculum' – a term that includes many of those things that occur in schools outside the formal classroom curriculum, for example at break-times, during school meals and extra-curricular activities. These broader issues encompass important elements of the moral, ethical and social dimensions of education that have been stressed by the government during the past decade and which apply to the teaching of all subjects, including science.

OBJECTIVES

By the end of this chapter you should be:

- familiar with aspects of school policies that deal with cross-curricular themes and dimensions;
- able to identify where and how cross-curricular themes and dimensions contribute to teaching and learning in science in your school;
- more aware of teaching strategies that are appropriate for teaching controversial issues.

CROSS-CURRICULAR ISSUES

The four cross-curricular themes identified in the introduction to this chapter form an important component of the curriculum and they should feature in the policy documents of your school. An introduction to this aspect of the National Curriculum appears in Chapter 2.

The current emphasis on league tables of examination success in England and Wales tends to make these components less visible than they should be. The cross-curricular themes may feature in your general school policy documents, mission statements and publicity materials for prospective parents and pupils, as well as in policy documents for curriculum subjects such as science. The themes are clearly identified in most Programmes of Study for PSE. Time for PSE may be allocated in your school's timetable or form part of your tutorial work during your school experience and in your first post.

TASK 11.1 CROSS-CURRICULAR THEMES: WHAT IS YOUR SCHOOL'S POLICY?

This task involves you in research by discussion with the member(s) of staff with responsibility for curriculum development.

1 Obtain copies of your school's policy documents (there should be policies for all curriculum subjects). Are there separate policy documents for:

   ● Education for economic and industrial understanding;
   ● Health education;
   ● Environmental education;
   ● Education for citizenship?

2 Is there a member of staff with responsibility for any, or all, of these four areas?

3 In the policy documents for the four cross-curricular themes, identify which aspects might be taught in science. (If such documents are not available, you may find the information in your school Schemes of Work for PSE or PSHE.)

4 Read the policy for science and identify where and how the four cross-curricular themes are introduced.

This information should help you to plan lessons that incorporate some elements of these cross-curricular issues. Keep a record during the year of where and when you incorporate the themes in your lessons. Record details of materials that you have found useful.

Education for economic and industrial understanding

The issue of how, as well as the extent to which, education in schools should or can prepare pupils for adult life, including employment, is one that continues to be debated. Hodkinson and Thomas (1991) argue that education for what they term 'economic awareness' is vital if pupils are to understand and make informed decisions about events and procedures that affect their lives.

The specification of knowledge, skills and attitudes for education for economic and industrial understanding by the NCC (1990a) provides a useful basis for thinking about the ways in which such understanding might be developed in your pupils. The NCC suggested that pupils required knowledge and understanding of a number of key economic concepts, including production, distribution and supply and demand. Pupils also needed to understand other issues such as:

- technological developments and their impact on lifestyles and workplaces;
- what it means to be a consumer, how consumer decisions are made and the implications of these decisions.

The skills identified include analytical, personal and social skills, which are common to all the cross-curricular themes. Many of these skills are similar to those that underpin the Science National Curriculum (DFE, 1995b), such as the ability of pupils to collect, analyse and interpret data and to distinguish between statements of fact and value. The attitudes identified are also familiar in the context of science. They include:

- respect for evidence and rational argument in economic contexts;
- concern for the use of scarce resources;
- sensitivity to the effects of economic choices on the environment;
- a sense of responsibility for the consequences of their own economic actions, as individuals and members of groups.

(NCC, 1990a, pp. 4–5)

Most of the suggestions made by the NCC appear sound. However, it has been noted that 'the task of defining economic awareness involves more than just listing key concepts, knowledge, skills; more than specifying useful contexts for investigations' (Hodkinson and Thomas, 1991, p. 43). Such education needs to draw on a number of subject areas, including science, and to encourage what Hodkinson and Thomas describe as a 'reflective stance'. Thus the way in which your school implements programmes related to economic and industrial awareness is crucial in determining their success. Science teachers have an important role to play in developing understanding through their work with pupils in science as well as their contribution to cross-curricular themes, extra-curricular activities and policy development. The Science National Curriculum makes explicit reference to issues related to economic and industrial understanding (see, e.g. DFE, 1995b, 'Applications of science', p. 24).

A further element of the recommendations made by the NCC was that pupils of all ages, from 5 to 16 years, should have direct experience of industry and what was termed the 'world of work' through visits and meetings with industrialists and others, as well as work experience by older pupils. The NCC was keen to involve pupils in business and community enterprises of the type reported by Bishop, which involved an industrial organisation, student teachers and local schools in developing science focused material in the area of economic and industrial understanding (Bishop, 1996). The initiative focused on three projects that ranged from an investigation of how a new product reaches the shops to one that studied the manufacture of tablets.

TASK 11.2 SCHOOL–INDUSTRY LINKS

There are a number of ways in which you can find out what school–industry links exist in your school. The range of industries used depends on the location of the school as well as demographic and economic factors.

1   If school–industry links are the responsibility of a member of staff in your school, find out what links there are and what possibilities there are for you to develop links with local industry yourself.
2   Find out whether representatives from local industry are school governors. (The teacher governors on the staff can help you find out.) Find out whether these governors work with pupils or give talks to pupils or whether they would be willing to do so.
3   Links with industry may also take place through work experience placements, for example in Year 10 or 11. Find out from the person with responsibility for placements which industries are involved.
4   Talk to colleagues in the geography and science departments about whether they have links with local industries and what relevant work they do with pupils in, for example, Year 9. What resources do they use?
5   Select one topic that you will be teaching to Year 9. Identify where and how you could introduce links to industrial processes and industries in the local area.

New materials for teaching science, including the Salter's Chemistry (Burton, Holman, Pilling and Waddington, 1994 a, b and c) and the SATIS materials produced by the Association for Science Education (ASE), show how issues related to economic and industrial understanding can

be tackled in science (ASE, 1991, 1994). There are also materials produced by industrial and commercial organisations, such as the power
industry, many of which are free of charge. Keep notes of any materials
that are being used in school, including names and addresses of the publishers. It is also a good idea to start collecting your own set of materials;
you could use the questions on pp. 218–19 as a basis for evaluating such
materials. A good source of information about available materials is the
annual ASE Meeting. The *School Science Review* (*SSR*), the journal published by the ASE, also contains useful articles and information about
industrial links (e.g. Bishop, 1996).

Some schools have Science and Technology Weeks or 'Fairs' to
encourage pupils to pursue scientific careers. Helping to plan and run
such an event is a good way of finding out more about local industries
(see Science and Technology Regional Associations and The National
SATRO in Appendix 5). See also Chapter 13.

Health education

> Health is a positive state of mental, physical and social well-being
> and not merely the absence of disease or infirmity.
>   (World Health Organisation Constitution, 1946)

Current views about health education are based on ideas of the health
promoting school, which envisages a whole school approach to health
promotion that includes:

- the taught curriculum;
- the 'hidden' curriculum;
- the active participation of parents and governors, teachers and pupils.

At the present time, as part of the move towards developing health promoting schools throughout Europe, health promotion programmes are
being developed as part of a joint initiative by the World Health Organisation (WHO) and the Council of Europe (CEC) which aims to:

> develop, and assess the effectiveness of, strategies for changing and
> shaping pupils' patterns of behaviour, with the aim of safe-guarding
> their long-term health.
>   (Department of Health, 1992, p. 27)

It is still too early to judge whether such aims are realistic or achievable.
However, the programme should help to raise the profile and importance
of health education in schools.

This section of the chapter focuses on one aspect of the whole school approach to health education, namely the taught curriculum. Aspects of the hidden curriculum and the participation of parents and other adults in the health promoting school will be discussed later.

Health education has long had a place in the school curriculum, despite the fact that its presence has not always been acknowledged, as was noted by HMI in 1978:

> health education is unavoidable, even if its presence is denied.
>
> (DES, 1978a, p. 29)

So what is health education? (Try writing your own definition before you read the next paragraph.) The answer to this question is not a straightforward one. One group of students on an initial teacher education course came up with responses that included the following. Health education is about:

- people and their ways of life;
- learning how to take responsibility for one's own health and that of the family and community;
- mental, as well as physical health;
- teaching and learning about disease and disease prevention;
- becoming aware of the internal and external environment and the relationship between these.

These ideas, which acknowledge the diversity of knowledge, skills and attitudes about health, are a useful starting point for developing an agreed definition of health education. The list also indicates how views about health education have changed during the last thirty years. In the past, the basis of health education was considered to be the transmission of information:

Information → Knowledge → Attitudes → Behaviour → Better health

This model assumes that if people are provided with information, they will change their behaviour, if appropriate, and thus become healthier. The model ignores a number of important features about learning and behaviour, including the importance of motivation in learning and the value systems and beliefs of the individual. Current views about health education are very different; they are based on a model of 'self-empowerment' that seeks to promote what Tones (1987) describes as genuinely informed decision making. The model is premised on the provision of knowledge and skills, including social skills. However, the model seeks also to enhance and develop self-esteem. Self-esteem, and the recognition by individuals that they can have control over their lives, is an essential pre-requisite of self-empowerment.

A model for health education in schools, based on the self-empowerment model, that was developed in consultation with teachers, is shown in Figure 11.1. An important element of this model is the recognition that health education builds on experiences in a planned way. Furthermore, the skills identified are very similar to those regarded as important in teaching in science.

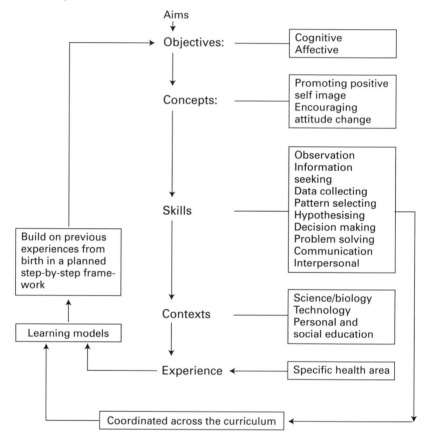

Figure 11.1   A model for health education
Source: based on Secondary Science Curriculum Review, 1984

The NCC identified nine components of health education:

1   substance use and misuse;
2   sex education;
3   family life education;
4   safety;

5 health-related exercise;
6 food and nutrition;
7 personal hygiene;
8 environmental aspects of health;
9 psychological aspects of health.

(NCC, 1990b)

All of the topics listed above feature in Personal Social and Health Education (PSHE) programmes, although only certain aspects will be covered in science. However, health education is an intrinsic element of the work of all science teachers, through their contribution to pastoral work and/or PSHE programmes in addition to the aspects of health education that form part of science.

TASK 11.3 WHAT IS TAUGHT IN HEALTH EDUCATION IN YOUR SCHOOL?

Look at the programmes of study for science and PSE in your school. Create a summary table that shows:

- the topics covered in health education each year;
- which department is responsible for teaching each topic.

The table, which might look something like the one below, provides you with insights into the scope and provision for health education in your school that may be useful when you are planning to teach science topics that have links with health education.

Health education areas	Year group					PSE topics	Science topics	Other subjects
	7	8	9	10	11			
1 Substance use and misuse								
2 Sex education								
3 Family life education								
4 Safety								
5 Health-related exercise								
6 Food and nutrition								
7 Personal hygiene								
8 Environmental aspects of health								
9 Psychological aspects of health								

Teaching about health education is not always straightforward because topics may be controversial, impinging on personal beliefs and feelings. Such teaching must take place in ways that are consistent with the statutory provisions of the 1988 Education Reform Act, which placed a duty on schools to 'promote the spiritual, moral and physical development of pupils'. There is also legislation that covers teaching about sex education in schools that should be identified in school policy documents (DFE, 1993). Governors of maintained schools are required to provide sex education, including education about HIV/AIDS, to all registered pupils. However, parents have the right to withdraw pupils from all, or part, of sex education outside the National Curriculum. In order to comply with this last requirement, schools normally teach sex education as part of PSHE. However, biological aspects of sex education can be taught in science. You need to be aware of how the science curriculum integrates with the PSHE programme.

Teaching strategies that can be used in teaching about controversial issues are discussed in a later section of this chapter; they include discussion and role play and the use of audio-visual material, including videos.

There is a wide variety of materials available to support teaching about health education, some of which are produced by commercial organisations and need to be used with discretion. In recent years, for example, food manufacturers and retailers have begun to develop a range of educational materials that are targeted at schools and teachers. Concern has been expressed by many people about the information in these materials and the way in which products are marketed. Recently the Department of Health convened a Project Team as part of its Nutrition Task Force to review educational materials and to produce guidelines for those using and writing such materials. The *Guidelines on Educational Materials concerned with Nutrition* (GEMPT, 1996) contains a helpful checklist, for evaluating materials, which is designed to be used in conjunction with the guidelines. The checklist is:

- Does the material take account of current government health policy and reflect recent overviews of scientific thinking?
- Does the material acknowledge the main sources on which it is based?
- If there is controversy about any issue covered in the material, is this acknowledged?
- Is the material misleading?
- Are any comments or statements about nutrition placed in the context of a balanced and healthy lifestyle?
- Is the name and address of the producer and the name of any sponsor clearly stated? Have contact names and addresses been given for further information and comment?

- Is the date of the publication clearly marked and is the material up-to-date?
- Are abbreviations and acronyms explained in full the first time they are used?
- Are the pages numbered?
- Is there an index? Would an index be helpful?
- Is there any guidance about other sources of information on the same subject?
- Is there a glossary of technical terms used or words that are likely to be unfamiliar?
- Are logos and trade names in text and illustrations used sparingly and in a relevant context?
- Is the material appropriate for its intended users?
- Has consideration been given to the level of understanding required, the language used and the complexity of the ideas put forward?
- Is the layout and presentation appropriate for the target users?
- Have materials been pre-tested?
- Have the materials been referenced to the National Curriculum, where appropriate?
- Is the material sensitive to the needs of all groups in society?
- Does the material recognise the complexity of the social and cultural messages attached to foods and the effects that certain messages have on those who are most vulnerable?

Many teachers have already found the checklist useful to evaluate science materials in addition to those related to health and nutrition education.

TASK 11.4 DOES THE LOGO MATTER? EVALUATING TEACHING AND LEARNING MATERIALS IN HEALTH EDUCATION

Select one or two examples of materials produced by food manufacturers or retailers to support teaching about food and use the checklist shown above to decide:

1 whether you would use these materials for teaching;
2 whether you would advise colleagues to use, or buy, the materials;
3 how and when you would use the materials;
4 how you could adapt the materials to make them more appropriate for use with a Year 7 group.

Environmental education

> The objective of environmental education is to increase awareness
> to the problems in this field, as well as possible solutions, and to lay
> the foundations to a fully informed and active participation of the
> individual in the protection of the environment and the prudent use
> of natural resources.
>
> (The Council and the Ministers of Education Meeting
> within the Council, 1988)

Issues concerning the environment are ones with which your pupils identify closely and which receive widespread media attention; they range
from concerns about the effect of oil spillage on sea birds to the long
term effects of the destruction of rain forests. These concerns are justified and are widely recognised, as is the importance of environmental
education by international organisations, agencies and governments. The
publication of Agenda 21, as an outcome of the UN Conference in Rio
de Janeiro in 1992 (United Nations, 1992), is helping to promote environmental education for sustainable development at local level through
partnerships, such as those between community and voluntary groups
and schools.

Despite the publication of Agenda 21, and the perceived importance of
environmental education in schools, it appears that environmental education is not a high priority in many schools at the present time. The issues
related to environmental education are explored by Gayford, who stresses
the importance of identifying the nature and purposes of environmental
education and its place in the curriculum (Gayford, 1996).

The NCC conceived environmental education as being composed of
three linked components:

- education **about** the environment;
- education **for** the environment;
- education **in** or **through** the environment.

(NCC, 1990c, p. 7)

The environment, as is evident from the previous chapter, which explored
ways of teaching pupils in the environment through first-hand experience, provides a relevant context for learning and a starting point for
consideration of wider issues related to the environment. Education **for**
the environment, as defined by the NCC, is concerned with education
about the protection, care and responsible use of the environment and
involves consideration of values and attitudes. Ideas such as these can be

linked to the earlier discussion of the health promoting school; they involve aspects of the taught curriculum as well as those of the 'hidden' curriculum. This model of environmental education is an influential one. However, as Gayford points out, it is open to criticism (ASE, 1993). Environmental education, in the same way as health education, can be problematic as it deals with values, attitudes and behaviour and can involve emotive issues. Achieving balance and presenting unbiased views when teaching is essential.

Guidance about developing school policies and teaching about environmental issues is available from a number of sources including the ASE (ASE, 1993) and the Council for Environmental Education (CEE, 1995) and voluntary organisations such as the Royal Society for the Protection of Birds (RSPB, 1996). The CEE, in common with other organisations, suggests that schools should carry out an environmental audit of all aspects of the school environment. Ideally everyone in school should be involved in such an audit, which might include a number of areas that are particularly relevant to science teachers, for example:

- energy and energy efficiency;
- development of the school grounds including conservation areas;
- building and materials.

TASK 11.5 AN ENVIRONMENTAL AUDIT TRAIL

1 Take photographs (or make sketches) of different areas around the school; include buildings and artefacts as well as features such as trees and shrubs, car parks and rubbish collection points.

2 Using the photographs as a starting point, devise an environmental trail that would help to raise pupils' awareness of environmental issues.

3 Look at the schemes of work for science and geography and identify ways in which the trail could be used with different year groups to enhance the teaching of specific topics, such as the variation in growth in plants. See also Figure 10.5, which relates to the use of materials in the built environment.

4 Try out your trail!

One starting point for studying the local environment is to ask your pupils for their views and suggestions about ways in which the environment of the school might be improved. This idea is one that has been tried very successfully in schools, when pupils have been given a map of the school building and grounds and asked to suggest ways in which specific areas might be improved. The suggestions frequently reveal both understanding of the issues and imaginative responses to specific problems. However, there need to be mechanisms in place by which pupils' suggestions can be acted upon. Some schools have had competitions judged by governors and parents and representatives from the local community, including garden centres and local authority parks departments. The 'winning' design has then been used as a basis for implementing planned changes.

Approaches to teaching that start with the familiar environment are important. Some of your pupils may never have stood underneath a tree on a hot summer's day or visited a wood and, as a consequence, may find it difficult to comprehend the implications of the large scale, and indiscriminate, felling of trees in a tropical rain forest. Planned and carefully structured experiences that begin in your classroom and school grounds can then move on to consider the locality and, ultimately, the global environment.

Environmental education can incorporate long term studies or projects that monitor, for example, atmospheric pollution in the locality of the school. Such studies can collect data that can be compared with national, and international, records. Pupils in a number of schools throughout Europe have been involved since 1995 in a project that is monitoring nitrogen dioxide and sulphur dioxide levels at the roadside near the schools and in the school grounds. The project began in 1994 with seventeen schools in the London area. Pupils measured nitrogen dioxide, carbon monoxide and pH levels of rain water at regular intervals during 1995; their results were compared with sites in central London and elsewhere. Details of this study and the findings have been published (Job, 1996) and should prove a valuable resource for teachers undertaking similar projects. Further data about acid rain and air quality is available in a resource guide produced by the Atmospheric and Research Centre (ARIC) (Hare, 1995). The data in these resource guides highlight the need for urgent action to control atmospheric pollution in cities.

Education for citizenship

The NCC identified the main aims of education for citizenship as follows:

- to establish the importance of positive, participative citizenship and provide the motivation to join in;

- to help pupils to acquire and understand essential information on which to base the development of their skills, values and attitudes towards citizenship.

(NCC, 1990d, p. 2)

Whilst these aims may be laudable, achieving them provides challenges both in the context of cross-curricular themes and in teaching and learning in science.

The NCC (1990d) identified a basic framework for education for citizenship based on eight components:

1 community;
2 democracy in action;
3 the citizen and the law;
4 work and employment;
5 public services;
6 a plural society;
7 leisure;
8 being a citizen.

It is probably easier to visualise how these components might contribute to the cross-curricular themes discussed earlier in the chapter than to understand their contribution to specific science topics. Consideration of topics related to economic and industrial understanding can provide opportunities to explore all of these components, as does study of environmental or health education.

Suggestions for classroom activities that enable links to be made between education for citizenship, other cross-curricular themes and individual curriculum subjects can be found in publications such as those by the Centre for Citizenship Studies in Education, University of Leicester (Edwards and Fogelman, 1993). One example cited in this book is that of designing and testing new materials for a playground. Such a project involves systematic enquiry and the application of knowledge about materials and their properties, allied to study of physical processes, such as forces. It also involves consideration of health and safety issues, needs and costs (economic and industrial understanding) and public and community service, local government and legislation (citizenship).

Ideas for ways in which issues related to citizenship might be addressed in science are also implicit in some of the issues considered in the earlier sections of this chapter. Discussions about the environment and the causes of pollution, for example, provide opportunities to explore issues about individual and collective responsibilities for the environment. Science lessons also provide opportunities for promoting knowledge and skills related to education for citizenship through the use of strategies such as collaborative group work, the critical evaluation of evidence and pupils taking responsibility for their own learning.

The approaches described above help pupils to work with other people by developing their sensitivity and insight about issues, which is part of helping pupils themselves to cope with sensitive issues.

TASK 11.6 HOW MIGHT SCIENCE CONTRIBUTE TO TEACHING FOR CITIZENSHIP AT KEY STAGE 4?

1   For this task you need a copy of:

- the Science National Curriculum (DFE, 1995b);
- the GCSE syllabus in your teaching subject;
- your science department's Scheme of Work.

2   Find the Programmes of Study for Key Stage 4 in Science NC, including the section on 'Experimental and investigative science'.

3   Identify two topics that you are teaching at Key Stage 4. Create a table like the one below:

Skill area	Topic 1	Topic 2
Systematic enquiry		
Application of science		
Nature of scientific ideas		
Communication		
Health and safety		
Planning experimental procedures		
Obtaining evidence		
Analysing evidence and drawing conclusions		
Evaluating evidence		

4   Complete the table by noting what opportunities your chosen topic provides to develop specific skills listed in the table. For example, under 'Evaluating evidence', note whether the topic provides opportunities for pupils to consider whether the evidence collected is sufficient to enable firm conclusions to be drawn (DFE, 1995b, p. 27, 4a).

5   The completed table should help you to identify at least five ways in which your topic contributes to aspects of education for citizenship. An example might be arguing a case clearly and concisely for, or against, changes in the local environment, using evidence obtained from field work.

Task 11.6 will have indicated that issues of citizenship are linked closely to other cross-curricular themes discussed in the earlier sections of this chapter. The activity may also have made you ask questions about the nature and value of the topics that are taught as part of the science curriculum. Such issues are particularly important in the context of possible future developments in the science curriculum and are the subject of ongoing debate (see, e.g. Millar, 1996).

TEACHING CONTROVERSIAL ISSUES

Many of the issues identified earlier concerning teaching about cross-curricular issues, for example those related to personal behaviour, are sensitive ones, particularly for pupils in their teens. Care needs to be taken to select teaching approaches that are appropriate and do not cause individual pupils distress or create anxiety. Such approaches demand sensitivity and understanding of the needs of individuals and groups, their stage of physical and emotional development, their social and family background. Guidance about approaches you can use can be found in *Learning to Teach in the Secondary School* (Capel, Leask and Turner, 1995, Chapter 4) and *Exploring Health Education: A Growth and Development Perspective* (Williams, Roberts, Hyde, Wetton and Moon, 1990).

Ways to introduce controversial issues to pupils, such as the use of nuclear power, can be found in, for example, Wellington (1986). There may also be suggestions in the PSE and tutorial programmes used by your school.

Approaches that can be valuable include the use of discussion and role play and simulation. These strategies require careful planning and orchestration if they are to be successful. If you have not used a role play before, try observing a more experienced colleague, particularly someone who teaches English or drama, before you try a role play yourself (see Task 11.7). Then try using the strategy with a non-controversial issue, such as the journey of a red blood corpuscle round the body. A role play such as this can be devised by pupils themselves – such a strategy is a good way of helping them to understand particular concepts – or can be directed by you.

TASK 11.7 OBSERVING ROLE PLAY AND DRAMA

1   Talk to colleagues in the English and drama department, as well as colleagues in science and language departments, about when

continued . . .

and where they use role play in their teaching. Ask if you can observe, or help, with a role play, particularly with a class that you teach.

2   During the lesson(s), note how the role play is introduced, how parts are assigned, how pupils are organised before and during the role play and what happens at the end of the role play (the important debriefing).

3   Discuss the outcomes with the colleagues involved.

4   For each year group that you teach, identify one topic where you could use a role play.

Information about developing and using role plays and simulations in science can be found in *Teaching Science* (Frost, 1995, Chapter 11). Figure 11.2 summarises the stages in planning and using role play in science teaching. Like most teaching strategies, role plays need careful preparation if they are to be successful; you also have to allow time for debriefing discussions with pupils after the activity. You will find further ideas, plus teacher and pupils' notes for role plays, as well as other teaching strategies including discussions, in the Science and Technology in Soci-

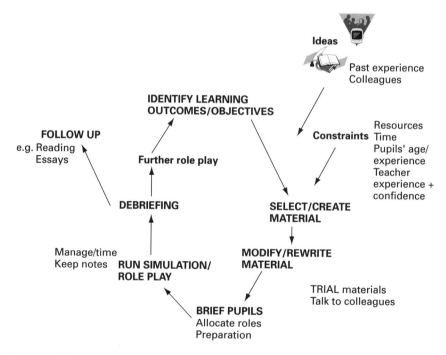

Figure 11.2   Using role play in science

ety (SATIS) materials produced by the ASE for various age groups (ASE, 1991, 1994).

TASK 11.8 USING ROLE PLAY IN SCIENCE

1 Choose a topic that you intend to teach to Year 12 that involves teaching about a controversial issue (for example the siting of a wind power station, the use of DNA 'fingerprinting', ways of reducing particulates in the air).
2 Identify where you could use a role play to enhance pupils' understanding of the topic.
3 What sort of role play would be most appropriate, for example a debate, a public meeting?
4 Identify your objectives.
5 Find out whether there are published materials that you could use, such as SATIS 16–19 (ASE, 1991).
6 Try out the role play; remember to allow time for your pupils to plan what they have to do and for the debriefing discussion after the session.
7 After the lesson, evaluate the success of the activity, referring to your objectives. What did your pupils learn and what did they think about the activity?
8 How might you modify the materials for a different group of pupils?

THE 'HIDDEN' CURRICULUM

The term 'hidden curriculum', as was mentioned earlier, is used frequently to describe many things that happen in school both inside and outside the classroom but may not appear in the formal subject curriculum or school prospectus. The hidden curriculum encompasses issues related to the whole environment and the spiritual and moral ethos of the school. First impressions of schools often provide clues about some of these dimensions:

- Is the school a welcoming place?
- Is the environment aesthetically pleasing and well cared for?
- Are there examples of pupils' work around the school?
- How do pupils and staff relate to each other?

The answers to questions such as these provide important clues about your school as a dynamic entity, including whether it is an environmentally sound, health promoting school of the type identified earlier. These aspects of your school have a direct influence on the curriculum as a whole and how and what pupils learn inside and outside the classroom. Making links between the taught and the hidden curriculum is important, but may be something that is not fully acknowledged or recognised by pupils or staff. One example of the hidden curriculum is the relationship, if any, between what is taught about food in science and technology lessons and the reality of the school dining room or canteen.

Ideally, messages about diet and health that are promoted in your lessons should be linked to the type of food that is available during the day from the canteen and other food and drink outlets in the school, including vending machines. One of the risk factors identified by government (Department of Health, 1992) and the World Health Organisation (1990) is the high intake of foods high in fat and sugar in the population as a whole. Surveys of the diets of pupils have highlighted the increasing consumption of such foods by pupils (Department of Health, 1989) and there are concerns about their future health. What pupils choose to eat is governed by a number of factors, including peer group pressure, physiological needs, likes and dislikes, religious beliefs and health knowledge. However, schools do have an important responsibility for helping pupils to reach sensible and informed decisions about their diets, and this means ensuring that the way in which food is served and eaten at lunch time in your school is consistent with current guidelines about diet and health.

TASK 11.9 SCHOOL MEALS AND SCIENCE – MAKING LINKS

1   Spend one lunch break observing what happens in your school dining room – what foods are most commonly selected and eaten?
2   Do staff eat with pupils?
3   Talk to pupils about their views about the food that is on offer.
4   Collect pupils' suggestions about ways in which the dining room and the food might be improved.
5   What do catering staff feel about the food served and the dining area?

This initial survey could be used as a basis for work that involves pupils in surveys of food consumption, wastage and analysis of the nutrients in a typical meal. The School Meals Assessment Project computer analysis program could be used for the analysis (Cawdron, 1995).

SUMMARY

This chapter has examined cross-curricular themes in the context of the whole curriculum as well as science. Aspects of the 'hidden curriculum' that are particularly relevant to science teaching, such as school meals, have also been identified. Links between academic subjects have not been considered in depth, although these links are important and are perhaps made less frequently than they should be. Pupils tend to view subjects as separate entities and do not always recognise when links are being made. Comments such as the following are rare: 'In some geography projects we have done bits of science' (Year 9 pupil).

Your pupils require help if they are to make the links between subjects and the cross-curricular themes that should underpin the curriculum subjects. Although less visible, the themes are important. Science teachers have a responsibility to ensure that these wider curriculum issues are identified and addressed as part of their teaching. The materials developed for projects such as Salters Chemistry and the ASE SATIS materials provide examples of how such links could be made in science.

When you prepare your Career Entry Profile make sure you include any work that you have done that goes beyond the science curriculum. See Appendix 4, especially 'Subject knowledge' and 'Subject application' and 'Further professional development' and your national set of required standards for NQT.

FURTHER READING

Edwards, J. and Fogelham, K. (1993) *Developing Citizenship in the Curriculum*, London: David Fulton Publishers.
    The papers in this book include general articles that look at the contribution of other cross-curricular themes to developing citizenship, as well as discussion of the role of subjects such as science.

Frost, J. (ed.) (1995) *Teaching Science*, London: Woburn Press.
    This book includes helpful and detailed guidance on strategies for teaching, including ideas on how to organise and run discussions and simulations in science lessons.

Harris, G. and Blackwell, C. (eds) (1996) *Environmental Issues in Education*: *Monitoring Change in Education*, Aldershot: Arena.
    This book provides ideas about the ways in which different habitats can be used as a teaching and learning resource by pupils of different ages as well as information about support systems that are available for environmental education from, for example, non-government organisations.

Wellington, J.J. (ed.) (1986) *Controversial Issues in the Curriculum*, Oxford: Basil Blackwell.

Contains useful advice on how to handle controversial issues as well as ideas of resources and teaching approaches to topics such as education for employment and unemployment and the use of nuclear power.

Williams, T., Roberts, J., Hyde, J., Wetton, N. and Moon, A. (1990) *Exploring Health Education: A Growth and Development Perspective*, London: Health Education Authority. (See also associated publication *Exploring Health Education: Materials for Teacher Education*).

A very useful resource that contains ideas for approaches to teaching about health related topics with pupils of different ages.

Whitehead, D. and Dyer, D. (eds) (1991) *New Developments in Economics and Business Education*, London: Kogan Page in association with the Institute of Education, University of London.

Contains useful papers on economic and industrial understanding as a cross-curricular theme, ideas for teaching and links with science.

12 Using Information Technology in teaching and learning science

INTRODUCTION

It is no accident that computers are everyday objects in laboratories, be they in schools, research or industry. They have more than justified their existence in an environment that revolves around making and recording measurements, manipulating information and communicating the results to others.

Bill Gates captured the essence of IT when he said:

> some fear that technology will dehumanise formal education. But anyone who has seen kids working together around a computer, the way my friends and I first did in 1968, or watched exchanges between students in classrooms separated by oceans, knows that technology can humanise the educational environment. The same technological forces that will make learning so necessary will also make it practical and enjoyable. Corporations are reinventing themselves around the flexible opportunities afforded by information technology; classrooms will have to change as well.
>
> (Gates, 1995, p. 184)

He continues

> Technology will not, however, isolate students. One of the most important educational experiences is collaboration. In some of the world's most creative classrooms, computers and communications networks are already beginning to change the conventional relationships among students themselves, and between students and teachers, by facilitating collaborative learning.
>
> (Gates, 1995, p. 200)

The National Curriculum for Information Technology (IT) specifies the use of computers in schools so that pupils are able to work competently with them (DFE, 1995a). As a prospective teacher, you are expected to demonstrate competence in the use of IT in your teaching. Refer to the appropriate national standards and Appendix 4 for details. It is essential that such skills are taught within the subject areas and not in the isolation of IT lessons. Using IT in your teaching provides an ideal opportunity to meet many of these requirements and for pupils to develop IT competence; see DFE (1992) and OFSTED (1994).

OBJECTIVES

By the end of this chapter you should be confident in using a personal computer (PC) to:

- understand some of the basic concepts in relation to the use
  - as a word processor,
  - with databases,
  - with spreadsheets,
  - for desktop publishing and graphics,
  - with multimedia,
  - for interfacing with the environment,
  - with the Internet;
- improve your teaching;
- help with lesson planning and in your day to day routines.

TERMINOLOGY

The following abbreviations are used throughout this chapter:

CD	Compact Disc
CD-ROM	Compact Disc – Read Only Material
DTP	Desktop Publishing
FTP	File Transfer Protocol
ISDN	Integrated Services Digital Network
IT	Information Technology
PC	Personal Computer
WP	Word Processor
WWW	World Wide Web

COMPUTERS IN SCIENCE

Schools vary in the extent to which computers are used in science teaching. In some laboratories a computer is available all the time; in other schools the computer has to be booked as you would a video player and monitor. In yet other schools, computers are kept in a special room to which you have to take your pupils. Much depends on the attitude of your head of department, or the presence of a keen teacher. Does your department's Scheme of Work write in the computer as part of the teaching programme?

TASK 12.1 INFORMATION TECHNOLOGY (IT) IN YOUR SCHOOL EXPERIENCE SCHOOL

Make sure you know where the departmental computers are kept and how you can access them for teaching and personal use.

Obtain a copy of the Scheme of Work in your school science faculty. Identify ways in which IT is being used and suggest further possibilities for its use. Summarise your findings on one side of A4 and discuss them with your school tutor.

Using your PC as a word processor

Most computer users spend more time word processing than anything else. Using a computer to produce documents has many advantages over the traditional typewriter. For example:

- documents can be saved to disk (if they are saved to a floppy disk, they may then be transferred to other compatible computers);
- a wide range of text styles (fonts) are available to improve presentation; text may be edited with cut, copy and paste functions. Any chunks of text that need to be used again may simply be copied and inserted without the need for re-typing. This is useful for drafting and editing of documents;
- graphics (pictures, charts and graphs, etc.) may be included in documents;
- documents can be spell and grammar checked;
- it is easy to amend material for differentiated teaching.

It is also a useful 'thinking' tool, enabling drafting and editing of ideas for both teachers and pupils.

The older DOS based WP programs have been replaced by 'Windows', which is much easier to learn and use, arguably more powerful and offers a facility known as WYSIWYG (what you see is what you get). This means that what you see on the screen is what you will get out of the printer.

Many different WP programs exist. Although most share similar functions, you will have to familiarise yourself with the ones available. Consult a friendly or knowledgeable teacher. It is important for you to locate the IT co-ordinator in your school and to find the facilities available and how you gain access to them.

Word processing may be used for:

- writing essays;
- making posters;
- keeping records such as lesson plans, teaching notes, programmes of study, etc.;
- producing worksheets;
- writing reports;
- writing a homework, or a report of an investigation, etc. Working in this way can greatly motivate the less able or disaffected student. The spell check facility is helpful to everyone.

BASIC CONCEPTS

This section is for any student teacher who has not used a computer before. Skip this section if you are familiar with basic word processing. Move on to the next section on spreadsheets.

Many of the details given below will apply to other software programs. You should become thoroughly familiar with these concepts before moving ahead.

Making a start

Having double clicked with the mouse on the appropriate icon, the word processing program will load. When this process is completed, you will usually be presented with a blank work screen known as a document. You can then start typing directly into this. If you want to open an existing document, you need to select the Open command from the File menu display. You will be presented with a list of existing files. Click on the one you want using the mouse, and select 'OK'.

The keyboard enables you to enter text on the screen. Upper case characters may be obtained by pressing the shift key in conjunction with the appropriate letter. Look at the menu and toolbar and search through the options. You should find that you are able to select different fonts, font sizes, bold, underlined and italic text and so on; experiment with the menus and icons to become familiar with their functions.

Navigating a document

There are two main ways of moving around in a document. The first is simply to use the mouse, clicking where you wish the insertion point to go, or clicking on the scroll arrows in the corner of the screen. Alternatively, you can use the keyboard arrows, page down and page up keys, home and end keys.

Selecting text

Text can easily be selected by using a mouse. A single word can usually be selected by double clicking on it with a mouse. A line can usually be selected by clicking beside the line in the left margin. A sentence can usually be selected by holding down the ctrl key, and clicking inside the sentence. Double clicking in the left hand margin beside a paragraph will usually select the paragraph. Perhaps the most straightforward way though is simply to position the mouse pointer to the left of the first character you want to select, hold down the left hand mouse button, and then drag the mouse over the text.

Editing text

Having selected text, you can delete it by pressing the delete key. If you wish to copy it, select Copy from the Edit menu, position the insertion point where you want the copied text to appear, and then select the Paste command in the Edit menu.

If you want to move text elsewhere in the document, select the Edit menu's Cut command, position the insertion point where you want the text to appear, and then select Paste from the Edit menu.

You can spell check your document. Search through the menu, or look at the toolbar to find a spell checking option.

Importing graphics

Most PCs allow you to import pictures of objects into your word processed documents. This adds visual appeal to your work. In most cases, select 'Insert' from the menu bar and look for Picture.

Saving your document

Look at the File menu and select the Save command. If you're saving a new document, the Save dialogue box will appear and you are prompted to enter a name. If you are using any version of Windows prior to Windows 95, you must not use more than eight characters in your name.

Printing your document

Select the Print command from the File menu and the print dialogue box appears. You are asked whether you want to print all of your document, or just a selection. Select OK when you are happy with your choice.

These skills cover the basics of word processing, but you may need to look further for extra help; consult the appropriate manual or a colleague experienced in word processing.

Most programs have a Help menu, usually located towards the right of the Menu Bar. Access this if you want advice. This advice applies equally to other types of software mentioned later in the chapter.

TASK 12.2 PRACTISING WORD PROCESSING SKILLS

Practise basic WP skills and produce some simple information or worksheets for your classroom use. If you are feeling ambitious, try to find out how to incorporate a table, picture or graph in your document. A useful facility is the Border command which enables you to put a box around text on worksheets. Try the Format menu on the toolbar. With the confidence behind you of your acquired skills, encourage and enable pupils to write up a practical activity or a piece of research on a word processor. You will see for yourself how using computers can increase pupil motivation. Most pupils are computer literate, so need relatively little help. Be sure to seek out the IT co-ordinator for help.

Having completed the above tasks and become familiar with the available WP packages, you should be able to:

- create, save and open a document;
- select appropriate fonts;
- search for and replace text;
- produce effects such as columns in documents;
- underline text;
- check your spelling;
- import graphics and tables.

USING A SPREADSHEET

Bill Gates made clear the advantages of spreadsheets when he said:

> When the first electronic spreadsheets appeared in 1978, they were a vast improvement over paper and pencil. What they made possible was putting formulas behind each element in a table of data. These formulas could refer to other elements of the table. Any change in one value would immediately affect the other cells, so projections such as sales, growth, or changes in interest rates could be played with (in order to) to examine 'what if' scenarios, and the impact of every change would be instantly apparent.
>
> (Gates, 1995, p. 139)

The use of spreadsheets is not confined to business. Spreadsheets are, as suggested above, powerful manipulators of all sorts of numerical data. A spreadsheet is like a giant table or grid made up of a number of rows and columns. It is often referred to as a worksheet. Each section within a table is known as a cell and can be referenced by a letter and a number. For example, the first cell is A1. The code A1 is also known as an address. You can select a cell using the mouse. When you have done this, the cell is said to be active; you can now enter information.

TASK 12.3 USING A SPREADSHEET

Use a spreadsheet as a register and mark sheet for your classes. Record relevant marks as well as attendance. Use the spreadsheet to calculate average marks, deviations, etc. Most spreadsheets use a formula such as ' = average (a1:a19)' to average figures in this range of cells.

Demonstrate to pupils how to use a spreadsheet to produce results tables after a practical activity and produce an appropriate graph or chart.

A spreadsheet is useful for storing numerical data. A simple example would be a class list of test and exam results. Text as well as numbers can be inserted into cells. An example is shown in Figure 12.1.

This facility alone does not give a spreadsheet much advantage over word processing applications, which could equally well be used for storing such information. A spreadsheet, however, allows you to manipulate numerical data and is capable of performing complex calculations.

As with word processing applications, a wide range of spreadsheets are available. Many enable you to produce graphs and charts directly from

		Forces	Energy		Deviation from
	Surname	Firstname	test %	test %	Average %	class mean
Brown	John	55	59	57	-2.5
Higgs	Fiona	76	68	72	12.5
Jones	Racheal	34	41	37.5	-22
Smith	James	54	60	57	-2.5
Taylor	Iain	76	72	74	14.5
			Mean	59.5	

		Forces	Energy		Deviation from
	Surname	Firstname	test %	test %	Average %	class mean
Brown	John	55	59	'=SUM(C13:D13)/2	'=E13-E19
Higgs	Fiona	76	68	'=SUM(C14:D14)/2	'=E14-E19
Jones	Racheal	34	41	'=SUM(C15:D15)/2	'=E15-E19
Smith	James	54	60	'=SUM(C16:D16)/2	'=E16-E19
Taylor	Iain	76	72	'=SUM(C17:D17)/2	'=E17-E19
			Mean	'=SUM(E13:E17)/5	

Figure 12.1   Using a spreadsheet to record test results. The second table gives examples of some typical formulae. For example, the average mark for John Brown was obtained by adding the contents of cell C13 and D3 together, and dividing by 2.

the information in them. The methods for doing this vary. With some you need only highlight the appropriate section and select 'graph' from the menu. There are often a wide range of graphs and charts available from which to select. An example of this facility is shown in Figure 12.2.

Time taken (s)	Distance travelled (m)	Average speed (m/s)
0	0	0
1	0.5	0.5
2	1.0	0.5
3	1.5	0.5
4	2.0	0.5

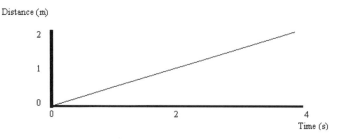

Figure 12.2   Using a spreadsheet to display results and plot graphs

In Figure 12.3 we show how pupils can be helped to calculate enthalpies of combustion. This activity is appropriate for pupils at A level or GNVQ or for more able pupils at KS4. For further uses of spreadsheets in science see Brosnan (1992).

You may, from time to time, have to consult a manual or a friendly computer user for detailed help. If you have completed the above tasks and familiarised yourself with the available spreadsheet package(s), you should be able to:

- create, save and open a document;
- enter text and numbers into cells;
- write simple formulae into cells;
- produce graphs and charts.

Table 12.1 shows how a spreadsheet can be constructed to calculate the enthalpy of combustion for any hydrocarbon, in this case methane.

The bond energies are taken from a book of data. The equation for combustion of methane in air is

$$CH_4 + 2O_2 = CO_2 + 2H_2O$$

There are four C–H bonds and two O=O bonds broken; and one C=O bond and four O–H bonds made. Columns B and C show the number of bonds broken and the energy associated with each bond. The total energy input needed to break all bonds is shown in column D. The number of bonds made and the energy output is shown in columns E and F.

The instruction for:

- cell 9D is 'multiply 9C by 9B';
- cell 10F is 'multiply 10E by 10B' (note the negative sign);
- cell 15D is 'sum of all D cells';
- cell 15F is 'sum of all F cells';
- cell 17F is 'sum of cells 15D and 15F'.

You can adapt this spreadsheet for the combustion of many compounds. Try setting up a spreadsheet to show a calculation of the enthalpy of combustion of ethanol in air (see Table 12.1).

Figure 12.3   Using a spreadsheet to calculate the enthalpy of combustion of alkanes
Source: adapted from Burton, Holman, Pilling and Waddington (1994a, b and c)

Table 12.1   Enthalpy changes of combustion

	A	B	C	D	E	F
1						
2			REACTION			
3	COMPOUND	CH4	CH4 + 2O2 = CO2 + 2H2O			
4						
5	BOND TYPE	BOND ENERGY	NUMBER	ENERGY IN	NUMBER	ENERGY OUT
6		KJ/MOL-1	BROKEN	KJ/MOL-1	MADE	KJ/MOL-1
7						
8	C–C	347	0	0	0	0
9	C–H	413	4	1652	0	0
10	C–O	805	0	0	2	−1610
11	O–O	498	2	996	0	0
12	O–H	464	0	0	4	−1856
13						
14						
15			Total energy in	2648	Total energy out	−3466
16			KJ/MOL-1		KJ/MOL-1	KJ/MOL-1
17	ENTHALPY CHANGE, COMBUSTION OF METHANE					−818

USING A DATABASE

A spreadsheet is a very good tool for storing and manipulating numerical data, but is of less use for doing the same with written data. This is where a database comes into its own.

Record cards were used widely for storing information such as names and addresses. In a database, each 'card' is known as a record. Each record contains a number of fields such as surname or telephone number. When you call up a new record, these fields will be blank, allowing you to enter the appropriate information. Different database programs vary in the number of fields contained in a single record.

Any database can have only one layout. This is what you see on the screen in front of you when you enter or access data. A layout can contain text linked to the fields (to help identify them) as well as the fields themselves. When you create a field in a database, you must specify data type, in other words whether you are entering characters, numbers, etc. Databases inevitably grow large. However, unlike a telephone directory which itself is a form of database, a computerised database allows you to search easily through the records to obtain information.

Whilst it is relatively easy to produce a word processed document using a PC, or to enter simple formulae into a spreadsheet, a database requires more effort because, rather than being a program in its own right, it is really a programming tool that you can develop to your own specifications. Each database needs setting up in its own way and some databases are easier to master than others. A simple database is shown in Figure 12.4 which comprises five fields and can be used to contain all the elements. More fields could be added if needed.

Records on a database can be indexed and sorted. When you sort records, you must decide which fields you want to include in the search. For example, you may wish to search college records using the field 'surnames' in order to trace an individual. This field is then called the index of the file. You can create a number of indexes. Your choice will determine how the information is presented.

It would be useful to produce a database of test questions and other resources for teaching. Having completed the above tasks and become familiar with the available database programs, you should be able to:

● create (define), save and open a database;
● create fields;
● enter information;
● search a database.

Element	Symbol	Group	Period	Characteristics
Chlorine	Cl	7	3	Greenish-yellow gas, heavier than air and poisonous
Potassium	K	1	4	Reactive metal, floats on water, low melting point for meta
Carbon	C	4	2	Found in two main forms; diamond and graphite
Helium	He	0	1	Unreactive colourless gas
Sulphur	S	6	3	Brittle yellow solid. Non-metal with low melting point

Figure 12.4 Building a database of elements in the Periodic Table

TASK 12.4 SETTING UP A DATABASE

Conduct a survey of one of your classes on eye colour, weight, height and sex. Enter the data into a database. You will need to enter appropriate field names and details before entering the data. Show the pupils how to conduct a search using the database. Once confident in the operation of a database, use it as a teaching aid. Find out if there are any databases in school that contain information about the Periodic Table or the solar system. If not, perhaps you could try to create one.

DESKTOP PUBLISHING (DTP) AND GRAPHICS

Graphics programs come under many banners. At the advanced end of the spectrum are those that allow you to manipulate images such as scanned photographs. At the other end are relatively simple drawing or painting programs.

Simple drawing programs of this type allow you to draw the outlines of an object, adding colour, or to produce images as if you were quite literally using a paintbrush. They also allow you to add text to any diagrams. This is useful if you are drawing equipment and want to label it. The example in Figure 12.5 shows a drawing that can easily be produced. The document can be saved and incorporated into a WP or DTP document.

Desktop publishing software is designed to replace the job of the type-setter and page make-up artist in the preparation of documents. A typical document contains text, pictures and graphic elements.

At first glance, a DTP and a good WP program seem to offer similar functions. However, WP programs focus on text and its manipulation (although images can be included), whereas DTP programs focus on page design rather than text. To this end, many layout and graphics tools are available on DTP programs. A good DTP program enables a greater control of text and images. A finished document will have a quality look and provide added impact to the reader. It is worthwhile trying to produce worksheets with a DTP to see if presentation can be improved. It is also a good idea to encourage the use of DTP software by pupils in relation to the preparation of presentations etc.; see, for example, Figure 12.6.

To use a DTP program effectively, you will need to find out how to position text and pictures within the document. Programs differ widely in their commands and methods of working. You have to search through the Menu options for the tools you want, or consult a manual.

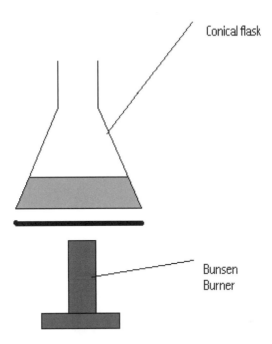

Figure 12.5   Using a simple drawing program to produce diagrams

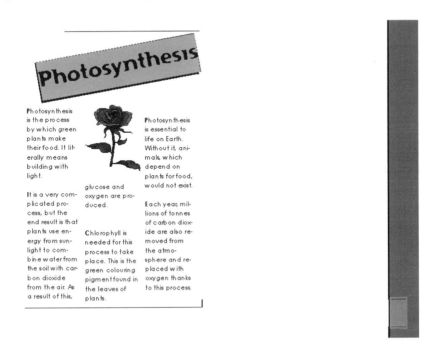

Figure 12.6   An example of an information sheet produced using a DTP program

Your school may possess a **scanner**. This allows photographs or similar images to be 'captured' and stored on disk, and these may be manipulated and incorporated in your documents.

Through the completion of the above tasks and becoming familiar with the graphics and DTP packages, you should be able to:

- plan a document layout in rough;
- create and position frames;
- add text and pictures and other graphical elements;
- edit a document;
- save, open and print a document;
- scan and save a photograph to disk.

MULTIMEDIA

Multimedia is simply the combination of sound, graphics, animation and video. It is most typically associated with CD-ROM discs which are basically the same as those used by CD audio players. A single CD-ROM can store as much information as some 400 floppy disks.

Multimedia applications allow you to interact with the computer to a greater degree. Information presented in this way can therefore be highly stimulating. It may be particularly useful when teaching a subject that offers little opportunity for practical work; see Figure 12.7. A number of very good CD-ROMs exist that provide stimulating material, for example, on the solar system.

Multimedia is linked with hypermedia, which combines multimedia with hypertext (see the section on the World Wide Web).

Look out for some of the following titles:

- Microsoft Encarta encyclopaedia (Microsoft 0345 002000);
- Body Works (Softkey International 0181 246 4000);
- Secondary Edition Electricity and Magnetism (Yorkshire International Thompson Multimedia 0113 2438283);
- Physics 'A' level Revision Software (ScreenActive 0181 3322132);

There are, of course, many more CD-ROMs to choose from.

Many of the encyclopaedic CD-ROMs are very useful for research, either for pupils or for staff. Information and diagrams may often be printed directly, or cut and pasted into WP or DTP programs. Beware, though, of copyright infringements; **read the guidance on copyright** provided with the resource.

TASK 12.5 USING CD-ROMs

Prepare a list of the science based CD-ROMs available in the school. You may need to visit the school library, IT department or other areas of the school to access them all. Try to find time to preview and familiarise yourself with one or more of them. List titles and underneath make suggestions of lessons etc. into which the more suitable ones could be incorporated. If possible, arrange for a computer equipped with a CD-ROM drive to be available in a lesson. Plan to incorporate a CD-ROM into one of your lessons, e.g. as a demonstration or an aid to research.

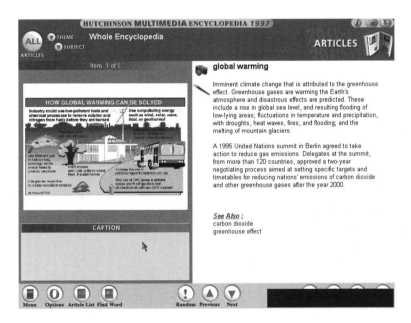

Figure 12.7   A typical view of an encyclopaedic CD-ROM
Source: Hutchinson Multimedia Encyclopedia 1997

It may be possible, if the hardware is available, to connect a television to the computer. This facility enables a greater number of pupils to share the experience.

Completion of the above tasks and becoming familiar with the CD-ROM material in your school and college should enable you to:

- operate a CD-ROM drive;
- access information on a variety of CD-ROMs;
- design ways of incorporating them into lessons.

INTERFACING WITH THE ENVIRONMENT

Computers can be used to monitor experiments or conditions outside. Many weather stations within schools and colleges are now linked directly to computers. Many combinations of hardware and software are available, depending upon requirements. You need a computer with a serial port, sensors, interface equipment and appropriate software; see Figure 12.8.

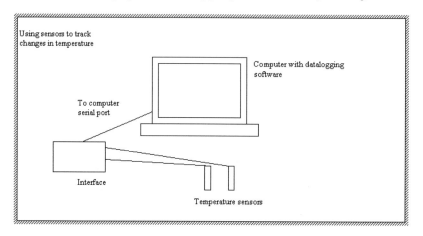

Figure 12.8   An example of a typical set-up for using sense and control equipment to monitor temperature changes

At some time you will perform an experiment that generates results that can be handled by a computer. Using a computer means that:

- results can be seen immediately;
- results can be processed automatically so that emerging patterns can be almost instantly observed;
- greater precision is possible;
- events that take place extremely rapidly can easily be monitored;
- a print-out of the results is easily obtainable for all to use.

For a computer to be 'aware' of its surroundings, it needs to be connected to sensors via an interface or data logger connected to the serial port of the computer. Many different sensors are available commercially. Check with your own school as to what is available. Different types of sensors include:

- movement;
- pH;
- pulse;
- sound;

- humidity;
- light sensors and gates;
- oxygen;
- pressure.

Computers can also be used to control external devices. Various control boxes are also available that attach to the interface box, enabling the computer to control lights, motors, buzzers, etc.

TASK 12.6 USING SENSORS

Produce a lesson plan that incorporates the use of sense and/or control equipment for a class you expect to teach. For example, you could use temperature sensors to conduct an investigation on the insulating abilities of different types of cups. As extension work, you could look at the effects of stirring, use of a lid, etc. on energy loss. Evaluate the lesson and identify the advantages and disadvantages of using this strategy. Make a record of other experiments that could be conducted or monitored using a computer and appropriate resources to help you.

Selection of the appropriate sensors helps pupils to identify variables more clearly, motivates them to predict results and enhances their abilities to observe, measure and analyse results. Most software enables results to be displayed graphically. For further guidance, see Cosgrove (1994), Dolsma (1995) and Frost (1996).

Completion of the above tasks and becoming familiar with the available hardware and software should enable you to:

- understand the basic applications of sense and control software and hardware;
- understand the different types of sensors that are available;
- connect the sensors to the computer via the interface;
- collect, display, manipulate, store and print data.

THE INTERNET

The Internet is probably going to be the single most important computer application for education in the years to come. It is possible to envisage a day when schools as we know them may no longer exist. Pupils will be able to access multimedia style course material on the World Wide Web (WWW) and be able to communicate with tutors via e-mail (electronic mail) or voice-mail.

The Internet is a world wide connection of computer networks. At present, some 50,000 networks and 5 million computers are connected via the Net. This number is growing at some 9 per cent per month. Current projections estimate that 100 million computers will be connected by the end of the century.

At present in the UK, the potential of the Net is somewhat limited by the speed at which data can be transmitted through our telephone lines. We have to connect via a modem which converts the computer's digital signals into analogue signals for transmission. The 'receiving' computer also has a modem, which turns these analogue signals back into digital signals. However, with the development of high speed fully digital links, the Integrated Services Digital Network (ISDN), data transmission will be considerably improved. This will allow the multimedia aspects of the Web to be developed to its potential.

The Net gives access to an unimaginably wide range of information. Already, there is very little that you could not successfully research on the Net. The Internet offers many services. Those most commonly used are e-mail, the WWW, File Transfer Protocol (FTP), Usenet and Telnet. For further discussion about the Internet, see Capel, Leask and Turner (1997, Chapter 14) and Herz (1994).

E-mail

This enables users to write messages and send them to other computers connected via the Net. You are usually connected to an access provider such as Compuserve or Zetnet via a local telephone call. You can e-mail anywhere in the world for the cost of a local call. This is possible because the providers lease telephone lines that always remain open.

TASK 12.7 USING E-MAIL

Find out the e-mail addresses of other schools around the world. Encourage your pupils to communicate with them so that they can find out about different aspects of life and schooling in other countries. You could use education and other newsgroups (see later section) to request such addresses, or to conduct research. Two school science faculties can share an investigation such as measuring the angle of elevation of the Sun at noon at two different locations on the Earth and use the data to compute the diameter of the Earth (see Chapter 10).

Before sending mail, you must know the address of the person to whom you are writing. The common form of address is *name@location.organisation.type.country*. For example, my personal address is *ian.hogg@*

zetnet.co.uk and the science faculty at Swakeleys School is *chem01 @swakeleys.u-net.com*. All e-mail addresses are case specific, i.e to gain access you must use the the specified upper or lower case letters in the address.

World Wide Web (WWW)

When people talk about the Internet, they are usually referring to the World Wide Web which is what the Net is famous for. The WWW consists of many hypermedia pages that contain lines of text on which you can point and click in order to navigate through vast amounts of information on other pages. These lines of text are called links.

Pages of information are displayed in a window on the monitor. In order to access this information, you need special **browser** software such as Netscape or Explorer. When reading through the information you will notice that certain words are displayed in a different colour or are underlined. The words marked in this way are hypertext links. Clicking on them with the mouse pointer will bring up another Web page. As you browse through the Web, pages may originate from anywhere in the world.

Web information can be of poor quality, because there is not the same external editing as exists for academic books. As a user, you may need to rely on sites set up by known institutions. You can easily produce your own web site. Many teachers, pupils and schools have already done this. Doing so is fairly straightforward. If you lack experience, obtain one of the many Web authoring software packages, which take you through the process step by step. You then send your page to your access provider (many of whom provide space for sites free of charge) who sets it up for you. Your web site can then be accessed by anyone in the world who is suitably equipped. Examples of Web pages are given in Figures 12.9 and 12.10.

With so many pages of information on the Web, it might seem almost impossible to find specific information. However, this is not necessarily the case, though searching the Web can be rather frustrating. A number of search tools exist. Many Web browsers have a 'search Web' button that will automatically take you to a **search engine**. All you then need do is enter a key word or phrase, and in a few seconds you will be presented with a list of search results. You then simply select the one that seems the most appropriate and click on its hypertext link.

A greater problem than searching for information is the slowness of the Internet due to the sheer number of people using it. If you are using the

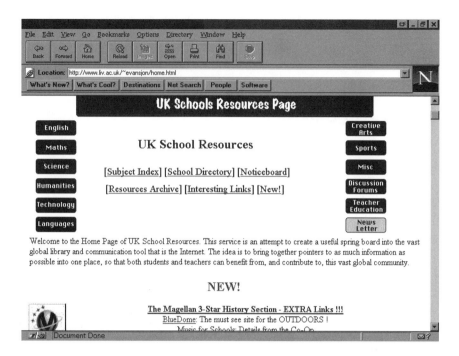

Figure 12.9   The UK School Resources page on the WWW. This is viewed in Netscape 3 and provides useful information for all subject areas. To access this resource you need a browser (e.g. Netscape or Internet Explorer) to help. The address of the page is given by 'Location'. This may be typed in directly. Clicking on 'links' within the page will enable you to explore to resource to the full.

WWW in the afternoon, when many Americans come on-line, or in the early evening, when many British and European users log on, congestion is inevitable. Sites involving heavy use of graphics can be particularly slow.

One of the best known search tools is YAHOO, which can be found at the address *http://www.yahoo.com/search.html*. Useful Web sites are listed at the end of this chapter.

As you conduct your own searches on the WWW, it is worthwhile noting the location of good sites for future reference. Most Web browsers will allow you to store locations so that they can be directly accessed.

If you are using the Web for research purposes, it is worthwhile having your word processing application open in the background. Relevant text can then simply be cut and pasted into the application as required. This

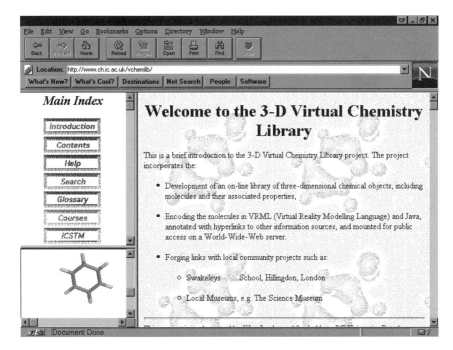

Figure 12.10 The 3D Virtual Chemistry Library Project. This is a project involving Imperial College and Swakeleys School and is well worth a visit. Viewed in Netscape 3, this is a prime example of how schools and universities can forge links. See p. 254 for web site addresses.

is a quick and efficient way of making up information sheets. Many Web pages enable you to download software. You may, for example, find programs that demonstrate Newton's Laws of Motion, or the Periodic Table; see also Erb (1996).

TASK 12.8 USING THE WWW

- Conduct research on a topic of your choice using the WWW. Show and enable pupils to use it as a research tool.
- Access some of the educational sites and see if you can find any teaching tips or even ready prepared worksheets.
- Find relevant software (shareware or freeware) and download it for use in the classroom or lab.

Usenet

This facility allows access to thousands of user groups called newsgroups. You can find newsgroups relating to almost any topic you wish to mention. A small selection is listed below; italics indicate location:

Science and aeronautics	Aerospace simulation technology
sci.aeronautics	*sci.aeronautics.simulation*
Agriculture	Anthropology
sci.agriculture	*sci.anthropology*
Astronomy	Biology
sci.astro	*sci.bio*
Evolutionary biology	Chemistry
sci.bio.evolution	*sci.chem*
The Science of Education	Physics
sci.edu	*sci.physics*

If you are unable to find relevant information on the WWW, you can try posting questions to a relevant newsgroup. Someone will be in receipt of your message and may be in a position to offer you help. With newsgroups, a reply is obviously not instantaneous. It is necessary to access your computer over a period of days to see if you have a reply. Further, you can specify whether you wish someone to reply via the newsgroup itself or via e-mail.

Newsgroups are also excellent tools for research. Staff in my science faculty recently 'posted' on to the WWW pupils' questionnaires on asthma. Such questions then became available to a world wide audience. In this particular case, we received many detailed replies and much relevant information from a professor of pharmacology in America.

File Transfer Protocol (FTP) is used for retrieving programs from the Internet. There are many software and hardware manufacturers and public FTP sites, which are basically the Internet's version of the files section of a Bulletin Board.

SUMMARY

Computers are here to stay. Their power will increase as will their ability to communicate due to the installation of such things as ISDN links. It is increasingly important for you to be computer literate. We suggest you buy a computer magazine regularly and keep in touch with developments. If you are not aware of the latest developments, you can be sure that an increasing number of your pupils are up to date. For further discussion on IT in the National Curriculum, see National Council for Educational Technology (1995).

If you have mastered most of the basics included in this chapter, look out for other types of educational software. Follow developments on the WWW, as teaching resources displayed here will become much more advanced in years to come. It is possible to imagine a time when an entire course can be taught over the Internet (indeed some colleges and universities already offer this option for distance learning). In due course you might like to find out how to write and publish your own Web pages and produce school or science faculty Web pages, or use the WWW for pupils to publish their own work.

This chapter has provided you with some basic IT skills necessary to teach in schools today. At the end of each section of this chapter there is short checklist of IT skills. Go back and check your development against these as well as against the course requirements. Include your achievements in your personal portfolio or Career Entry Profile.

This chapter cannot, by its very nature, be fully comprehensive. You should consult other resources to obtain further information, including IT specialists within schools, software manuals and books included in the Further Reading section at the end of this chapter. Two good books are Haydn and Macaskill (1996a, 1996b).

You need to equip yourself with at least a minimum working knowledge of today's operating systems from DOS and Windows 3.11 through to Windows 95 and, in the future, various versions of Windows NT (the operating system that is destined to replace Windows 95). Further, some schools may be using IBM's OS2 operating system. The more knowledge you have of these, the easier it will be to set up, configure, rectify problems and modify computers. For further discussion we recommend you read Beynon and Mackay (1993); Northwood (1991) and Norton (1993). Distance learning materials can be obtained from John Backwell (tel 0181 265 1994; e-mail: *backwell@mail.bogo.co.uk*).

FURTHER READING

Beynon, J. and Mackay, H. (eds) (1993) *Computers in the Classroom: More Questions Than Answers*, London: The Falmer Press.
The role of computers in teaching are examined in these papers.

Department for Education (DFE) (1992) *Information Technology in Secondary Schools: A Review by HMI*, London: HMSO.
Looks at the use of IT in specific subjects within the National Curriculum.

Frost, R. (1996) *The 'IT in Science' Book of Datalogging and Control*, Hatfield: Association for Science Education.
Latest version updated April 1996. Excellent resource for the use of IT in science, with details of how to use IT in science activities.

Hadyn, T. and Macaskill, C. (1996a) *Making the Most of Information Technology in the PGCE Year*, London: The Institute of Education, University of London.

Hadyn, T. and Macaskill, C. (1996b) *Information Technology and Initial Teacher Education: Bridging the Gap Between What Is and What Might Be*, London: The Institute of Education, University of London.

Herz, J.C. (1994) *Surfing on the Internet: A Net-Head's Adventures On-line*, London: Abacus Books.
Gives an insight into the 'Net'.

Norton, P. (1993) *Inside the PC*, New York: Brady Publishing.
Excellent book that helps you understand the workings of a computer.

WEB SITE ADDRESSES

Addresses do change but were correct at the time of writing.

British Medical Journal	*http://www.bmj.com/bmj*
History of Science/Science Studies reference sources	*http://gort.ucsd.edu/ds/initial.html*
Human Genome Mapping Project	*http://www.hgmp.mrc.ac.uk/home-page.html*
Nature	*http://www.nature.com*
New Scientist	*http://www.newscientist.com*
Reuters News	*http://www.yahoo.com/headlines/*
Swakeleys School	*http://www.users.zetnet.co.uk/swakeleys/*
Teacher Net UK	*http://www.teachernetuk.org*
The 3D Virtual Chemistry Library Project (see figure 12.10)	*http://www.ch.ic.ac.uk/vchemlib/*
The Met Office Home Page	*http://www.meto.govt.uk/*
The National Curriculum	*http://www.open.gov.uk/dfee/schurric.htm*
The Office of Science and Technology	*http://www.open.gov.uk/ost/osthome.htm*

UK School Resources Home Page   *http://www.liv.ac.uk/~evansjon/ home.html*

UK Schools: Other Educational Home Pages   *http://www.liv.ac.uk/~evansjon/ other_ed.html*

13 Professional development

INTRODUCTION

In this chapter we consider your professional development at the completion of your course of initial teacher education and ways in which you can build on progress. Throughout this book we have used the term 'reflective practitioner' as a kind of shorthand for ways in which you monitor and promote your own development. At the heart of this idea is the belief that improvement in your teaching comes about through the regular evaluation of your own teaching, with the support of your tutors and teachers. In your first post, the responsibility lies more with you as an emerging professional and autonomous teacher. We expect that, in your first post, you will be supported by a mentor or head of department who will help you both to utilise your new skills in the new environment and to build on them. Reflective practice can be used to assist you in evaluating your own performance and to set personal targets for future growth. Wisdom lies in the capacity to accept that you make mistakes and to learn from experience. Knowing when you have made mistakes, when you have been successful, and the reasons for both, enable you to develop professionally; this process is part of reflective practice.

In the companion volume to this book, *Learning to Teach in the Secondary School* (Capel, Leask and Turner, 1995) the task of getting your first post (Unit 8.1) and general issues about your further professional development (Unit 8.2) are addressed in detail. In this chapter we add to that discussion and focus on the particular concerns for you as an emerging science teacher.

OBJECTIVES

By the end of this chapter you should:

- know how to obtain your first post;
- be able to produce your portfolio and Career History Profile which summarises, with evidence, your progress as a science teacher;

- be aware of ways in which to keep up to date and to widen your professional horizons, through INSET, induction and other support in your NQT year;
- be aware of the opportunities of further educational qualifications;
- be considering ways to broaden your knowledge and understanding of education both as a practice and an academic discipline;
- be willing to continue reflective practice into your teaching career.

GETTING YOUR FIRST POST

Start looking for your post in January. You should review regularly the *Times Educational Supplement*, the education sections of the *Guardian*, *Times* and *Independent* newspapers for advertisements and know which day of the week they appear. Talk to colleagues in school about possible vacancies occurring in your school experience school and more widely. Other student teachers are sources of information.

When you read an advertisement, make sure you understand the descriptions of schools. The range of descriptions include:

- state maintained, voluntary aided or independent;
- local authority maintained or Grant Maintained;
- City Technology College (CTC) or a school with Technology status;
- grammar, comprehensive or secondary modern (rare);
- secondary (11–19, 11–16 or 14–19), or middle school;
- single sex or mixed;
- community college (or school);
- FE college or secondary school.

Find out how pupils are selected for entry to the school.

Practical information about schools can be obtained in the *Education Year Book* (see useful addresses, Appendix 5) and more detailed information through an OFSTED report of inspection; this is a public document and is on the Internet. An important decision in choosing a school is whether or not you wish to teach post-16 courses, such as GCE A level or GNVQ.

Send for further details of the post and ensure that you know how to apply, by form or personal letter. Complete the details, paying special attention to the specification of the post as advertised and the skills and qualities demanded by the position. You must address the requirements of the post and not assume that your qualities self-evidently meet the criteria.

Writing your application should reveal to the reader something about the schools in which you practised, their type and location; the number, Key Stage and level of classes taught and, where relevant, the examination board you taught towards at KS4. You cannot be expected to have taught everything in a Key Stage syllabus, but by mentioning areas of the curriculum you have taught, you indicate to the interviewers some areas of experience and invite questions on that subject, to your advantage.

If called for interview, try to arrange to visit the school before the event; if possible in advance of the day of interview. Walking round the school, meeting some of the staff, watching a science lesson, talking to a member of the technical staff, watching the pupils in the playground at break allows you get a feeling about the school, the staff and the way it 'runs'. As well as confirming your candidacy, such a visit can suggest questions to ask at interview or identify areas in which you may be asked questions.

Advertisements for teaching posts frequently cite the type of course or curriculum package being followed, e.g. Bath Science, Science Scene or Salter's A level Chemistry. If you intend to proceed with the application, make sure you know something about that course. Whereas it is not necessary to have taught a particular course to be considered for interview, interviewers may expect candidates to brief themselves about it. In a similar way, if you are expected to teach GCSE double science with a particular board, get an overall picture of the scheme before you attend for interview.

Candidates are sometimes asked to teach a class as part of the interview procedure. You should ask about this possibility prior to interview and check in advance what preparation is expected of you.

Many schools require their science teachers to teach all the sciences to Key Stage 3 and Key Stage 4; other schools direct science teachers into their specialist areas at Key Stage 4. Many independent schools teach the separate sciences from Year 7. Be prepared to respond to questions about your willingness to commit yourself in any of these ways. Your decision depends on your confidence, enthusiasm, personal philosophy and your curriculum knowledge. You should enquire about this aspect of school policy, in advance of the interview, if you have personal preferences for your first post.

Areas in which you can be asked questions are shown in Figure 13.1. You need to consider which of these apply to your situation and prioritise their importance when preparing for interview. Take a portfolio of your best work with you to the interview. This can be used to respond to some questions, e.g. 'How would you set about providing differentiated

A knowledge of subject	Direct question about your subject knowledge in your specialist subject, e.g. describe the forces acting on a ball thrown up in the air.
Application of your subject knowledge	How would you introduce Year 9 pupils to the concept of photosynthesis, or moments, or ions?
Curriculum or syllabus knowledge	I see you used the text *Active Science* on school experience. How did you make use of it in lessons and what criteria would you use to evaluate its usefulness?
Evaluation of lessons	Describe a lesson you have taught that was successful. Tell us about the lesson and the evidence for its success.
Safety, risk assessment and COSHH regulations	How would you set about assessing the safety issues involved in food tests for protein, sugars and starch in Year 8? What risk assessment procedures would you carry out?
Class management, differentiation and motivation	
Equal opportunities	
Special needs including statemented pupils in your class	
Your experience as a form tutor	
Contribution to the extra-curricular life of the school	
Your skills in IT	
Your ability to work with a team	

Figure 13.1 Preparing for interview questions

work for a middle set of pupils in Year 7?' A lesson plan showing evidence of planning for differentiation, that was reasonably successful and was evaluated by you (or a teacher) can be effective and provide a focus for discussion. We discuss portfolios later in this chapter.

TASK 13.1 PREPARING FOR INTERVIEW QUESTIONS

At interview for a first science post you may be asked questions in many areas. Some questions arise from the information in your CV or letter of application. When you write your application, think carefully about the experience or evidence you cite in support of your application so that you can respond confidently in interview.

In Figure 13.1, some areas of expertise are followed by questions. For these examples, prepare a response to these or similar questions.

Other areas of expertise in the table have no commentary. Identify the possible focus of a question in these areas and identify ways in which to respond.

For this task you could work with other student teachers; or the task could be the subject of a class seminar or for discussion with your tutors. Consider ways in which your portfolio can contribute to your response.

Interviews are often unpredictable and stressful, especially your first. Careful preparation encourages confidence and enables you to look business like, relaxed and to be polite. Arrive in good time (a trial journey is often wise). When interviewed, wait to be asked to be seated, get comfortable and put your notes or portfolio in a handy position. If you have prepared questions, make sure they are to hand. Do not fiddle with your pen or papers but try to sit still and look at the interviewer when questioned and when answering. Answer honestly to the best of your ability and do not be afraid to pause and think; if you do not understand the question, ask for it to be repeated. If you do not know the answer to a question, do not waffle but say 'I'm sorry, I do not have an answer to that question' (this is a rare event). Develop the right balance between humour and seriousness, but do not laugh away ignorance.

Following your successful interview, you need to prepare for your first appointment. We suggest you read Unit 8.1 in Capel, Leask and Turner (1995) about ways in which to prepare for this event.

YOUR PERSONAL PROFESSIONAL PORTFOLIO

By the end of your initial course of teacher education, you need to write a statement of your development, using the criteria set for the award of NQT status in England and Wales, or Scotland or Northern Ireland (Appendices 1, 2 and 3). In England and Wales, this statement is referred to as a Career Entry Profile (CEP). This statement may be part of a personal professional portfolio (PPP), which contains a summary and evidence of your achievements.

Your PPP should contain samples of your work throughout the year and include evidence from school experience and college; sources of evidence are shown in Figure 13.2. To help identify your achievements, a suggested list of the qualities needed by science teachers is given in Appendix 4; the list contains knowledge, skills and attitudes acquired by good, experienced teachers and therefore includes some qualities which you have not had the opportunity to demonstrate.

Select carefully for inclusion examples of your work that you could discuss at interview.

School experience	Details of your school experience with evidence of classes taught, by Key Stage and grouping. Also examination classes and post-16.
Lesson plans	Examples that show, e.g. risk assessment, planned learning objectives, differentiated lesson, evaluations of your work by you and others.
Assessment	Evidence of assessment material; investigations prepared and assessed. Assigning level statements to pupil work. Evidence of formative and summative assessment.
Materials produced by you	Worksheets, practical guidance, differentiated tasks, guidance for watching a video; transparency overlays.
Beyond the laboratory	Evidence of planning for field work, visits, out of school activities.
Personal diary	Extracts of a diary kept throughout the year, to show, e.g. personal development, insights, changing viewpoint, challenging circumstances, experience gained at a parents' evening.
Assignments	Written work produced for coursework or other requirements.
Extra-curricular involvement	Example of other activities in school.
IT skills	Evidence of your IT capability and ability to use IT to support your teaching.
Personal statement	A statement of your progress, achievements and personal understanding of science teaching. Evidence of your awareness of your progress in relation to the appropriate standards required of a NQT.

Figure 13.2 Examples of items for inclusion in your personal professional portfolio

Responding to the standards required of a NQT

To write a Career Entry Profile or other personal statement of your development, respond using the headings in the appropriate document (Appendices 1, 2 or 3). Also, refer to the lists in Appendix 4 as a checklist to stimulate thinking and to help identify your strengths and areas for development; see Task 13.2. It is necessary to respond to all the items in Appendix 4; but see also Chapter 1, pp. 12–13.

TASK 13.2 RESPONDING TO THE CRITERIA FOR STANDARDS REQUIRED OF A NQT

Write your personal statement of your development as a science teacher for inclusion in your portfolio. Refer to the appropriate national standards (Appendices 1, 2 or 3), the list of knowledge, skills and attitudes in Appendix 4 and Chapter 1, pp. 12–13.

Collect together a copy of:

- end of term reports from your school experience school;
- evaluations by teachers of your lessons;
- your own teaching file with lesson evaluations;
- the checklist in Appendix 4.
- the appropriate standards or competences (e.g. Appendices 1, 2 or 3).

With the help of the above documents assess your development using the main headings from your national requirements. You may find the four-point scale in Figure 13.3 helpful. Discuss your assessment with your tutors.

Your portfolio or Career Entry Profile, if kept up to date, is helpful in responding to appraisal in your first post.

FUTURE PROFESSIONAL SUPPORT

From student teacher to NQT

We advise that you join a **teaching union** either when you are a student teacher or as soon as you take up your first post. They give general professional advice and through their publications keep you up to date with educational issues and development. The addresses of unions are found in Appendix 5. Unions provide you also with both legal and professional support and they give advice on request.

Use the following guidelines to determine the extent to which you meet the standards, as suggested in Task 13.2. There are, of course, levels of experience and skill beyond 4 (Frost and Jennings, 1995). Decide whether you have:

•••• 4: a reasonably consistent level of skill performance; you feel in control and can make adjustments as necessary. You have a real understanding of the essentials and can apply them at an acceptable level, *given your limited experience*;

••• 3: some knowledge of a skill, through study or by watching other teachers; you have begun to 'have a go' but recognise the tentative nature of your efforts or the unexpected difficulty of the task;

•• 2: awareness of the issue but you have not really had the opportunity to engage with it;

• 1: not really considered this aspect of teaching.

Figure 13.3 Suggested levels of response to the list of knowledge, skills and attitudes needed by science teachers (Appendix 4)
Source: adapted from Frost and Jennings, 1995

We strongly recommend that you join the **Association of Science Education** (ASE). As well as being the major subject professional organisation for science teachers in the UK, it is an international organisation for teachers, advisers, technicians, industrialists and others contributing to science education. The ASE represents you legally in circumstances when, for example, you have an accident in the laboratory and you are sued for negligence – a very rare event; see Hull (1993, pp. 129–47).

The ASE provides a forum for the views of members on science education issues, advice on matters of health and safety, legal advice and conferences on educational issues. Equally important is its role in developing policy and practice in key areas of science education, both nationally and regionally. The ASE publishes journals for primary and secondary teachers as well as book reviews, newsletters and occasional publications on issues of importance, e.g. science investigations. The journals include:

• *Education in Science*;
• *School Science Review*;
• *Post Sixteen Science Issues*;
• *Science Teacher Education*;
• *Primary Science Review*.

The journals are a way of keeping up to date, widening your knowledge and understanding of science and science education. The ASE has annual meetings of international renown and regional meetings, both of which are a way of gaining support, advice and encouragement.

Valuable support and advice is given by a range of **professional and academic organisations**, some of which are listed below. The advice ranges from curriculum matters, publications, science journals, advice and, sometimes, financial grants for projects or curriculum initiatives. For example:

The Royal Society
The Institute of Physics
The Pupil Researcher Initiative
The Biochemical Society
British Association for the Advancement of Science
The Royal Society of Chemistry
The Institute of Biology
The Royal Institution
The Royal Academy of Engineering

These and other addresses are in Appendix 5.

The support such societies give schools is considerable. Many societies have supported developments in the science faculty of one of us (WD) over several years; many initiatives in schools would not have been possible without their financial support and invaluable advice.

Other links and sources of advice and support include IHE, further education colleges, other schools, local industries and neighbourhood engineers. Many institutions often provide speakers on specific topics for your pupils or support for curriculum development.

If your school is an **LEA** maintained school, i.e. not Grant Maintained or independent, you should receive, and be able to seek, advice from attached advisory science teachers or inspectors. Your head of science can advise you on this resource. Enquire about an active local support group, e.g. a regional ASE network, for the exchange of ideas or for INSET throughout your NQT year. Find out from other science teachers in your school where the best local support can be obtained.

The statutory probationary year for NQTs is no longer a national requirement; however, some governing bodies of schools employ staff on a probationary period. All schools have an **induction programme** for NQTs. The specific arrangements depend upon the school and the energy and commitment of the responsible member of staff. Many schools appoint a dedicated mentor to look after new staff. For further details about working with your **mentor** as a NQT, see Capel, Leask and Turner (1997, Chapter 3). You will receive continued support for professional development throughout your teaching career from your science colleagues, your line manager and as a result of appraisal procedures; see also Bolton (1996); McTiffin (1996).

As a NQT you will have increased pupil contact time and less time to concentrate on your own personal development, therefore before taking up your post make sure you find out as much as possible about your timetable, courses and commitment so that you can prepare in advance.

At the start of term you should be given a staff handbook, with details of:

- the induction scheme for new staff and NQTs;
- details of the appraisal process and target setting;
- INSET arrangements and staff development programmes.

You should find out how to apply for courses, if possible before the start of term so that you can seek support for attendance from your head of science. Many local IHE run **subject specific courses** for NQTs. Record both the details and dates in your diary and teacher planner.

TASK 13.3 IDENTIFYING TARGETS

Use your Career Entry Profile to identify the targets for your development in the next year or two. Use the Profile to identify the skills, knowledge and experiences that you wish next to target. Prepare a tentative list of priority areas.

In your first post, other priorities arise from the nature of the post, many of which cannot be anticipated. However, you may find it helpful to know where your priorities lie when planning your future development, e.g. for choice between INSET courses.

Teaching outside your specialist science area

Most science teachers in maintained schools are required to teach the sciences to Key Stage 3 and in some cases to Key Stage 4. A good Scheme of Work often provides enough insight into the topic for you to know where to look for support and recommend a text for you to consult. This text is often the one recommended for the pupils.

We suggest that, when necessary, you consult the subject specialists in your department for advice and clarification. It is important that you identify a text book that you can consult for knowledge and explanation. Many curriculum packages have a teacher's guide that is often useful but does not have the full explanation needed. Some examination boards and the NCC provide up to date information and guidance on particular science topics. Support for non-specialists teaching physics can be found in Osborne (1989).

Another way of widening your experience is to arrange visits for your pupils to local industry, museums and science centres. Involve your pupils in **Science Fairs**, pupil research projects or science theatre groups (Smail and Windale, 1996). Support for pupil research projects in schools can be obtained from the Royal Society, the British Association for Young Scientists and the Standing Council for School Science and Technology; see Appendix 5.

YOUR ROLE AS A FORM TUTOR

During your school experience you have probably been attached to a form in support of a form tutor. As a result of that experience you have developed ideas of your own about this role that you may want to put into practice in your first post. Some teachers say that a form takes on some of the personality of their form tutor. So what type of form tutor do you wish to be?

Your role as a form tutor is an important one in which you become close to many of your tutor group. A number of your pupils look to you for support, guidance and trust. You can have an influence on your pupils' self-esteem and their motivation. One way to support that role is to make time to talk to each pupil individually on a regular basis about their aspirations and difficulties.

As a form tutor, you are concerned with the academic and personal development of your pupils. You are expected to provide information for your pupils and, where appropriate, teach the PSHE programme. This can involve you in leading discussions, often on sensitive issues. Many schools run in-service training courses to help staff with this aspect of their work, especially with guidance on aspects of confidentiality. For further guidance see Chapter 11 and Jennings (1996, Chapter 8).

Of central concern to schools is the level of attainment of their pupils. School development programmes focus on this feature and often emphasise the role of the form tutor in raising attainment. Form tutors are increasingly seen as an important factor in improving academic attainment, and in your first teaching post you may be introduced to academic tutoring. The pastoral dimension to your work is part of the notion of the 'value added' dimension to school performance.

Value added is designed to modify the harsh picture shown by crude league tables based on SAT scores, GCSE grades and GCE A level results. Value added factors try to measure the progress made by a student attributable to the work of the school over and above expectation, for example as judged by the performance of the pupil on entry. The total picture given by examination results and value added is used to plan targets for future development of the school.

Value added analysis of examination performance of groups of pupils in the school takes into account other factors outside the control of the school (such as students' prior attainment and socially determined factors) that might have an impact on public examination results. By controlling these other factors, using statistical methods of analysis, the academic performance of pupils in a school can be presented against the background of expectation at entry. The extent to which the pupils exceed expectation, or not, is a measure of the value added by the school.

Value added data can make comparative performance tables more credible by presenting a clearer picture of pupil progress. The role of the form tutor in a programme of planned tutoring of her pupils contributes significantly to their performance and, in turn, to value added by the school. See Cowling and Gallear (1996); Jesson (1996); Fitz-Gibbon (1995).

The form tutor uses evidence of academic progress and performance provided by subject staff to support **academic tutoring**. Through a series of tutorials, she enables her pupils to develop targets for their own development. Targets are agreed, recorded and deadlines set for their achievement. A key feature of the programme is a monitoring process that provides regular checks on progress and gives support when needed. The process is designed to improve pupil performance, support teaching and enhance learning. Academic tutoring and monitoring can lead to improvement in pupils' performance, motivation and self-esteem. The procedures described are of benefit to pupils beyond school and help them to develop strategies useful in later career development.

By teaching others about taking responsibility for their development, you see two sides of the same coin. Throughout your own career you too need to appraise your progress and development at regular intervals, and, by helping your pupils, you strengthen the process for yourself. You can expect to be appraised by your line manager at regular intervals in your career. Appraisal followed by targeted support and in-service work is part of your professional development and one way in which your school supports you. The procedures described are all part of what 'being professional' is about and is actively supported by the Teacher Training Agency. We suggest you read 'Developing further as a teacher' for more details (Capel, Leask and Turner, 1995, Unit 8.2).

SUMMARY

Education is marked by continuous change and you need to prepare yourself for such a career. You need to be able to adapt to change in a world that is increasingly technologically based and an education system that has to be increasingly accountable to society. One area in which change is imminent is the post-16 curriculum and the extent to which vocational education develops in relation to the traditional academic curriculum. You should keep an eye open for developments in GNVQ courses.

The demands on a science teacher are often seen to be greater than in other subject areas, although colleagues will challenge that assumption. In the generic book *Learning to Teach in the Secondary School* (Capel, Leask and Turner, 1995), the authors address the task of 'developing further as a teacher' and 'your accountability, contractual and statutory duties'; we recommend you read those units before taking up your first post.

> A load of books does not equal one good teacher.
>
> (Hart, quoted in Styles, 1986, p. 42)

The most important resource is you. Retain a sense of humour, learn to relax and find time for yourself at the end of each day or week. Most pupils are enjoyable to teach and many pupils wish to understand science; teaching can be rewarding. Try not to worry about things you cannot change and focus instead on those that you can do something about. Maintain a sense of proportion between work and play. While building your career, do not lose sight of what you value most in your teaching, in your career in your personal life and what it means to be human.

FURTHER READING

Hoyle, E. and Johns, P. (1995) *Professional Knowledge and Professional Practice*, London: Cassell.
  A useful text that explores the issues surrounding professional knowledge and practice.

Woolnough, B.E. (1994) *Effective Science Teaching*, Buckingham: Open University Press.
A useful book that highlights good practice.

Wellington, J. (1994) *Secondary Science, Contemporary Issues and Practical Approaches*, London: Routledge.
A thorough guide, answering major questions on many aspects of science education, including sensitive and controversial issues.

Pring, R. (1996) 'The year 2000', in M. Wilkin and D. Sankey (eds) (1994) *Collaboration and Transition in Initial Teacher Training*, London: Kogan Page.
This chapter provides a useful discussion about the future of professional development of teachers.

Appendix 1 Standards of knowledge, understanding and skills required by newly qualified teachers in secondary schools in England and Wales

Extracts from: Annex A, Circular 10/97 *Teaching: High Status, High Standards: Requirements for Courses of Initial Teacher Training* (Department for Education and Employment (DFEE) 1997a)

Qualified Teacher Status (QTS) is a requirement for all those who teach in a maintained school. The standards for QTS are set out under the following headings:

A Knowledge and Understanding
B Planning, Teaching and Class Management
C Monitoring, Assessment, Recording, Reporting and Accountability
D Other Professional Requirements

The details for each standard for secondary teachers are set out below.

A   KNOWLEDGE AND UNDERSTANDING

For all courses, those to be awarded Qualified Teacher Status must, when assessed, demonstrate that they:

1 have a secure knowledge and understanding of the concept and skills in their specialist subject(s)[1] at a standard equivalent to degree level to enable them to teach it (them) confidently and accurately at

- KS3 for trainees on 7–14 courses;
- KS3 and KS4 and, where relevant, post–16 for trainees on 11–16 or 18 courses;
- KS4 and post–16 for trainees on 14–19 courses;

2 have, for their specialist subject(s), where applicable, a detailed knowledge and understanding of the National Curriculum programmes of study, level descriptions or end of key stage descriptions for KS3 and, where applicable, National Curriculum programmes of study for KS4;

3 for Religious Education (RE) specialists, have a detailed knowledge of the model syllabuses for RE;

4 are familiar, for their specialist subject(s), with the relevant KS4 and post-16 examination syllabuses and courses, including vocational courses[2]

5 understand, for their specialist subject(s), the framework of 14–19 course qualifications and the routes of progression through it[2];

6 understand, for their specialist subject(s), progression from the KS2 programmes of study[3];

7 know and can teach the key skills required for current qualifications relevant to their specialist subject, for pupils aged 14–19, and understand the contribution that their specialist subject(s) makes to the development of key skills;

8 cope securely with subject-related questions which pupils raise;

9 are aware of, and know how to access, recent inspection evidence and classroom relevant research evidence on teaching secondary pupils in their specialist subject(s), and know how to use this to inform and improve their teaching;

10 know, understand, for their specialist subject(s), pupils' most common misconceptions and mistakes;

11 understand how pupils' learning in the subject is affected by their physical, intellectual, emotional and social development;

12 have a working knowledge of information technology (IT) to a standard equivalent to level 8 in the National Curriculum for pupils, and understand the contribution that IT makes to their specialist subject[4];

13 are familiar with subject-specific health and safety requirements, where relevant, and plan lessons to avoid potential hazards.

B PLANNING, TEACHING AND CLASS MANAGEMENT

For all courses, those to be awarded Qualified Teacher Status must, when assessed, demonstrate that they:

Planning

A plan their teaching to achieve progression in children's learning through:

1 identifying clear teaching objectives and content, appropriate to the subject matter and the pupils being taught, and specifying how these will be taught and assessed;

2 setting tasks for whole class, individual and group work, including homework, which challenge pupils and ensure high levels of pupil interest;

3 setting appropriate and demanding expectations for pupils' learning, motivation and presentation of work;

4 setting clear targets for pupils' learning, building on prior attainment, and ensuring that pupils are aware of the substance and purpose of what they are asked to do;

5 identifying pupils who:

- have special educational needs, including specific learning difficulties;
- are very able;
- are not yet fluent in English;

and knowing where to get help in order to give positive and targeted support;

B provide clear structures for lessons, and sequences of lessons, in the short, medium and longer term, which maintain pace, motivation and challenge for pupils;

C make effective use of assessment information on pupils' attainment and progress in their teaching and in planning future lessons and sequences of lessons;

D plan opportunities to contribute to pupils' personal, spiritual, moral, social and cultural development;

E where applicable, ensure coverage of the relevant examination syllabuses and National Curriculum programmes of study.

Teaching and class management.

For all courses, those to be awarded Qualified Teacher Status must, when assessed, demonstrate that they:

F ensure effective teaching of whole classes, and of groups and individuals within the whole class setting, so that teaching objectives are met, and best use is made of available teaching time;

G monitor and intervene when teaching to ensure sound learning and discipline;

H establish and maintain a purposeful working atmosphere;

I set high expectations for pupils' behaviour, establishing and maintaining a good standard of discipline through well-focused teaching and through positive and productive relationships;

J establish a safe environment which supports learning and in which pupils feel secure and confident;

K use teaching methods which sustain the momentum of pupils' work and keep all pupils engaged through:

1 stimulating intellectual curiosity, communicating enthusiasm for the subject being taught, fostering pupils' enthusiasm and maintaining pupils' motivation;

2 matching the approaches used to the subject matter and the pupils being taught;

3 structuring information well, including content and aims, signalling transitions and summarising key points as the lesson progresses;

4 clear presentation of content around a set of key ideas, using appropriate subject-specific vocabulary and well-chosen illustrations and examples;

5 clear instruction and demonstration and accurate well-paced explanation;

6 effective questioning which matches the pace and direction of the lesson and ensures that the pupils take part;

7 careful attention to pupils' errors and misconceptions, and helping to remedy them;

8 listening carefully to pupils, analysing their responses and responding constructively in order to take pupils' learning forward;

9 selecting and making good use of textbooks, IT and other learning resources which enable teaching objectives to be met;

10 providing opportunities to pupils to consolidate their knowledge and maximising opportunities, both in the classroom and through setting well-focused homework, to reinforce and develop what has been learnt;

11 exploiting opportunities to improve pupils' basic skills in literacy, numeracy and IT, and the individual and collaborative study skills needed for effective learning, including information retrieval from libraries, texts and other sources;

12 exploiting opportunities to contribute to the quality of pupils' wider educational development, including their personal, spiritual, moral, social and cultural development;

13 setting high expectations for all pupils notwithstanding individual differences, including gender, and cultural and linguistic backgrounds;

14 providing opportunities to develop pupils' wider understanding by relating their learning to real and work-related examples;

L are familiar with the Code of Practice on the identification and assessment of special educational needs and, as part of their responsibilities under the Code, implement and keep records on individual action plans (IEPS) for pupils at stage 2 of the code and above;

M ensure that pupils acquire and consolidate knowledge, skills and understanding in the subject;

N evaluate their own teaching critically and use this to improve their effectiveness.

C MONITORING, ASSESSMENT, RECORDING, REPORTING AND ACCOUNTABILITY

For all courses, those to be awarded Qualified Teacher Status must, when assessed, demonstrate that they:

A assess how well learning objectives have been achieved and use this assessment to improve specific aspects of teaching;

B mark and monitor pupils' assigned classwork and homework, providing constructive oral and written feedback, and setting targets for pupils' progress;

C assess and record each pupil's progress systematically, including through focused observation, questioning, testing and marking, and use these records to:

1 check that pupils have understood and completed the work;

2 monitor strengths and weakness and use the information gained as a basis for purposeful intervention in pupils' learning;

3 inform planning;

4 check that pupils continue to make demonstrable progress in their acquisition of the knowledge, skills and understanding of the subject;

D are familiar with the statutory assessment and reporting requirements and know how to prepare and present informative reports to parents;

E where applicable, understand the expected demands of pupils in relation to each relevant level description or end of key stage description, and, in addition, for those on 11–16 or 18 and 14–19 courses, the demands of the syllabuses and course requirements for GCSE, other KS4 courses, and where applicable, post-16 courses;

F where applicable, understand and know how to implement the assessment requirements of current qualifications for pupils aged 14–19;

G recognise the level at which a pupil is achieving, and assess pupils consistently against attainment targets, where applicable, if necessary with guidance from an experienced teacher;

H understand and know how national, local, comparative and school data, including national curriculum test data, where applicable, can be used to set clear targets for pupils' achievement;

I use different kinds of assessment appropriately for different purposes, including national curriculum and other standardised tests, and baseline assessment where relevant.

D OTHER PROFESSIONAL REQUIREMENTS

For all courses, those to be awarded Qualified Teacher Status must, when assessed, demonstrate that they:

A have a working knowledge and understanding of:

1 teachers' professional duties as set out in the current School Teachers' Pay and Conditions document, issued under the School Teachers' Pay and Conditions Act 1991;

2 teachers' liabilities and responsibilities relating to:

- the Race Relations Act 1976;
- The Sex Discrimination Act 1975;
- Section 7 and Section 8 of the Health and Safety at Work etc., Act 1974
- teachers' common law duty to ensure that pupils are healthy and safe on school premises and when leading activities off the school site, such as educational visits, school outings, or field trips;
- what is reasonable for the purposes of safeguarding or promoting children's welfare (Section 3 (5) of the Children Act 1989);
- the role of the education service in protecting children from abuse (currently set out in DfEE circular 10/95 and the Home Office, Department of Health, DfEE and the Welsh Office guidance working together: a guide to arrangements for inter-agency co-operation for the protection of children from abuse 1991);

- appropriate physical contact with pupils (currently set out in the DfEE circular 10/95);
- appropriate physical restraint of pupils (Section 4 of the Education Act 1997 and DfEE Circular 9/94);
- detention of pupils on disciplinary grounds (Section 5 of the Education Act 1997)

B   have established, during work in schools, effective working relationships with professional colleagues including, where applicable, associate staff;

C   set a good example to the pupils they teach, through their presentation and personal and professional conduct;

D   are committed to ensuring that every pupil is given the opportunity to achieve their potential and meet the high expectations set for them;

E   understand the need to take responsibility for their own professional development and to keep up to date with research and developments in pedagogy and in the subjects they teach;

F   understand their professional responsibilities in relation to school policies and practices, including those concerned with pastoral and personal safety matters, including bullying;

G   recognise that learning takes place inside and outside the school context, and understand the need to liaise effectively with parents and other carers and with agencies with responsibility for pupils' education and welfare;

H   are aware of the role and purpose of school governing bodies.

NOTES

1   Required subject knowledge for those teaching science at secondary level will be specified when the ITT National Curricula are implemented.
2   This does not apply to trainees on 7–14 courses.
3   This does not apply to trainees on 14–19 courses.
4   Trainees may omit the 'control' element of the ITT National Curriculum Order if this is not relevant to their specialist subject. This standard does not apply until September 1998.

Appendix 2
Teacher competences for Scotland

Extract from: The Scottish Office Education Department (1993) *Teacher Competences 'Guidelines for teacher training courses'*, Edinburgh: The Scottish Office Department for Education.

2. THE COMPETENCES

2.1 Competences relating to subject and content of teaching

The new teacher should be able to:

- demonstrate a knowledge of the subject or subjects forming the content of his or her teaching which meets and goes beyond the immediate demands of the school curriculum
- plan generally, and in particular prepare coherent teaching programmes which ensure continuity and progression, taking into account national, regional and school curriculum policies and plan lessons within these teaching programmes
- select appropriate resources for learning, for example from radio and television broadcasts
- present the content of what is taught in an appropriate fashion to pupils
- justify what is taught from knowledge and understanding of the learning process, curriculum issues, child development in general and the needs of his or her pupils in particular.

2.2 Competences relating to the classroom

2.2.1 Communication

The new teacher should be able to:

- present what he or she is teaching in clear language and a stimulating manner

- question pupils effectively, respond and support their discussion and questioning.

2.2.2 Methodology

The new teacher should be able to:

- employ a range of teaching strategies appropriate to the subject or topic and, on the basis of careful assessment, to the pupils in his or her classes
- identify suitable occasions for teaching the class as a whole, in groups, in pairs or as individuals
- create contexts in which pupils can learn
- set expectations which make appropriate demands on pupils
- identify and respond appropriately to pupils with special educational needs or with learning difficulties
- take into account cultural differences among pupils
- encourage pupils to take initiatives in and become responsible for, their own learning
- select and use in a considered way a wide variety of resources, including information technology
- evaluate and justify the methodology being used.

2.2.3 Class management

The new teacher should have knowledge of the principles which lie behind the keeping of good discipline and should be able to:

- deploy a range of approaches to create and maintain a purposeful, orderly and safe environment for learning
- manage pupil behaviour by the use of appropriate rewards and sanctions and be aware when it is necessary to seek advice
- sustain the interest and motivation of the pupils
- evaluate and justify his or her own actions in managing pupils.

2.2.4 Assessment

The new teacher should:

- have an understanding of the principles of assessment and the different kinds of assessment which may be used
- be able to assess the quality of pupils' learning against national standards defined for that particular group of pupils

- be able to assess and record systematically the progress of individual pupils
- be able to provide regular feedback to pupils on their progress
- be able to use assessment to evaluate and improve teaching.

2.3 Competences relating to the school

The new teacher should:

- have some knowledge of the system in which he or she is working and in particular of the organisation and management systems of schools, of school policies and development plans and where they relate to his or her teaching
- know how to discuss with parents a range of issues relevant to their children
- be informed about school boards
- know how to communicate with members of other professions concerned with the welfare of school pupils and with members of the community served by the school, as well as with colleagues within the school and its associated schools
- be aware of sources of help and expertise within the school and how they can be used
- be aware of cross-curricular aspects of school work and able to make an input into these
- have interests and skills which can contribute to activities with pupils outside the formal curriculum.

2.4 Competences related to professionalism

The new teacher should:

- have a working knowledge of his or her pastoral, contractual, legal and administrative responsibilities
- be able to make a preliminary evaluation of his or her own professional progress.

However, professionalism implies more than a mere series of competences. It also implies a set of attitudes which have particular power in that they are communicated to those being taught:

- a commitment to the job and to those affected by the job
- a commitment to self-monitoring and continuing professional development

- a commitment to collaborate with others to promote pupil achievement
- a commitment to promoting the moral and spiritual well-being of pupils
- a commitment to the community within and beyond the school and to promoting a responsible attitude towards the needs of the environment
- a commitment to views of fairness and equality of opportunity as expressed in multi-cultural and other non-discriminatory policies.

Appendix 3
Competences expected of newly qualified teachers in Northern Ireland

Extract from: Department of Education Northern Ireland (1996) *Arrangements for Initial Teacher Training in Northern Ireland from 1st September 1996*, London: HMSO.

AREAS OF COMPETENCE

The competences are grouped around five areas (see below). A set of key competences for Newly Qualified Teachers are recognised for reporting purposes and it is these which are listed below. In the document these key competences are expanded into 89 statements. This full set of competences apply to teachers in initial teacher education, induction and the early years of further professional development.

KEY COMPETENCES FOR NQTS

1 Understanding of the curriculum and professional knowledge

(The teacher):

- demonstrates understanding of the requirements of the Northern Ireland Curriculum, and in particular, of the areas of study and the educational themes embodied in it and of their interdependence.
- demonstrates knowledge of the range of resources available to support the curriculum, including Information Technology.
- demonstrates knowledge of child development and an understanding of how it can be promoted.
- demonstrates a knowledge of the various ways in which children learn, both generally and in particular subject contexts.

- demonstrates knowledge of the principles involved in fostering good discipline.

2 Subject knowledge and subject application

(The teacher):

- demonstrates understanding appropriate to the demands of the school curriculum for the relevant age phase, of the knowledge, concepts and skills of his or her specialist subject.
- demonstrates breadth of knowledge in all of the subjects forming the content of his or her teaching and an awareness of their contribution to areas of study.
- plans appropriate lessons within teaching programmes.
- demonstrates a knowledge of the particular methodologies and procedures necessary for effective teaching of the subject(s) being taught.
- shows awareness of potential areas of learning difficulty within the subject(s).
- plans schemes of lessons, taking account of continuity and progression (more experienced students only).

3 Teaching strategies and techniques and classroom management

(The teacher):

- plans and employs a wide range of teaching strategies (including the use of a whole class, group, pair or individual modes) appropriate to the age, ability, interests, experiences and attainment level of the pupils and to the objectives to each lesson.
- can justify the teaching methods being used.
- can identify and respond to relevant individual differences between pupils and sets appropriately demanding expectations for learning performance.
- is able to recognise pupils' special needs and provides appropriately for these.
- contributes to ensuring continuity and progression in children's learning within and between classes and subjects.
- establishes good classroom rapport; captures and maintains pupils' attention, interest and involvement.

- makes appropriate use of the range of resources available to support the curriculum, including Information Technology.
- establishes clear rules and expectations regarding pupils' behaviour and deals with inappropriate behaviour.
- manages his or her own time and that of the pupils effectively.
- seeks advice when necessary.

4 Assessment and recording of pupils' progress

(The teacher):

- assesses and records pupils' performance in a systematic manner, using attainment targets and level descriptions where applicable.
- uses different methods of assessment as appropriate, in order to monitor the progress of individual children.
- uses the outcomes of assessment, as appropriate, in order to evaluate teaching and plan for the future.
- provides feedback with regular, thorough feedback on their progress in a constructive manner which fosters their self confidence and self esteem.

5 Foundation for further professional development

(The teacher):
- shows a pastoral concern for pupils.
- develops effective working relationships with teachers and other colleagues within the school and, where applicable, in associated schools.
- contributes to activities with pupils outside the formal curriculum.
- demonstrates awareness of the importance of informed, critical reflection in evaluating his or her professional practice.

Appendix 4
The knowledge, skills and attitudes required by effective science teachers

The statements in this Appendix were developed by members of a research project investigating ways of using the DFE Statements of competence (Department for Education and the Welsh Office (DFE/WO, 1992) with science teachers during their initial teacher education course. The authors of this book are indebted to Arthur Jennings, Jenny Frost and Alastair Cuthbertson, Science and Technology, Institute of Education, University of London for permission to reproduce their work. See Frost and Jennings (1995, 1996).

Readers should note that the statements of competence (DFE/WO, 1992) have been replaced in England and Wales by a set of statutory standards (DFEE, 1997a); see Appendix 1. In addition, not all statutory or non-statutory general course requirements leading to QTS are necessarily met by the material in this appendix.

In Appendix 4, under 'Subject Knowledge' the abbreviation 'AT' refers to Attainment Target of the National Curriculum (NC) Science pre-1995 in England and Wales. In the current NC Science (DFE, 1995b) the former sections AT1–AT4 are now described under the 'Programme of Study' at each key stage and referred to by teachers as Sc1, Sc2 etc.; see chapter 2, pp. 34–5.

USING THE STATEMENTS

The lists that follow represent much of the knowledge, skills and attitudes that good science teachers need to develop. We suggest that they apply not only to you as a new teachers in school but throughout your career. Although we make reference to the statutory standards that relate to England and Wales, the modified list can be applied to standards or competences in other contexts; see Appendices 1, 2 and 3. In the context of the DFE Circular (DFE/WO, 1992), competence to teach referred to attainment at 'a level appropriate to newly qualified teachers'. To many teachers in school this working definition, despite its imprecision, has meaning. It accommodates diversity while implying minimum standards.

Not all teachers display the knowledge, skills and attitudes in the same way and not all teachers have acquired them. This list of statements should be treated as a guideline for your development, as a means of dialogue with colleagues, especially with your tutors as well as at a personal level as a means of reviewing and reflecting on your professional development. The list is not a checklist to be ticked off as 'done'. One way of using them is described in Figure 13.3.

Your development as a teacher on your course of initial teacher education is rapid but some skills develop before others, e.g. attention to classroom management precedes assessment of pupil learning. Thus we have left columns headed term 1, 2 and 3 to suggest that you should identify some qualities early in the first term on which to concentrate. The rate and order in which these qualities develop depends on you, the demands of your course, your school placements and the opportunities they bring. Discuss this list of knowledge, skills and attitudes regularly as part of evaluation of your teaching, reflection on your progress and as a way of interpreting your national requirements referred to above. It has at its heart a formative function, to provide you with the means of evaluating and diagnosing your own progress. It can be helpful also in constructing your Career Entry Profile; see Chapter 13.

Ways of using this list are given in the text, especially in Chapter 1 and Chapter 13.

Subject knowledge

This includes **knowledge** *of* science, and **knowledge** *about* science – both as a discipline in itself and its place in the curriculum.

Newly qualified teachers should:

		Term 1	2	3
Kn1	know and understand the scientific facts, concepts and principles associated with ATs 2, 3 and 4 of National Curriculum Science up to and including Key Stage 3;			
Kn2	know and understand the scientific facts, concepts and principles for at least **one** science subject at Key Stage 4, and **one** science subject at A level;			
Kn3	understand the procedures required for AT1 and the relation of AT1 to ATs 2, 3 and 4;			
Kn4	know the standard laboratory procedures and the standard laboratory apparatus applicable to standards Kn1, 2 and 3;			
Kn5	appreciate the extent of specialist language used in science;			
Kn6	be familiar with different views on the relation between science and society;			
Kn7	be familiar with contemporary views on the nature of scientific knowledge and of the scientific endeavour;			
Kn8	understand thinking about links between science and technology.			

Subject curriculum knowledge

SCK1	know the different applications of microcomputers for science teaching;			
SCK2	know and understand the relevant health and safety regulations and practices;			
SCK3	know at least basic aspects of care and maintenance of equipment and materials (including living material) within the areas appropriate to Kn1 and 2;			
SCK4	have a working knowledge of the resources available for science teaching, including museums visits and field work;			
SCK5	understand the place of science in the whole curriculum, its relationship to other subjects including mathematics, technology and geography, and its relationship to cross-curricular themes such as sex education, health education and environmental education;			
SCK6	understand the implications of, and arguments for, science education as an entitlement of every pupil in school;			
SCK7	have some familiarity with the history of science education and details of present models of organisation of science in the curriculum.			

Subject application

Making science teaching alive and effective in the classroom and laboratory.

Newly qualified teachers should be able to:

		Term		
		1	2	3
App1	translate scientific knowledge into explanations appropriate to pupils at different ages and levels;			
App2	use appropriate language for pupils of different ages, levels, abilities, interest;			
App3	apply knowledge of the role of language in learning to their science teaching;			
App4	develop pupils' language and communication skills through science;			
App5	produce coherent lesson plans with clearly defined aims and learning objectives;			
App6	produce coherent lesson plans that take account of NC programmes of study in science, the department's Scheme of Work, school curriculum policies, safety regulations, and pupils' existing knowledge, skills and learning capabilities;			
App7	produce coherent topic plans that take account of NC programmes of study in science, the department's Scheme of Work, school curriculum policies, safety regulations, and pupils' existing knowledge, skills and learning capabilities;			
App8	plan lessons that relate science to technology and society and which may involve consideration of controversial issues;			
App9	prepare schemes of work and topic plans which take account of pupils' experiences in geography, mathematics, and technology;			
App10	evaluate the way teaching of key scientific skills and concepts are linked in schemes of work from one year to the next;			
App11	plan so as to provide for a range and balance of science topics over a whole school year;			
App12	appraise science education resources and give reasons for the selection of materials that take account of gender and cultural origins and which reflect the global nature of scientific endeavour;			
App13	demonstrate practical techniques and use laboratory equipment clearly, correctly and safely;			
App14	create and maintain a stimulating and interesting environment in the classroom.			

Teaching strategies, class management and evaluation

Organising the lesson content and creating the environment for orderly and purposeful learning of science. Monitoring the effectiveness of teaching and management.

a. Pupils' learning

Newly qualified teachers should:

		Term		
		1	2	3
PL1	be aware of, and understand, the substantial body of evidence about how children learn science and the ideas about science that they develop;			
PL2	understand how development of pupils' intellectual abilities relates to learning science;			
PL3	understand study skills and encourage their development in pupils;			
PL4	plan and conduct lessons that apply an understanding of the way children learn science.			

b. Teaching strategies

Newly qualified teachers should:

		Term		
		1	2	3
TS1	choose and use appropriate teaching strategies for specific purposes and pupil groups;			
TS2	plan and conduct lessons for different age and ability groups that have discrete periods of different activities;			
TS3	plan and conduct lessons that over a period of time involve many different learning strategies and consequent management techniques, e.g. discussion, role play, field work, use of texts and videos, exposition, practical work, theory lessons, etc.;			
TS4	select appropriate practical activities consistent with the learning approach, ensuring that the equipment is appropriate for the characteristics (including behaviour) of the teaching group;			
TS5	use audio-visual resources effectively in teaching;			
TS6	use Information Technology appropriately in lessons.			

c. Management

Newly qualified teachers should:

Term

		1	2	3
Man1	observe school procedures for ordering apparatus and equipment;			
Man2	carry out risk assessment for laboratory lessons reliably;			
Man3	organise classroom and practical work with due regard to safety and care of pupils and apparatus;			
Man4	achieve harmonious working by grouping pupils appropriately for the teaching strategy chosen (small groups, pairs, whole class, etc.);			
Man5	achieve the distribution and collection of equipment in an orderly and efficient manner;			
Man6	ensure that pupils are appropriately instructed on the procedures for use of equipment;			
Man7	use their awareness of the differences amongst pupils in attitudes to science, in confidence with apparatus, in interest, etc. to organise classes so as not to reinforce stereotypes, such as those associated with gender;			
Man8	ensure that rooms are maintained as orderly scientific working environments;			

d. Lesson evaluation

Newly qualified teachers should be able to:

Term

		1	2	3
LE1	evaluate the extent of achievement of lesson objectives;			
LE2	evaluate the lesson in terms of a range of pupils' learning;			
LE3	make constructive suggestions for improvement to the lesson.			

Assessment, recording and reporting

Making accurate and informative judgements about pupils' progress.

Newly qualified teachers should:

		Term		
		1	2	3
Ass1	appreciate the merits and limitations of a wide range of assessment techniques applicable to science;			
Ass2	understand the characteristics of norm and criterion referenced assessment and the use of assessment for formative, diagnostic and summative purposes;			
Ass3	select and use reliably appropriate assessment techniques to monitor pupils' knowledge of facts, processes and concepts;			
Ass4	select and use reliably appropriate assessment techniques to monitor pupils' achievements in application of science, comprehension and their awareness of the social and economic consequences of science;			
Ass5	select and use reliably appropriate assessment techniques to assess pupils' practical skills;			
Ass6	select and use reliably appropriate assessment techniques to monitor pupils' planning and performance of investigations;			
Ass7	value, use and record oral and other ephermeral evidence for assessment;			
Ass8	apply assessment techniques to identify learning failure and to diagnose the point of difficulty (this applies to all pupils, from those classified as 'slow learner' to those classified as 'gifted');			
Ass9	provide constructive (formative) feedback to pupils through oral and written comments;			
Ass10	maintain detailed records of pupils' assessments;			
Ass11	understand the principles applying to pupil profiles and records of achievement;			
Ass12	contribute appropriately to pupils' profiles and assist pupils' in their own self-assessment and record making;			
Ass13	communicate positive achievement of pupils to parents, teachers, employers and HE;			
Ass14	understand the difficulties of assessing attitudes and the place of attitude judgements in reporting on pupils;			
Ass15	understand and participate in moderation procedures;			
Ass16	critically evaluate the effectiveness of different modeels of assessment;			
Ass17	make planning for assessment an intrinsic part of lesson planning.			

Personal skills

Aspects of personality that are apparent when teaching and which can be consciously cultivated.

Newly qualified teachers should be able to:

		Term	
		1	2	3

		Term 1	Term 2	Term 3
PS1	create and maintain a purposeful, safe and supportive environment for pupils' learning;			
PS2	communicate clearly with pupils through questioning, instructing, explaining and feedback;			
PS3	develop and sustain good, collaborative working relationships with pupils 1 at Key Stage 3 2 at Key Stage 4 3 post-16;			
PS4	incorporate motivational material into the start of lessons and sustain the motivation throughout lessons;			
PS5	generate enthusiasm, motivate pupils and maintain their interest;			
PS6	manage time effectively;			
PS7	maintain a live personal interest in science as a flourishing and active discipline.			

Further professional development

Newly qualified teachers should have acquired the foundation necessary to become active and informed members of a science department and a whole school staff and readiness to develop

		Term		
		1	2	3
FPD1	a working knowledge of their contractual, legal, administrative and pastoral responsibilities as teachers, and the particular issues that relate to science teaching;			
FPD2	an ability to discuss, critically and constructively, curriculum content and applications with colleagues, so that they can contribute to course development and planning;			
FPD3	collaborative and effective working relationships with the technical and other support staff;			
FPD4	a particular interest in an aspect of science education which they can contribute to a science department, e.g. science and drama, IT in science, field studies;			
FPD5	the ability to evaluate pupils' learning and recognise the effects on that learning of teachers' expectations and actions;			
FPD6	an awareness of governor influence and control, especially with respect to sex-education policy;			
FPD7	a recognition of the legislative framework for the curriculum and the processes for curriculum change;			
FPD8	awareness of the role of the Association of Science Education in the promotion of science in schools;			
FPD9	their knowledge on special education needs in relation to science teaching;			
FPD10	their ability to promote the spiritual, moral, social and cultural development of pupils through teaching science.			

Appendix 5
Useful addresses

GOVERNMENT OFFICES

Curriculum Council for Wales
Castle Buildings
Womanby Street
Cardiff CF1 9SX
Telephone: 01222 375 400

Department for Education and
    Employment
Sanctuary Buildings
Great Smith Street
London SW1P 3BT
Telephone: 0171 925 5000

Department for Education for
    Northern Ireland
Rathgael House
Balloo Road
Bangor
Co Down BT19 7PR
Telephone: 01247 279 279

Northern Ireland Curriculum
    Council (NICC)
29 Clarendon Road
Belfast
BT1 3BG
Telephone: 01232 261 200

Qualifications and Curriculum
    Authority (QCA)
Newcome House
45 Notting Hill Gate
London W11 3JB
Telephone: 0171 229 1234

Scottish Office Education and
    Industry Department
Victoria Quay
Edinburgh
EH6 6QQ
Telephone: 01315 568 400

Scottish Consultative Council for the
    Curriculum (SCCC)
Gardyne Road
Broughty Ferry
Dundee DD5 1NY
Telephone: 01382 455 053

Welsh Office Education
    Department
Crown Building
Cathays Park
Cardiff
CF1 3NQ
Telephone: 01222 825 111

TEACHING UNIONS

Association of Teachers and
    Lecturers
7 Northumberland Street
London WC2N 5DA
Telephone: 0171 930 6441

National Union of Teachers
Hamilton House
Mableton Place
London WC1H 9BD
Telephone: 0171 388 6191

National Association of
Schoolmasters Union of Women
Teachers
Hillscourt Education Centre
Rednal
Birmingham B45 8RS
Telephone: 0121 453 6150

PROFESSIONAL ASSOCIATIONS, SOCIETIES AND SUPPORT SERVICES

The Association for Science
Education
College Lane
Hatfield
Hertfordshire AL10 9AA
Telephone: 01707 267 411

British Association for the Advancement of Science (BAAS)
23 Saville Row
London W1X 1AB
Telephone: 0171 973 3500

The Biochemical Society
59 Portland Place
Piccadilly
London W1N 3AJ
Telephone: 0171 580 5530

The British National Space Centre
151 Buckingham Palace Road
London SW1 9SS
Telephone: 0171 215 0704

British Society for the History of
Science
31 High Street
Stanford in the Vale
Farringdon
Oxon SN7 8LH
Telephone: 01367 718 963

CLEAPSS School Science Service
Brunel University

Uxbridge UB8 3PH
Telephone: 01895 251 496

Council for Environmental Education
University of Reading
London Road
Reading
Berkshire RG1 5AQ
Telephone: 01189 756 061

Earth Science Teachers Association
61 Hazelmere Road
Liphook
Hants GU30 7BN
Telephone: 01420 475 548

The Engineering Council
10 Maltravers Street
London WC2R 3ER
Telephone: 0171 240 7891

Field Studies
Field Studies Council
Central Services
Preston Montford
Montford Bridge
Shrewsbury SY4 1HW
Telephone: 01743 850 674

The Geological Society
Burlington House
Piccadilly
London W1V 9HG
Telephone: 0171 434 9944

The Institute of Biology
20 Queensway Place
London SW7 2DZ
Telephone: 0171 581 8333

The Institute of Physics
76 Portland Place
London W1N 3DH
Telephone: 0171 470 4800

The Natural History Museum
Cromwell Road
South Kensington

London SW7 5BD
Telephone: 0171 938 8723

National Council for Educational
    Technology (NCET)
Milburn Hill Road
Science Park
Coventry CV4 7JJ
Telephone: 01203 416 994

National Foundation for Educational
    Research (NFER) see Educational
    Authorities Directory, below.

The National SATRO (Science and
    Technology Regional Organisa-
    tions) Co-ordinator
Science, Design and Technology
    Centre
Middle Lane
Kingsly, Frodsham
Cheshire WA6 6TZ
Telephone: 01928 788 854

Neighbourhood Engineers
The Engineering Council
Trinity Centre
Block B1
Franhams Road
Ware
Herts SG12 7PT
Telephone: 01920 888 161

The Royal Academy of Engineering
29 Great Peter Street
London SW1 3LW
Telephone: 0171 222 2688/227 0500

The Royal Institution
21 Albemarle Street
London W1X 4BS
Telephone: 0171 409 2992

The Royal Society
6 Carlton House Terrace
London SW1Y 5AG
Telephone: 0171 839 5561

The Royal Society of Chemistry
Burlington House
Piccadilly
London W1V OBN
Telephone: 0171 437 8656

Royal Society for the Protection of
    Birds
The Lodge
Sandy
Bedfordshire ST19 2DL
Telephone: 01767 680 551

Science Line
Broadcasting Support Service
252 Western Avenue
London W3 6XJ
Telephone: 0345 600 444

The Science Museum
Exhibition Road
London SW7 2DD
Telephone: 0171 938 8222

Science and Technology Regional
    Organisations (SATRO)
c/o Standing Conference on School
    Science and Technology (SCSST)
1 Giltspur Street
London EC1A 9DD
Telephone: 0171 294 2431

INDUSTRIAL AND RELATED ORGANISATIONS

British Broadcasting Corporation
    (BBC)
BBC Education
British Broadcasting Corporation
White City
201 Wood Lane
London W12 7TS
Telephone: 0181 752 5252

BP Educational Service
PO Box 934

Bournemouth
Dorset BH8 8YY
Telephone: 01202 669 940

British Telecom (BT)
BT Centre
81 Newgate Street
London EC1A 7AJ
Telephone: 0171 356 5000

British Nuclear Fuels Ltd (BNFL)
BNLF Education Unit
PO Box 10
Wetherby
West Yorkshire LS23 7EL
Telephone: 01937 840 209

British Steel Plc
British Steel Education Service
PO Box 10
Wetherby
West Yorkshire LS23 7EL
Telephone: 01937 840 243

Creativity in Science and Technology
(CREST)
1 Giltspur Street
London EC1A 2DD
Telephone: 0171 294 3099

Electricity Association
30 Millbank
London SW1P 4RD
Telephone: 0171 963 5839

ESSO Information Service
PO Box 46
Hounslow
Middlesex TW4 6NF
Telephone: 0181 759 0939

Glaxo Welcome plc
Gunnels Wood Road
Stevenage
Hertfordshire SG1 2NY
Telephone: 01438 745 745

Health and Safety Executive
  Information Centre
Broad Lane
Sheffield S3 7HQ
Telephone: 0114 289 2000

Health and Safety
Health and Safety Executive
Rose Court
2 Southwark Bridge
London SE1 9HS
Telephone: 0171 717 6000

Imperial Chemical Industries (ICI)
ICI C&P Ltd
Education and Ecology Area
PO Box 54
Wilton
Middlesborough TS90 8JA
Telephone: 01642 433 542

Science and Plants for Schools
Homerton College
Cambridge CB2 2PH
Telephone: 01223 411 216

Shell Education Service
Shell UK Limited
Shell-Mex House
Strand
London WC2R 0DX
Telephone: 0171 257 1774

TEACHER EXCHANGES AND VISITS

The Central Bureau for Educational
  Visits and Exchanges
10 Spring Gardens
London SW1A 2BN
Telephone: 0171 389 4004

Central Bureau for Educational Visits
  and Exchanges
3 Bruntsfield Crescent

Edingburgh EH10 4HD
Telephone: 0131 447 8024

Central Bureau for Educational
  Visits and Exchanges
1 Chlorine Gardens
Belfast BT9 5DJ
Telephone: 01232 664 418

OTHER

Classroom Action Research Network
  (CARN)
School of Education
University of East Anglia
Norwich NR4 7TJ
Telephone: 01603 456 161

National Association for Special
  Educational Needs
Units 4 and 5
Amber Business Village
Amber C1
Amington Tamworth
Staffordshire B77 4RP
Telephone: 01827 311 500

The Pupil Researcher Initiative
Centre for Science Education
School of Science
Sheffield Hallam University
City Campus

Pond Street
Sheffield S1 1WB
Telephone: 01142 532 211

Special Educational Needs National
  Advisory Council
Department for Education
The University
Liverpool L69 3BX
Telephone: 01517 942 500

Voluntary Services Overseas
317 Putney Bridge Road
London SW15 2PN
Telephone: 0181 780 7200

For addresses of the following:

- Examination boards
- Institutes of higher education
- Further education institutions
- Teacher centres
- Local education authorities
  (LEAs)
- Schools (Maintained and indepen-
  dent)

please refer to *The Educational Auth-orities Directory and Annual*, The School Government Publishing Company Ltd, which is available in schools and libraries.

Bibliography

Adey, P, and Shayer, M. (1994) *Really Raising Standards: Cognitive Intervention and Academic Achievement*, London: Routledge.

Adey, P., Shayer, M. and Yates, C. (1989a) 'Cognitive acceleration: the effects of two years of intervention in science classes', in P. Adey, J. Bliss, J. Head and M. Shayer (eds) *Adolescent Development and School Science*, Lewes: The Falmer Press, pp. 240–9.

—— (1989b) *Thinking Science, the Curriculum Materials of the Case Project*, London: Macmillan.

Archenhold, W.F., Bell, J.F., Donnelly, J., Johnson, S. and Welford, G. (1988) *Science at Age 15: A Review of APU Findings 1980–4*, London: HMSO.

Association for Science Education (ASE) (1981) *Education Through Science: A Policy Statement*, Hatfield: ASE.

—— (1991) *SATIS 16–19*, Hatfield: ASE.

—— (1992) *Change in Our Future: A Challenge for Science Education*, Hatfield: ASE.

—— (1993) *Environmental Educational Policy Statement*, Hatfield: ASE.

—— (1994) *SATIS 8–14 Key Stages 2 and 3*, Hatfield: ASE.

Association for Science Education: Laboratory Safeguards Committee (1988) *Safety in the School Laboratory*, Hatfield: ASE.

Avison, J., Bailey, M. and Hill, G. (1995) *Science Scene: Investigations and Assessment Book*, London: Hodder & Stoughton.

Bell, B.F. and Brook, A. (1984) *Children's Learning in Science Project: Aspects of Secondary Students' Understanding of Plant Nutrition*, Leeds: Centre for Studies in Science and Mathematics Education, University of Leeds.

Beynon, J. and Mackay, H. (eds) (1993) *Computers in the Classroom: More Questions Than Answers*, London: The Falmer Press.

Bishop, P. (1996) 'Education and industry links: a tripartite model', *School Science Review*, 77, 281, pp. 27–33.

Black, P. (1987) 'Deciding to teach', *Steam*, 8, Middlesborough: ICI, p. 1.

—— (1990) 'APU science – the past and the future', *School Science Review*, **72**, 258, September, pp. 13–28.

—— (1993) 'The purposes of science education' in R. Hull (ed.) *The Science Teachers' Handbook: Secondary*, Hemel Hempstead: Simon & Schuster for the Association for Science Education, pp. 6–22.

Bolton, H. (1996) 'A teacher? What, me? No, never!', *Science Teacher Education*, 17, September, pp. 12–13.

Borrows, P. (1984) 'The Pimlico Chemistry Trail', *School Science Review*, 66, 235, pp. 221–33.

Bownas, G. and Thwaite, A. (1964) *The Penguin Book of Japanese Verse*, London: Penguin Books.

Brooks, C. and Hawes, P. (1995) 'Using lichens as air pollution monitors: a new approach', *School Science Review*, 76, 277, pp. 7–12.

Brosnan, T. (1992) 'Spreadsheets – of swans and swimming (modelling a titration)', *Education in Chemistry*, March, pp. 50–2.

Bruner, J. (1960) *The Process of Education*, New York: Vintage Books.

Bulman, L. (1984) *Teaching Language and Study Skills in Secondary Science*, London: Heinemann Educational Books.

Burgess, T. (1997) 'Language in the classroom and curriculum' in S. Capel, M. Leask and T. Turner (1997) *Starting to Teach in the Secondary School: A Companion for the Newly Qualified Teacher*, London: Routledge, Chapter 10.

Burton, G., Holman, J., Pilling, G. and Waddington, D. (1994a) *Salter's Advanced Chemistry: Chemical Storylines*, Oxford: Heinemann, p. 18 DF2 Getting energy from fuels.

—— (1994b) *Salter's Advanced Chemistry: Chemical Ideas*, Oxford: Heinemann, p. 18 Section 4.2 Where does energy come from?

—— (1994c) *Salter's Advanced Chemistry: Activity Sheets; Activity DF2.1 Using a spreadsheet to calculate enthalpy changes of combustion*, Oxford: Heinemann, pp. 24–5.

Capel, S., Leask, M. and Turner, T. (1995) *Learning to Teach in the Secondary School: A Companion to School Experience*, London: Routledge.

—— (1997) *Starting to Teach in the Secondary School: A Companion for the Newly Qualified Teacher*, London: Routledge.

Carey, J. (ed.) (1995) *The Faber Book of Science* (paperback edn), London: Faber & Faber.

Carre, C. (1981) *Language, Teaching and Learning: 4 Science*, London: Ward Lock Educational.

Cawdron, G. (1995) *School Meals Assessment Project*, London: Health Education Authority.

Chalmers, A.F. (1982) *What is This Thing Called Science?* (2nd edn), Milton Keynes: Open University Press.

Chant, C. (1989) *Science, Technology and Everyday Life, 1870–1950*, London: Routledge.

Chaudhary, V. (1997) 'Parents sue heart transplant hospital', *Guardian*, 15 April, p. 4, column 3.

CLEAPSS School Science Service/SSSERC (1981) '*Hazcards*', CLEAPSS, Brunel University, Uxbridge UB8 3PH.

Cosgrove, F. (1994) 'Use of data-logging to determine internal resistance', *School Science Review*, 76, 275, December, pp. 87–8.

Council for Environmental Education (1995) *Develop an Environmental Policy: A Call to Action for Schools*, Reading: CEE.

Cowling, L. and Gallear, B. (1996) 'Demonstrating value added', *Education in Science*, 170, November, pp. 24–5.

Davies, F. and Greene, T. (1984) *Schools Council: Reading for Learning in the Sciences*, London: Oliver & Boyd.

Davies, H. (1996) 'The Sphereactor: an experimental sewage and waste water treatment', *Guardian Education*, 12 November.

Dawkins, R. (1991) *The Blind Watchmaker*, London: Penguin Books.

Dearing, R. (1994) *The National Curriculum and its Assessment, Final Report*, London: School Curriculum and Assessment Authority.

—— (1996) *Review of Qualifications for 16-19 Year Olds: Issues for Consideration*, London: School Curriculum and Assessment Authority.

Dee, L. with Emmerson, P. (1995) *Special Educational Needs in the Secondary School*, Occasional Papers in Teacher Education and Training (OPTET), London: Initial Teacher Education, Institute of Education, University of London.

Denton, C. and Postlethwaite, K. (1985) *Able Children: Identifying Them in the Classroom*, Slough: NFER-Nelson.

Department for Education (DFE) (1992) *Information Technology in Secondary Schools: A Review by HMI*, London: HMSO.

—— (1993) *Great Britain Education Act 1993 (Section 241) Sex Education in Schools*, London: DFE.

—— (1995a) *Information Technology in the National Curriculum (1995 revision)*, London: HMSO.

—— (1995b) *Science in the National Curriculum*, London: HMSO.

Department for Education and the Welsh Office (DFE/WO) (1992) *Circulars 9/92 and 35/92 Initial Teacher Training (Secondary Phase)*, London and Cardiff: DFE/WO.

Department for Education/Department for Employment (DFE/ED) (1991) *Education and Training for the Twenty First Century*, London: DFE/ED.

Department for Education and Employment (DFEE) (1996) *Safety in Science Laboratories* (4th edn), London: HMSO.

—— (1997a) *Circular 10/97 Teaching: High Status, High Standards. Requirements for Courses of Initial Teacher Training*, London: DFEE.

—— (1997b) *Maximising Achievement: The National Framework for Education and Training*, London: DFEE.

Department of Education and Science (DES) (1978a) *Primary Education in England: A Survey by HM Inspectors*, London: HMSO.

—— (1978b) *Special Educational Needs*, London: HMSO Cmnd. 7212 (The Warnock Report).

—— (1979) *Aspects of Secondary Education: A Survey by HMI*, London: HMSO.

—— (1980) *A View of the Curriculum*, HMI Series: Matters for Discussion, London: HMSO.

—— (1981) *Great Britain Education Act 1981*, London: HMSO.

—— (1985a) *Science 5–16: A Statement of Policy*, London: HMSO.

—— (1985b) *The Curriculum from 5–16 (Curriculum Matters No. 2)*, London: HMSO.

—— (1985c) *Better Schools*, London: HMSO.

—— (1988a) *National Curriculum Task Group on Assessment and Testing: A Report*, London: HMSO.

—— (1988b) *Science in the National Curriculum: The Orders*, London: HMSO.

—— (1989) *Safety in Outdoor Education*, London: HMSO.

Department of Education Northern Ireland (1996) *Arrangements for Initial Teacher Training in Northern Ireland from 1st September 1996*, London: HMSO.

Department of Health (1989) *The Diets of British Schoolchildren Sub-Committee on Nutritional Surveillance. Committee on Medical Aspects of Food Policy. Report on Health and Social Subjects No.36*, London: HMSO.

—— (1992) *The Health of the Nation*, London: HMSO.

Dillon, J., Watson, R. and Tosulungu, C. (1993) *Chemistry and the Environment*, London: Royal Society of Chemistry.

Dixon, B. (1973) *What is Science For?*, London: Collins.

—— (1989) *The Science of Science: Changing the Way We Think*, London: Cassell.

Dobson, K. (1992) 'Creating a monster in the lab', *Guardian Education*, 31 March, p. 25.

Dobson, K. and Sunley, C. (eds) (1996) *Co-ordinated Science*, London: Collins.

Dolsma, K. (1995) 'Recording an ECG and heart sounds with a BBC microcomputer', *School Science Review*, 76, 277, June, pp. 54–6.

Dorling, G., Hunt, A. and Monger, G. (1988) *Nuffield Co-ordinated Sciences*, Harlow: Longman.

Dove, J. (1994) 'Headstones, local churches and Sc3', *School Science Review*, 75, 272, pp. 43–50.

Driver, R. and Bell, B. (1990) 'Students thinking and learning of science: a constructivists' view', *School Science Review*, 67, 240, pp. 443–56.

Driver, R., Guesne, E. and Tiberghien, A. (1988) *Children's Ideas in Science*, Milton Keynes: Open University Press.

Driver, R., Leach, J., Millar, R. and Scott, P. (1996) *Young People's Images of Science*, Buckingham: Open University Press.

Driver, R., Squires, A., Rushworth, P. and Wood-Robinson, V. (eds) (1994) *Making Sense of Secondary Science*, London: Routledge for the Open University.

Dunbar, R. (1995) *The Trouble with Science*, London: Faber & Faber.

Dunne, D. (ed.) (1996) *The New Science 1 Book: Experimental and Investigative Science*, Northampton: Northampton County Council (The Science Centre).

Edwards, J. and Fogelman, K. (1993) *Developing Citizenship in the Curriculum*, London: David Fulton Publishers.

Engineering Council (1992) *Neighbourhood Engineers: Practical Support for Schools*, London: Engineering Council.

ERA (1988) *Education Reform Act 29 July 1988; Section 1 and 2 Aims of the School Curriculum*, London: HMSO.

Erb, C. (1996) 'Science pages on the World Wide Web', *School Science Review*, 77, 280, March, pp. 125–7.

Fitz-Gibbon, C. (1995) *The Value Added National Project: Interim Report*, London: SCAA.

Follett, B. (1997) 'From animal behaviour to DNA and back again: in praise of molecular biology', *School Science Review*, 78, 284, March, pp. 15–22. The Presidential Address to members of the ASE, Birmingham, January.

Foster, S. (1989) 'Streetwise physics', *School Science Review*, 71, 254, September, pp. 15–22.

Frost, J. (ed.) (1995) *Teaching Science*, London: Woburn Press.

—— (1996/97) 'School based science tasks', in *PGCE Science Handbook for Students*, London: Science and Technology Group Institute of Education, University of London, appendix.

Frost, J. and Jennings, A. (1995) 'The use of statements of competence in the professional development of science teachers'. Paper read at the inaugural conference, Science Education Research in Europe, University of Leeds, April.

—— (1996) 'Competence, progression and partnership in ITE', *Science Teacher Education*, 18, (December) p. 9.

Frost, R. (1996) *The 'IT in Science' Book of Datalogging and Control*, Hatfield: The Association for Science Education (latest version updated April 1996).

Froufe, J. (1990) *Measurement in School Science*, London: Schools Examination and Assessment Council.

Gates, B. (1995) *The Road Ahead*, London: Viking Penguin Books.

Gayford, C. (1996) *The Nature and Purposes of Environmental Education*, in G. Harris and C. Blackwell, *Environmental Issues in Education*, Aldershot: Arena, pp. 1–20.

GEMPT (1996) *Guidelines on Educational Materials concerned with Nutrition. NTFP Team*, London: Department of Health, p. 13.

Gipps, C. and Stobbart, G. (1994) *Assessment: A Teacher's Guide to the Issues*, London: Hodder & Stoughton.

Goldberg, J. (1989) *Anatomy of a Scientific Discovery* (1st edn), London: Bantam Books.

Goodfield, J. (1982) *An Imagined World: A Story of Scientific Discovery*, London: Penguin Books.

Gould, S.J. (1989) *Wonderful Life: The Burgess Shale and the Nature of History*, London: Hutchinson Radius.

Haber, L. (1970) *Black Pioneers of Science and Invention*, San Diego: Harcourt, Brace & Company.

Hall, W. (1973) *Schools Council Integrated Science Project Teachers' Handbook*, Harlow: Longman (known as SCISP or 'Patterns')

Hardie, J. and Hale, M. (1993) 'Science and environmental education', in R. Hull (ed.) (1993) *Science Teachers' Handbook: Secondary*, Hemel Hempstead: Simon & Schuster.

Harding, J. (1994) 'Swimming pool chemistry teaching', *School Science Review*, 76, 275, pp. 45–9.

Hare, S. (1995) *Acid Rain and Air Quality: A Resource Guide*, Manchester: Manchester Metropolitan University.

Hargreaves, D. (1984) *Improving Secondary Schools. Report of the Committee on the Curriculum & Organisation of Secondary Schools*, London: ILEA.

Harlen, W. (1986) *Planning Scientific Investigations at Age 11*, London: Department for Education and Science and Welsh Office.

Harris, G. and Blackwell, C. (eds) (1996) *Environmental Issues in Education: Monitoring Change in Education*, Aldershot: Arena.

Harris, J. (ed.) (1985) *Revised Nuffield Advanced Science, Physics*, Harlow: Longman.

Havard, N. (1996) *Student Attitudes to Studying A Level Sciences*, London: Public Understanding of Science.

Hawking, S. (1988) *A Brief History of Time*, London: Bantam.

Haydn, T. and Macaskill, C. (1996a) *Making the Most of Information Technology in the PGCE Year*, London: The Institute of Education, University of London. In the series 'Occasional Papers in Teacher Education and Training (OPTET)'.

—— (1996b) *Information Technology and Initial Teacher Education: Bridging the Gap Between What Is and What Might Be*, London: The Institute of Education, University of London. In the series 'Occasional Papers in Teacher Education and Training (OPTET)'.

Haytor, D. (1997) 'Measuring the Earth from observations of the Sun', *School Science Review* 79, 286, pp. 123–4.

Hazell, A. (1996) 'Teaching practice', *Science Teacher Education*, 17, September, pp. 17–18.

Health and Safety Commission (1989) *Control of Substances Hazardous to Health (COSHH) Guidance for Schools*, London: HMSO.

Herz, J.C. (1994) *Surfing on the Internet: A Net-head's Adventures On-line*, London: Abacus Books.

Hill, T. (undated) *Differentiating the Secondary Curriculum: Base Lining (12)*, Wiltshire: Wiltshire County Council. See section 1: science, waves and vibrations.

Hodkinson, S. and Thomas, L. (1991) 'Economics education for all', in D. Whitehead and D. Dyer (eds) (1991) *New Developments in Economics and Business Education*, London: Kogan Page in association with the Institute of Education, University of London.

Hollins, M. (1986) 'Stones and structures', *ILEA Science News*, 33, July, pp. 16–17.

Horton, R. (1993) *Patterns of Thought in Africa and the West: Essays on Magic, Religion and Science*, Cambridge: Cambridge University Press.

Hoyle, E. and Johns, P. (1995) *Professional Knowledge and Professional Practice*, London: Cassell.

Huff, T. (1993) *The Rise of Early Modern Science*, Cambridge: Cambridge University Press.

Hull, R. (ed.) (1993) *Science Teacher's Handbook: Secondary*, Hemel Hempstead: Simon & Schuster for the Association for Science Education.

Ingle, R. and Jennings, A. (1981) *Science in Schools: Which Way Now?*, London: Institute of Education, University of London.

Institute of Biology (1990) *Safety in Biological Fieldwork*, London: Institute of Biology.

Jenkins, E. (1979) *From Armstrong to Nuffield*, London: John Murray.

Jennings, A. (1986) *Science in the Locality*, Cambridge: Cambridge University Press.

—— (1992) *National Curriculum Science: So Near and Yet So Far*, London: The Tufnell Press.

—— (1995) 'Discussions', in J. Frost (ed.) *Teaching Science*, London: Woburn Press.

Jesson, D. (1996) *Value Added Measures of School GCSE Performance*, London: DFEE.

Job, D. (1996) *Schools Network on Air Pollution: A School Based Monitoring Project on London's Air Quality. Report of Findings 1995*, London: Geography Education and Earth Science Process Centre, Institute of Education, University of London.

Johnson, K. (1991) *Physics For You*, Cheltenham: Stanley Thornes.

Johnson, S. (1988) *National Assessment: The APU Science Approach*, London: HMSO.

Jones, A.T., Simon, S.A., Black, P.J., Fairbrother, R.W. and Watson, J.R. (1992) *Open Work in Science: Development of Scientific Investigations in Schools*, Hatfield: Association for Science Education (the OPENS Project).

Jones, S. (1996) *In the Blood*, London: Harper Collins.

King, S. (1996) *Classroom Observation*, London: Institute of Education, University of London. In the series 'Occasional Papers in Teacher Education and Training (OPTET)'.

Lakin, L. (1995) 'Environmental education, a challenge to the ASE from mastermind', *Education in Science*, 163, June, pp. 8–10.

Lambert, D. and Gough, L. (1994) *Differentiated Learning*, London: Institute of Education, University of London. In the series 'Occasional Papers in Teacher Education and Training (OPTET)'.

Laws, P.M. (1996) 'Investigative work in the National Curriculum', *School Science Review*, 77, 281, pp. 17–25.

Layton, D. (1993) *Technology's Challenge to Science Education*, Buckingham: Open University Press.

Learning Through Landscapes (1994) *The School Grounds Resource Directory*, Winchester: Learning Through Landscapes.

Levine, J. (ed.) (1990) *Bilingual Learners and the Mainstream Curriculum*, London: The Falmer Press.

Lightbody, P. and Durndell, A. (1996) 'The masculine image of careers in science and technology: fact or fantasy', *British Journal of Educational Psychology*, 66, 2, June, pp. 231–46.

Lucas, N. (1997) 'The changing sixth form: the growth of pre-vocational education', in S. Capel, M. Leask and T. Turner *Starting to Teach in Secondary School: A Companion for the NQT*, London: Routledge.

Macaskill, C. and Ogborn, J. (1996) 'Science and technology', *School Science Review*, 77, 281, pp. 55–61.

McGrath, C. (1994) 'SATIS 8–14 resources', *Education in Science*, 159, September.

McTiffin, L. (1996) 'The first year of teaching', *Science Teacher Education*, 18, December, p. 7.

Major, J. (1997) 'Advanced GNVQ Science; our first cohort', *School Science Review*, 78, 284, March, pp. 41–8.

Medawar, P. (1974) 'Lucky Jim', in P.B. Medawar (ed.) *The Hope of Progress*, London: Wildwood House.

Midland Examining Group (1996) *Science: Double Award Syllabuses A (Nuffield), B (Suffolk) and C (Salters)*, Cambridge: Midland Examining Group.

Millar, R. (1996) 'Towards a science curriculum for public understanding', *School Science Review*, 77, 280, pp. 7–18.

Monk, M. and Dillon, J. (1995) *Learning to Teach Science: Activities for Student Teachers and Mentors*, London: The Falmer Press.

Moon, B. and Shelton Mayes, A. (1991) *Teaching and Learning in the Secondary School*, Buckingham: Open University Press.

National Commission for Education (1993) *Learning to Succeed: A Radical Look at Education Today*, London: Heinemann for the Paul Hamlyn Foundation.

National Council for Educational Technology (NCET) (1995) *Approaches to IT Capability Key Stage 3*, Coventry: NCET.

National Curriculum Council (NCC) (1989) *Curriculum Guidance 2: A Curriculum for All: Special Needs in the National Curriculum*, York: NCC.

—— (1990a) *Curriculum Guidance 4: Education for Economic and Industrial Understanding*, York: NCC.

—— (1990b) *Curriculum Guidance 5: Health Education*, York: NCC.

—— (1990c) *Curriculum Guidance 7: Environmental Education*, York: NCC.

—— (1990d) *Curriculum Guidance 8: Education for Citizenship*, York: NCC.

—— (1992a) *Curriculum Guidance 9: The National Curriculum and Pupils with Severe Learning Difficulties*, York: NCC.

—— (1992b) *Curriculum Guidance 10: Teaching Science to Pupils with Special Educational Needs*, York: NCC.

—— (1992c) *Science: Non-Statutory Guidance*, York: NCC. (Separate guidance is issued by the Curriculum Council for Wales.)

Northwood, J. (1991) *Computing in the National Curriculum – PC Compatibles*, London: Sigma Press.

Norton, P. (1993) *Inside the PC*, New York: Brady Publishing.

Nuffield Science in Practice (1994a) *GNVQ Science: Advanced Assignments Pack*, Oxford: Heinemann.

—— (1994b) *GNVQ Science: Advanced Student Book*, Oxford: Heinemann.

O'Hear, P. and White, J. (1991) *A National Curriculum for All: Laying the Foundations for Success*, London: Institute for Public Policy Research.

OFSTED (1994) *Information Technology in Schools Initiative: Final Report*, London: HMSO.

—— (1995) *Science: A Review of Inspection Findings 1993/94*, London: HMSO.

Ogborn, J., Kouladis, V. and Papadopetrakis, E. (1996) 'We measured the Earth by telephone', *School Science Review*, 77, 281, June, pp. 88–90.

Ogborn, J., Kress, K., Martins, I. and McGillicuddy, K. (1996) *Explaining Science in the Classroom*, Buckingham: Open University Press.

Osborn, J. (1986) 'Physics in the field', *ILEA Science News*, 33, July, pp. 11–14.

Osborne, R. (1989) *Teaching Physics: A Guide for Non-specialists*, Cambridge: Cambridge University Press.

Osborne, R. and Freyburg, R. (1985) *Learning in Science*, Auckland: Heinemann.

Parkinson, J. (1994) *The Effective Teaching of Secondary Science*, Harlow: Longman.

Postlethwaite, K. (1993) *Differentiated Science Teaching*, Buckingham: Open University Press.

Pring, R.A. (1995) *Closing the Gap: Liberal Education and Vocational Preparation*, London: Hodder & Stoughton.

—— (1996) 'The year 2000', in M. Wilkin and D. Sankey (eds) (1994) *Collaboration and Transition in Initial Teacher Training*, London: Kogan Page.

Ramsden, P. (1995) 'Science education for the year 2000 and beyond', *Education in Science*, 164, September, p. 22.

Reiss, M. (1993) *Science Education for a Pluralist Society*, Buckingham: Open University Press.

Richards, R. (1972) *Time: A Unit for Teachers, Science 5–13 Project*, London: Macdonald Education.

—— (1989) *An Early Start to Nature*, Hemel Hempstead: Macdonald Educational. (Although written for primary teachers, the ideas and techniques are suitable or easily adapted to secondary school.)

—— (1991) *An Early Start to the Environment*, London: Simon & Schuster. (Although written for primary teachers, the ideas and techniques are suitable or easily adapted to secondary school.)

Richards, R., Collis, M. and Kincaid, D. (1987) *An Early Start to Science*, Hemel Hempstead: Macdonald Educational. (Although written for primary teachers, the ideas and techniques are suitable or easily adapted to secondary school.)

Roach, T., Smith, D. and Vazquez, M. (1990) *Bilingual Pupils and Secondary Science*, Hounslow: Community Languages Support Services Secondary Team, London Borough of Hounslow.

Ronan, C. (1966) *The Ages of Science*, London: Harrap.

Ronan, C. and Needham, T. (1978/1981) *The Shorter Science and Civilisation in China*, Cambridge: Cambridge University Press.

Rosen, D. and Rosen, S. (1994) *London Science*, London: Prion.

Rowlands, D. and Snape, G. (eds) (1992) *Science at Work*, Harlow: Longman.

Royal Society for the Protection of Birds (RSPB) (1996) *Our World – Our Responsibility. Environmental Education – A Practical Guide*, Sandy: RSPB in association with the Council for Environmental Education.

Russell, T., Black, P., Harlen, W., Johnson, S. and Palacio, D. (1988) *Science at Age 11: A Review of the APU Findings 1980–1984*, London: HMSO.

Sagan, C. (1977) *The Dragons of Eden*, London: Hodder & Stoughton.

Sanderson, P.L. (1987) 'Environmental chemistry in action', *Education in Chemistry*, 24, 1, pp. 16–18.

Schofield, B., Black, P., Bell, J.F., Johnson, S., Murphy, P., Qualter, A. and Russell, T. (1988) *Science at Age 13: A Review of the APU Findings 1980–4*, London: HMSO.

School Curriculum and Assessment Authority (SCAA) (1995/6) *Exemplification of Standards in Science*, London: SCAA.

—— (1996) *Standards at Key Stage 3: Science*, London: SCAA.

——/Curriculum and Assessment Authority for Wales (1995) *Mandatory Code of Practice for the GCSE (revised)*, London: SCAA.

Science Faculty (1996) 'Handbook', Swakeleys School, Clifton Gardens, Hillingdon, Uxbridge UB10 OEJ.

Secondary PGCE Subject Handbook, Science (1996/7) Science and Technology Group, Institute of Education, University of London.

Secondary Science Curriculum Review (1984) *Health and Science Education: Proposals for Action and Consultation*, London: SSCR.

SEN policy document (1996) Swakeleys School, Clifton Gardens, Hillingdon, Uxbridge UB10 OEJ.

Shipstone, D. (1988) 'Understanding of simple electrical circuits', in R. Driver, E. Guesne and A. Tiberghien (eds) *Children's Ideas in Science*, Milton Keynes: Open University Press.

Smail, B. and Windale, M. (1996) *Celebrating Science*, London: Pupil Research Initiative and the British Association.

Smith, D. (1997a) 'Materials and their properties (AT3): an activity pack for Key Stages 3 and 4 (The SPEAL Project)', London: London Borough of Islington, The Barnsbury Complex, Offord Road, London N1 1FQ.

—— (1997b) 'Life processes (AT2): an activity pack for Key Stages 3 and 4 (The SPEAL Project)', London: London Borough of Islington, The Barnsbury Complex, Offord Road, London N1 1FQ.

Smith, R. (1996) 'Physical science trails', *Primary Science Review*, 43, June, pp. 17–19.

Smithers, A. (1994) *Impact of Double Science*, London: Engineering Council.

Solomon, J. (1993) *Teaching Science, Society and Technology*, Buckingham: Open University Press.

—— (1996) 'Student learning on a GNVQ course: motivation and self-esteem', *School Science Review*, 77, 280, March, pp. 37–44.

Solomon, J., Duveen, J., Scott, L. and Hall, S. (undated) *Science Through Sc1 Investigations*, Hatfield: Association for Science Education (about 1995).

Spurgin, B. (1994) 'Reaction time in athletics', *School Science Review*, 76, 274, pp. 35–43.

Staff Handbook (1996) Swakeleys School, Clifton Gardens, Hillingdon, Uxbridge UB10 OEJ.

Stern, J. (1995) *Learning to Teach*, London: David Fulton Publishers.

Stoll, L. and Fink, D. (1996) *Changing Our Schools*, Buckingham: Open University Press.

Styles, M. (1986) *You'll Love This Stuff*, Cambridge: Cambridge University Press.

Sutton, C. (1981) *Communicating in the Classroom*, London: Hodder & Stoughton.

—— (1992) *Words, Science and Learning*, Buckingham: Open University Press.

The Council and the Ministers of Education Meeting within the Council (1988) 'Resolution on environmental education', *Official Journal of the European Communities* (No. C177/8).

The Good Resources Guide, Chemical Industry Education Centre, Department of Chemistry, University of York, Heslington, York YO1 5DD.

The Scottish Office Education Department (1993) *Teacher Competences 'Guidelines for Teacher Training Courses'*, Edinburgh: The Scottish Office Department for Education.

Thorp, S. (ed.) (1991) *Race, Equality and Science Teaching: An Active Inset Manual for Teachers and Educators*, Hatfield: Association for Science Education.

Thorp, S., Deshpande, P. and Edwards, C. (1994) *Race, Equality and Science Teaching: A Handbook for Teachers*, Hatfield: Association for Science Education.

Tones, K. (1987) 'Health promotion, affective education and the personal-social development of young people', in K. David and T. Williams *Health Education in Schools*, London: Harper & Row.

Turner, S.A. (1995) 'Simulations', in J. Frost (ed.) (1995) *Teaching Science*, London: Woburn, Figure 7.1.

United Nations (1992) *UN Conference on Environment on Development, Agenda 21 Rio Declaration*, Paris: UNESCO.

University of York Science Education Group (1994) *Salters Advanced Chemistry*, Oxford: Heinemann.

Versey, J., Fairbrother, R., Parkin, T., Bourne, J., Dye, A. and Watkinson, A. (undated) *Managing Differentiated Learning and Assessment in the National Curriculum (Science)*, Hatfield: Association for Science Education; appeared in 1995.

Vincent, R. and Wray, J. (1988) 'Safety in out-of-school science', *School Science Review*, 70, 250, September, pp. 55–60.

Welford, G., Harlen, W. and Schofield, B. (1985) *Practical Testing at Ages 11, 13 and 15*, London: Department for Education and Science.

Wellington, J. J. (ed.) (1986) *Controversial Issues in the Curriculum*, Oxford: Basil Blackwell.

—— (1994) *Secondary Science: Contemporary Issues and Practical Approaches*, London: Routledge.

Whitehead, D. and Dyer, D. (eds) (1991) *New Developments in Economics and Business Education*, London: Kogan Page in association with the Institute of Education, University of London.

Williams, T., Roberts, J., Hyde, J., Wetton, N. and Moon, A. (1990) *Exploring Health Education: A Growth and Development Perspective*, London: Health Education Authority.

Wolpert, L. (1992) *The Unnatural Nature of Science*, London: Faber & Faber.

Woolnough, B. (1994) *Effective Science Teaching*, Buckingham: Open University Press.

World Health Organisation (1990) *Diet, Nutrition and Prevention of Chronic Disease*, Geneva: World Health Organisation.

Author index

Subject index